T0314049

HOW MANY LANGUAGES DO WE NEED?

HOW MANY LANGUAGES DO WE NEED?

THE ECONOMICS OF LINGUISTIC DIVERSITY

Victor Ginsburgh

Shlomo Weber

PRINCETON UNIVERSITY PRESS

PRINCETON AND OXFORD

CONTENTS

ACKNOWLEDGMENTS

We are grateful to our editor, Richard Baggaley, for his patience. Our running behind schedule was fortunately mitigated by the speed of his own reactions to any of our requests. His suggestions and ceaseless encouragement were indispensable, as were those of Seth Ditchik.

We thank two anonymous referees, as well as Antonio Estache and Georg Kirchsteiger, who provided extremely careful comments on an earlier version of the manuscript. Some joint papers with our co-authors, Klaus Desmet, Jan Fidrmuc, Jean Gabszewicz, Didier Laussel, Michel Le Breton, Abdul Noury, Ignacio Ortuño-Ortín, Juan Prieto-Rodriguez, Sheila Weyers, and Israel Zang, are discussed in the book. We are grateful to all of them for sharing the joy of joint research.

Our thanks also go to Professor Paul Demaret, rector of the College of Europe in Bruges, who welcomed us to spend three months in a beautiful old building located on one of the many canals. We are also most indebted to Eric de Souza, Xavier Estève, Dominik Hanf, Valérie Hauspie, Marc Mermuys, Marie-Jeanne Vandenberghe, Clara Verbeke, and Ann Verlinde for having made our visit to Bruges so friendly and enjoyable.

Last but not the least, we wish to thank Sanjeev Kumar, who introduced us to the intricacies of linguistic challenges on the Indian subcontinent; Maryam Kharaishvili, for her help with editing the manuscript; Yuval Weber, for his very useful comments and suggestions; Marjorie Pannell, who translated our Globish into English; and Brigitte Pelner, who made a manuscript become a book.

The support one of us received from the Spanish Ministry of Science and Innovation (grant ECO2008-01300) is gratefully acknowledged.

Language is a ford through the river of time,
It leads us to the dwelling of those gone before;
But he cannot arrive there,
Who fears deep water.

—Vladislav Illich-Svytich[1]

---

[1]Vladislav Illich-Svytich (1934–1966), Russian linguist and one of the fathers of Nostratics, an Urlanguage in which he composed this short poem, which is inscribed on his headstone.

HOW MANY LANGUAGES DO WE NEED?

INTRODUCTION

THE TITLE OF THE BOOK, *How Many Languages Do We Need?*, reflects a difficult choice that was pervasive in many multilingual societies over the course of human history, and still is today. The problem is very much on the agenda of a large number of countries, regions, and international unions that must address various aspects of multilingualism. The desire to avoid an excess of societal fragmentation in our rapidly globalizing environment narrows the focus to a relatively small number of "core" languages. But such restrictions inevitably disenfranchise speakers of "non-core" languages. In this book, we analyze the trade-off between the quest for efficiency that a small number of languages is thought to foster and a reduction in disenfranchisement, which calls for more languages.

Linguistic policies vary across the globe. The European Union adopts the policy of twenty-three official languages,[2] India has instituted the famous "three-language policy," a variant of which was also considered in Nigeria. The range is wide, and obviously much depends on the way policies are implemented. The EU's policy has its problems, but has not led to wars. Nor do the 207 languages in Australia, or the 364 languages in the United States. In Sri Lanka, however, two languages were one too many, and thousands of people died as a consequence.

The search for an "optimal" number of languages is implicitly linked to a second question about which languages to choose. Languages differ from each other; some are close, others are distant, but we can easily admit that however we measure distance, Spanish and Italian seem closer than English and Greek. That fact will play an important role in our analysis.

DIVERSITY COULD BE GOOD, BUT IT IS NOT FREE

Economists are two-handed. One hand immediately recognizes that the diversity of existing cultures and languages, which often cannot be dissociated, is important. Limiting the number of languages creates a

---

[2]One per country, with the exception of Luxembourg. Some countries—Germany and Austria, for example—share a common language.

disenfranchisement that even developed and democratic countries sometimes cannot support. History, including that of the contemporary era, shows how oppression or suppression of languages or cultures may lead to bloody wars. It is shocking and horrifying to think of the cost of linguistic policies in terms of human lives, but failure to do so ignores the passion and violence generated by the defense of or attack on one's own culture and language. Languages have evolved over the course of human history, sometimes for smooth reasons, at other times for brutal ones. The following few questions (there are many others) are extremely interesting: (1) Why did some languages survive and even grow? (2) Why are some languages spoken by millions or even billions of people, and others by a few hundred or even less? (3) How do languages change, and why (for linguistic reasons such as phonetics or syntax; for imposed reasons such as invasions, migrations, or colonization)? These questions have been dealt with by linguists, historians and archaeologists, and more recently by biologists. We brush up against some in the chapters of the book, but space considerations unfortunately prevented us from a more detailed examination.[3]

The importance people and countries attach to their native language and culture can also be illustrated by the substantial resources devoted to advertising and promoting their culture, language, and literature. Some (Great Britain and its British Council, France and the Alliance Française, the German Goethe Institut, the Italian Società Dante Alighieri, or the Spanish Instituto Cervantes, to cite a few) have institutes in many other countries to teach their language and culture. Countries subsidize translations both into and from their own language.[4]

For many, the protection of linguistic diversity is especially important in our globalized environment, often dominated by English. This issue is discussed later, but here we would like to point out that what seems to be the relentless march of English can breed strong feelings of disenfranchisement. Here is what the American–Chilean literature professor and author Ariel Dorfman (2002, 92) has to say:

---

[3]The interested reader is referred to chapter 7 of Cavalli-Sforza and Cavalli-Sforza (1995), as well as Cavalli-Sforza (2000) on prehistorical times and ancient human diasporas, Janson (2002) and Ostler (2005) on antiquity and more recent times, and McWhorter (2001) on pidgins and creoles. Renfrew (1987) examines links between archaeological discoveries and languages.

[4]The list of countries that offer subsidies for translations is large. See http://portal.unesco.org/culture/en/ev.php.

The ascendancy of English, like so many phenomena associated with globalization, leaves too many invisible losers, too many people silenced. ... Do you come from a place ... that does not control a language that commands respect? Do you reside in a language ... whose existence does not have the kind of value in the marketplace that can get you a good job and help you in [the] everyday struggle to survive?

While one hand supports the virtues of linguistic diversity, the other hand would discreetly point out that they do not come for free. A host of economic studies suggests that too much diversity, whether linguistic, ethnic, religious, cultural, or genetic, breeds institutional wastefulness, bureaucratic inefficiency, and corruption. This so-called fractionalization may reduce political stability and hamper economic growth, as shown by the sad and painful example of postcolonial Africa. Cameroon has 279 languages, the Democratic Republic of Congo has 217, Nigeria 527, Sudan 134, and Tanzania 129. These staggering numbers—especially if they also represent ethnic groups— have often led to the argument that to accelerate economic progress, a country or a region may have to consider limiting the number of languages used for official, commercial, or legal purposes to a manageable and reasonable few.

The costs of linguistic diversity are not always direct and are some- times the consequence of poor translations and miscommunication. History is full of episodes in which these factors played an essential role in various international conflicts.[5] A well-known example is Article (i) of UN Security Council Resolution 242 of November 22, 1967, which requires the "withdrawal of Israeli armed forces from territories occu- pied in the recent conflict." The omission of the definite article before "territories" has been often interpreted to imply that the withdrawal refers to some but not all territories covered by the resolution. This delicate but crucial distinction was lost in the French and Russian versions. Indeed, no definite article exists in Russian, whereas French requires inclusion of the article. The Arabic version includes the article, but Arabic was not an official UN language at the time.

WHAT THE BOOK IS ABOUT

The purpose of our book is to use economic and to some extent linguistic and sociological reasoning to balance the benefits and costs

---

[5] See Lewis (2004) for more examples.

of various linguistic situations and policies. While extolling diversity, we must recognize that it may come with institutional wastefulness and inefficiency, corruption, legal and communication barriers, and lack of interest on the part of citizens about what happens in their country or region, or may lead to unrest, riots, and even wars. So also does restricting diversity, which results in disenfranchisement. It is a difficult challenge to decide on a "sensible" number of languages. That number is generally not one. It is probably not forty-two, the answer given by the computer in *The Hitchhiker's Guide to the Galaxy* to the question, "What is the answer to life, the universe and everything?"[6] And it is certainly not 527, the number of languages spoken in Nigeria today. Our contribution is to show that in the recipe, linguistic distances, which the reader will encounter in many chapters, are an important ingredient.[7]

The two opening chapters discuss the importance people attach to their native language and culture, and describe how linguistic policies have led to the alienation and disenfranchisement of various groups or individuals restricted in their linguistic rights.

Some very basic notions about linguistic and other types of distances are introduced in the next chapter and used throughout the book, especially in chapter 4, which illustrates the importance of linguistic or cultural distances in issues as diverse as bilateral international trade, the choice of immigration destination, translations of literary works, and the voting behavior of countries along linguistic and cultural lines. Smaller distances (or a common language) between countries have a positive impact on their trade. In many cases, immigrants are attracted by countries with which they had former contacts—through colonization, for example—and so gained some exposure to the culture and language. More literary works are translated from source languages (and cultures) that are close to the destination language. And the winners in a popular song contest in Europe are elected by those with whom they share cultural traits, including language.

But languages also evolve over time. In particular, learning foreign languages may alter the linguistic repertoire of various communities.

---

[6]We owe this reference to Richard B. Thank you, Richard, for this, and for so much more.

[7]Our goal has nothing, or very little, in common with the book by Ariel Rubinstein (2000), *Economics and Language.* Although the title is somewhat similar to ours, Rubinstein is mainly concerned with the links between the formal language of mathematical models and natural language. As important as they are, those issues are far removed from our main interests.

To evaluate the patterns of investment in human capital and private returns from learning foreign languages, in chapter 5 we use the theory of communicative benefits introduced by Nobel Prize winner Reinhard Selten and American linguist Jonathan Pool (1991) and link it to linguistic diversity. Distances again play a prominent role, since the decision to learn a new language strikes a balance between costs (the difficulty of learning it, which correlates with distance) and benefits. Will it pay to learn a language?

The next two chapters address the issues and the consequences of linguistic and ethnolinguistic diversity, fractionalization, and polarization, as well as disenfranchisement. Diversity, fractionalization, polarization, and disenfranchisement indices that measure these phenomena have a long history in linguistics and sociology, starting with the contribution of Joseph Greenberg (1956) and its later extension by Stanley Lieberson (1964), two distinguished representatives in their respective disciplines. Such indices have more recently been used by economists, who have underlined the important role they play in explaining economic growth, redistribution, income inequality, corruption, political stability, and bureaucratic (in)efficiency in many developing countries and regions in which democracy is little more than a buzzword. We also stress the fact that in empirical work, indices that account for linguistic distances perform better than those that do not.

The last chapter is devoted to a case study of linguistic policies in the EU. Linguistic policies should achieve a delicate balance, taking into account efficiency considerations without forgetting the will of the people. We suggest that though the English-only solution may yield greater efficiency and save on costs, it could generate too large a degree of disenfranchisement that leads to less political unity and citizens' loss of interest in a true European Union. We point to several alternative solutions that include the political feasibility of altering the extent of translation to some core languages, the provision of compensating transfers for countries that would be ready to cover their own translation needs, and some fair methods of sharing the global cost of translation and interpretation, which could be of use in other parts of the world.

SOME HINTS FOR A PIECEMEAL READING

Though we have tried to make the presentation as simple and accessible as possible, it is unavoidable that some chapters of the volume are more technical than others. Linguistics is a difficult topic, and so are economics and sociology, even when discussed in isolation. Here, all three disciplines are combined. Chapters 1 and 2 are of a purely descriptive nature. Chapter 3, on distances, uses linguistic concepts, and the reader, unless familiar with the field, should devote some time to reading this chapter, which lays out the basic insights used in all the other chapters. Chapter 5 uses game-theoretic concepts, and chapter 6 defines diversity, fractionalization, polarization, and disenfranchisement indices, which need some mathematical formulation. The reader who is not interested in technicalities may skip the first section of chapter 5 and chapter 6. Chapters 4 and 7 are devoted to the many empirical studies whose object is to estimate the impact of linguistic distances and ethnolinguistic diversity on economic outcomes. They include many tables devoted to econometric results, but these results are also discussed in simple terms, and both chapters can thus be read without relying on the detailed tables. The second part of chapter 7 and chapter 8 are devoted to a case study of linguistic policies, and most of it is easy reading. The last part of chapter 8, devoted to showing how the financial burden of the more than one billion euros spent every year by the EU on translation could be shared in a fair (or fairer) way, is a little more demanding.

Having given these warnings, we briefly address the question of the potential readership of the book. Both authors are economists, and it is obvious that their fellow economists who have had some basic training in game theory and econometrics, even if it is somewhat rusty, should be able to read the book without any difficulty. Students with a background in sociology or linguistics will probably face more problems, though they may skip the more technical chapters without losing the flavor of our arguments. A very basic economic training will permit following most of the discussion. The same is true for the lay reader. After all, as economists, we were also—and still are—lay readers in sociology and linguistics but had to grapple with some difficult concepts that we felt were necessary for our thesis.

Chapter 1

MY LANGUAGE IS MY HOMELAND

> Minha pátria é minha lengua.[1]
> —*Fernando Pessoa*

RUSSIAN AND SWAHILI. *The authors of this book have two different native languages, Swahili and Russian. A few years ago, the Russian native speaker accompanied the Swahili native speaker on a trip to Belarus in search of traces of the latter's father, born in Vitebsk (as was Marc Chagall, at approximately the same time). The hotel receptionist was totally confused by the fact that the traveler with a Russian–Jewish name (the Swahili speaker) could not utter a word of Russian, while the other, with a German name, spoke fluent Russian. This was without the receptionist's knowing that the visitor with whom she was unable to communicate was a native Swahili speaker. The fruits of globalization, as we say.*

We live in a world where individuals, families, and communities often uproot themselves, voluntarily or involuntary, and move to another place, country, or even continent. In fact, both of the authors have gone through this experience at different stages of their lives. One of us was given less than a week to collect his belongings before leaving his native country. What does one take on a journey to a distant, unfamiliar land? Books, memories, records? A very moving response to that dilemma is given by Ariel Dorfman, whose work was mentioned in the introduction. Dorfman (2002, 89) recalls Gabriel García Márquez's story of entire Colombian villages that migrated:

> Fleeing from catastrophes, plagues perhaps, or recurrent floods, or merely the desolation of being caught in the middle of civil wars, inhabitants of these villages decided, at some point in history, to uproot themselves, moving to a remote location in search of peace. As they packed every belonging that could be transported, they did not forget what was most important to them: their dead. According to García

[1] "My homeland is my language."

Márquez, these villagers, on the verge of becoming nomads, dug up the bones in the cemetery and, in effect, carried their ancestors into the unknown, probably animated by the need to defy the fluctuations of time and geography with the illusion that something from the past permeates the present, forming a hard physical link to memory at a time of devastating change.

Even though the desire to sustain links with the past is not always expressed in such a dramatic form, an important part of cultural history and heritage is invariably linked with language. The sensitivity of linguistic identity is forcefully underlined by Henry Bretton (1976, 447):

> Language then may indeed be the most explosive issue universally and over time. This mainly because language alone, unlike all other concerns associated with nationalism and ethnocentrism ... is so closely tied to the individual self. Fear of being deprived of communicating skills seems to raise political passions to a fever pitch.

When moving to distant lands, migrants take with them their language and begin a never-ending romance with it. Dorfman (2002, 90) continues:

> That language, which contains the seeds of their most intimate identity, will be put to the test when the voyage is over, especially if the migrants are moving to a foreign land. This is because those who await them at the new location have their own dead, their own ceremonies and cemeteries, and, of course, their own tongue.

The voyage, even if accomplished successfully (whatever this means), leaves deep marks and scars. We learn different languages, assume different linguistic identities that may confuse others and sometimes ourselves.

The threat to the survival of values, practices, and history that is posed by migrations is not limited to individuals and communities. History is full of examples (and we discuss some of them in subsequent chapters) of linguistic groups and regions whose experiences include language conflict, inherent incompatibilities between language communities, reluctance of the majority group to concede linguistic rights to minorities, the power of civil servants to protect their linguistic privileges, and the important and unpredictable material and symbolic consequences of linguistic choices (Pool 1991).

Even entire countries can feel insecure about their linguistic survival under threats coming from outside. Consider Iceland, one of the few monolingual countries in the world and practically the only surviving example in Europe of a linguistically homogeneous nation-state. Almost every Icelander speaks Icelandic as a first language and uses it as the dominant language in all spheres of life (Vikor 2000). Even without an internal linguistic issue, however, the country still felt compelled to protect its own identity, closely linked with its language. For about four hundred years there were numerous attempts to purge the Icelandic language of foreign, mostly Danish, influence. More recently, the dominance of English has become a serious threat to Icelandic identity, which developed through centuries of isolation, literary works, and the fostering of independent cultural values. The protection of their language included the successful attempt by Icelanders to persuade Microsoft to add Icelandic to the list of languages supported by Windows. It took more than six years of persistent lobbying by Icelandic authorities to overturn an initial refusal by Microsoft, but in 2004 the company produced an Icelandic version of Windows XP and the Office Packet of associated programs (Corgan 2004). In the beginning of the twenty-first century Iceland was still spending about 3 percent of its gross domestic product on activities related to the promotion and defense of its language, including translating and printing an astonishing number of foreign textbooks and fiction. Recently, Iceland engaged in serious attempts to become a member of the EU. While the survival of the language is not usually listed as a reason for the European shift in the country's foreign policy, one can notice, nevertheless, that the language's protection would receive a tremendous boost from the EU's multilingualism policy.

Iceland notwithstanding, almost all countries are multilingual. Indeed, the 2009 edition of *Ethnologue* lists 6,909 distinct living languages spoken all over the world, and since there are only 271 nations, dependencies, and other entities, the issue of linguistic diversity appears almost everywhere. Even though many of these nearly seven thousand languages are spoken in small and often remote and isolated communities, ethnic and linguistic heterogeneity is not an exclusively Third World phenomenon. Despite a long tradition of nation-states in Western Europe, most countries there are multilingual, with a plethora of indigenous regional languages such as Welsh in the United Kingdom, Catalan, Basque, and Galician in Spain, Provençal, Breton, and Occitan in France, and Frisian in the Netherlands. Obviously, in the study of societies that consist of several groups of citizens, one has to take into account various aspects of diversity, including wealth, geography, history, religion, and ethnicity. Each of these factors has an effect on the strength of the country's economic and political institutions, its growth, its stability, and its patterns of wealth redistribution.

The preservation of linguistic diversity and respect for the cultural heritage of members of a society is an important and much-needed task. However, in making policy and operational decisions, one has to recognize two caveats in protecting an excessive degree of diversity:

There is no free lunch for diversity. Sustaining a high degree of societal diversity could require allocating substantial resources to creating educational institutions and developing communication and coordination between groups. The financial cost and communication barriers may have a negative impact on national unity and, in general, may heavily burden the proper functioning of the society's institutions. It is difficult to assign a precise cost to sustaining diversity, but this cost nevertheless exists and is, in some cases, far from negligible. As Harvard economist Martin Weitzman (1992, 363) points out:

> Often there is an implicit injunction to preserve diversity because it represents a higher value than other things, which by comparison are "only money." Yet laws of economics apply to diversity also. We cannot preserve everything. There are no free lunches for diversity. Given our limited resources, preservation of diversity in one context can only be accomplished at some real opportunity cost in terms of well-being forgone in other spheres of life, including, possibly, a loss of diversity somewhere else in the system.

When is the meal too salty? How much salt do we want in our meal? No salt is not good at all for most customers, but by gradually increasing the amount of salt, we may quickly move from tasteless to uneatable. Shouldn't there be an optimal amount of salt, not too little, not too much? Also, how many spoons of sugar are needed for our morning coffee or tea? Some do not use sugar at all, Russians put three or four spoonfuls in their tea and drink the tea with the spoon in the cup, continually stirring their sticky beverage. Again, an optimum has to be found somewhere between zero and four, five, or six. Some art lovers may find black-and-white paintings rather dull, but adding an excessive number of colors does not necessarily make a painting more attractive. In all these examples—salt, sugar, colors—there exists an optimal degree of diversity that ensures a tasty meal, a pleasant cup of coffee, or sometimes a beautiful painting.

A study of diverse societies may suggest that there is an upper bound to the degree of heterogeneity that still guarantees proper and sustainable functioning. If it is too diverse, the society may fail to develop and implement policies acceptable for large groups of its citizens, and even the basis of societal existence could be questioned and threatened. The challenges of making everybody happy or even obedient are tremendous, and the eventual collapse of the Macedonian, Roman, Ottoman, and Mongolian empires was in large part caused by the inability of their rulers to keep all diverse and distant parts of their kingdoms under a unified rule. This happened not that long ago with the Russian empire, and it is happening now in China with Tibet and Xinjiang. One can wonder (as many do) whether the potential inclusion of countries such as Turkey and Ukraine in the EU would increase diversity within the EU to a degree that would rule out a reasonable compromise among its members.

Naturally, the determination of linguistic policies that reflect an "optimal" degree of diversity is a very challenging and delicate task. After all, language, like religion, "does not lend itself easily to compromise" (Laponce 1992, 599). Since language is an intimate part of individual and group identity, restricting linguistic rights may alienate and disenfranchise groups of individuals whose cultural, societal, and historical values and sensibilities are perceived to be threatened. The long and bloody ethnic conflict in Sri Lanka, the main roots of which lie in the complex relationship between two major linguistic groups, the Sinhalese and the Tamils, shows how emotional and explosive the restriction of linguistic rights may become.

The design of desirable linguistic policies in a multilingual society should also take into account the place of English in our current economic, social, scientific, educational, and cultural environment.[2] As Abram De Swaan (2001, 186) points out, "All societies in the contemporary world are being transformed by the spectacular increase of trade, transport and electronic communication. This 'globalization' proceeds in English." David Crystal (1999, 105) estimates that English is spoken by about one and a half billion people: 400 million use it as a mother tongue, 400 million as a second language, at least 150 million use it fluently as foreign language, and "four or five times this number with some degree of competence." Actually, the current role of English was accurately predicted by Alphonse de Candolle, a prominent Swiss scientist (not a linguist), in an essay written in French and published in 1873. Thus Candolle (1873):[3]

> [O]ne has to think why some languages are preferred to others. During
> the 17th and 18th centuries, there existed good reasons why French

---

[2] Also, looking at the not so distant past, we should not underestimate the role played by English in determining postcolonial linguistic policies in Asia and Africa.

[3] Our translation from the French. We are grateful to Dean Simonton for this reference.

succeeded Latin in Europe. At the time, French, a relatively simple and clear language, was spoken by a large proportion of educated people. It had the advantage of being close to Latin, which was well known. An Englishman or a German would know half of French if he knew Latin. A Spaniard or an Italian would know three quarters of it. A discussion or a paper written in French would have been understood by everybody.

During the 19th century, civilization has extended to the north [of France] and the population has increased more there than in the south. The use of English tripled as a consequence of the United States. Science is more and more cultivated in Germany, England, Scandinavia, and Russia.

The following conditions have to be satisfied for a language to become dominant: (1) it must include enough words, or Germanic and Latin forms, to be understood by both German and Latin populations; (2) it must be spoken by a large number of civilized people. It would also be convenient for such a language to be simple and clear.

English is the only language that could, within the next 50 or 100 years, offer all these conditions. The future predominance of the Anglo-American language is obvious.

Crystal (2003, xii) gives an excellent overview of the realities and reasons why English became a global language. It is worth quoting the opening words of the preface to his book, which show that Candolle's conjecture came true in about the length of time he had expected (fifty to one hundred years after 1873):

It all happened so quickly. In 1950, any notion of English as a true world language was but a dim, shadowy, theoretical possibility, surrounded by the political uncertainties of the Cold War, and lacking any clear definition or sense of direction. Fifty years on, and World English exists as a political and cultural reality.

Mario Vargas Llosa (2001), the 2010 Nobel Prize winner for literature, considers all this with more optimism:

There is no doubt that, with globalization, English has become the general language of our time, as was Latin in the Middle Ages. And it will continue to ascend, since it is an indispensable instrument for international transactions and communication. But does this mean that English necessarily develops at the expense of the other great languages? Absolutely not. In fact, the opposite is true. The vanishing of borders and an increasingly interdependent world have created incentives for new generations to learn and assimilate their cultures, not merely as a hobby but also out of necessity, because the ability to speak several languages and navigate comfortably in different cultures has become crucial for professional success.

Nevertheless, the role of English as a potential lingua franca has to be examined very carefully. English is spoken *almost everywhere* around the world, but it is still far from being spoken by *almost everyone*. In fact, even in the EU more than half the population does not speak it.[4] Mrinal Pande (2009) offers an interesting account of the dramatic decline in the circulation of English-language newspapers in India. After 1947, English newspapers were considered national outlets. While catering to a small part of the population, for about fifty years they collected the lion's share of advertising revenues. However, at the same time, India experienced the growth of the vernacular press, especially the Hindi press. Already in 1936, the Indian politician Madan Mohan Malviya had prevailed on the owners of the *Hindustan Times* to launch a Hindi daily to serve the common man. Pande (2009) describes this nicely as follows:

[T]he Hindi journalists underwent a unique expansion of the heart and mind as they began to report and write and absorb the fascinating reality of India beyond its big cities and the party headquarters offices. Their writings may have been less polished, their dailies less well-produced, but it was as though India had at last learnt to speak for itself. It is this aspect of the vernacular media, including in Hindi, which one finds the most beautiful and endearingly human. And with this, the Hindi newspapers, as in the case of their Tamil, Telugu, Kannada or Bengali counterparts, managed to create a republic for the humblest readers sitting far away in Samastipur or Farrukhabad or Almora.

At the beginning of the twenty-first century the readership in Uttar Pradesh, Bihar, and Jharkhand recorded a phenomenal annual growth of 14 percent. As Pande points out, news-hungry readers in Bihar were ready to spend five rupees a copy for a slim Hindi newspaper, almost three times the price of the (considerably fatter) English dailies. The 2009 Indian Readership Survey indicates that no English newspaper makes it into the top 10 Indian dailies, six of which are in Hindi. The total daily sales figures of India's largest-selling English daily, *The Times of India* (about 13 million copies a day), falls far behind that of the leading Hindi papers, *Dainik Jagran* (56 million), *Dainik Bhaskar* (34 million), *Amar Ujala* (29 million), and *Hindustan* (27 million).

[4]See chapter 7.

Vargas Llosa's optimism notwithstanding, one also has to recognize that to some extent, the ascent of English leads to a disenfranchisement of large sectors of the world community.

Assuming that a society can be and is kept together, our discussion indicates that the optimal degree of linguistic diversity will, in general, be reached when the society adopts more than one language, but possibly less than the entire set of languages spoken by all its members. In addition to the collective and public aspects of decision making in multilingual societies, which satisfy some efficiency criteria while bridging the "diversity gap," one of the goals of the book is to address individual decisions (such as acquiring foreign languages, making migration decisions, and choosing occupations) that are influenced by a society's linguistic diversity.

Recently the word *diversity* has became very popular in a wide range of contexts. There is an ever-growing number of diversity consultants, officers, and advisers whose role and function are to preserve and enhance diversity in political bodies, firms, federal and municipal offices, and universities. The University of Bologna in Italy, jointly with Austrian and Bulgarian universities, has created a new PhD program in diversity management and governance whose objective is to offer training in ethnic, cultural, linguistic, regional, religious, and other types of diversity. To train somebody in diversity, it would be good to have a precise meaning of the concept, which is also indispensable for a consistent quantitative analysis of linguistic or other types of diversity. We believe that diversity should not be considered a phenomenon outside the realm of social sciences, and hence it becomes necessary to assign a value to diversity and to offer theoretically and empirically sound ways to measure it. In short, we adopt Weitzman's (1992, 363–64) position: "If a value of diversity can be meaningfully postulated, then it can, at least in principle, be made commensurate with other benefits and costs."

One of the main goals of this book is to give a precise meaning to linguistic and to some extent ethnolinguistic diversity and to relate them to the notion of proximity or remoteness of groups associated with various languages. It is easy to agree that Italian and Spanish are linguistically closer to each other than either is to Polish or German. However, the notion of linguistic distance is often debated, and the question of its adequacy in representing dissimilarities between languages is still open. Indeed, the comparisons of vocabularies of various languages by Swadesh (1952) and later by Dyen, Kruskal, and Black (1992) fall short in accounting for the full complexities of linguistic proximity (or lack thereof). To address this issue, we extensively discuss what is meant and implied by linguistic, genetic, and cultural distances. We show further that distances and diversity play an important role in explaining a host of economic phenomena and situations.

Chapter 2

LINGUISTIC POLICIES, DISENFRANCHISEMENT, AND STANDARDIZATION

Les langues sont les étendards des peuples dominés.[1]
—Claude Hagège (2000), Le souffle de la langue

FROM RICHARD THE SECOND TO SRI LANKA AND YUGOSLAVIA. *Thomas Mowbray was exiled by Richard II to Venice, where he died, hopeless, because he could not master Venetian and could not use his native English. Likewise, many Sri Lankans died because some wanted to live their life in Tamil, while others were adamant about using Sinhalese. The pain of a language divide, artificial or real, was also visible in the break up of Yugoslavia.*

We start the chapter with a brief tour of linguistic challenges faced by mankind since what is known as the curse of the Tower of Babel. To guarantee cohesiveness and efficiency in a society, some compromising on language standardization, rooted in Max Weber's rationalization theory, becomes an essential part of public policies. Though standardization is appealing, it may have the undesirable consequence of disenfranchising various groups in a society. In this chapter we discuss both facets and describe various examples of standardization policies, as well as their intended and unintended consequences.

1. LINGUISTIC DIVERSITY: A BRIEF LOOK AT THE PAST

The challenge of linguistic diversity is not a creation of modern times. It is well documented over the course of human history, as well as in faiths and myths born out of human imagination. The most famous example is the consequence of the attempt of the people to build a

[1] "Languages are the flags of dominated peoples."

tower in Shinar, Babylonia, to be closer to the sky. God disliked the idea, descended, and, according to the Bible, "confuse[d] their speech, so that one person will not understand another's speech. God scattered them all over the face of the earth, and they stopped building the city" (Genesis 11:1–9).

Identical myths are also present in many other civilizations, though the tower to reach God is not always necessary. A Hindi myth tells a similar story featuring a wonder tree that reached heaven and was punished by Brahma, who cut off its branches, which fell to earth and created differences in languages. Iroquois Indians were guided by a god and directed to different areas, where their languages changed. In an Australian tribe with a unique language, diversity came about from eating an unfriendly woman who had died. But since the population ate from her at different times, they were led to speak diverse languages. In Greek mythology it was Hermes, the messenger of the gods, who confused languages. There are more down-to-earth examples as well. The Rosetta Stone is inscribed with three scripts: hieroglyphic, for priests; demotic, used for daily purposes; and Greek, the language of the administration.

It is somehow vexing that, in the past, multiplying the number of languages was considered a punishment or a curse sent by the gods (the Babelian curse), while today it is language disappearance that we are concerned with. In this sense, linguistic policies matter, since they may help to preserve languages, revive them (such as Hebrew, in Israel), or create new ones, as discussed in chapter 3.[2]

One should add that artificially constructed languages enjoy limited success in their attempts to gain official recognition and become leading players on the world's (or even the region's) linguistic scene. The most famous one, Esperanto, a Romance-German blend, was invented in 1867 by the Russian oculist Ludwik L. Zamenhof in the multilingual city of Bialystok, where, at the time, Polish, Russian, Yiddish, German, and Lithuanian were all widely spoken. At various points Esperanto enjoyed a wide following, and it still attracts some interest: as of January 3, 2010, the word "Esperanto" had received 66 million hits on Google. Esperanto counts several million speakers in various countries (the estimates vary), including the famous financier and philanthropist George Soros. Another Esperanto speaker, the Nobel Prize winner in economics and German game theorist Reinhard Selten, helped establish the Academy of Sciences in San Marino,

---

[2]Needless to say, policies, intentionally or otherwise, can sometimes also kill languages. North American native languages were replaced by English, French, Spanish, or Portuguese, while Coptic lost out to Arabic in Egypt.

the only institution in the world where Esperanto is the medium of instruction. Other examples of constructed languages include Slovio and Interlingua. Slovio is an artificial Slavic language created by Slovak linguist Marko Hucko about ten years ago to serve as a universal language easily understood by the 400 million speakers of Slavic languages. While it is too early to judge its success, it is evident that the hopes for Interlingua, an artificial language created by Giuseppe Piano and Edgar de Wahl in the first quarter of the twentieth century as the international language of science, have failed to materialize. The inability of the many—some say there are over 360—constructed languages to achieve the role and influence their creators aimed for can be attributed to the lack of broad international support and the unwillingness of large segments of the world's community to grant artificial languages the status and recognition needed for their growth and expansion.

2. Linguistic Standardization: Roots, Benefits, and Some Examples

The importance of linguistic policies is highlighted by the fact that about one-third of the world's nation-states have official language provisions in their constitutions. Public policies concerning linguistic diversity in various societies, countries, unions, and international organizations increasingly appear at the forefront of public debate. Linguistic diversity and, in particular, the treatment of minority languages are almost unparalleled in terms of their patriotic and emotional appeal. However, in searching for an optimal and sustainable degree of diversity, one inevitably has to examine public policies that, while entailing concessions and compromises, nevertheless impose, explicitly or implicitly, some degree of standardization, a part of Max Weber's rationalization theory.[3] The requirements of calculability, efficiency, predictability, and control over uncertainties lead to bureaucratization and the creation of a common legal system and a common language used for administrative purposes.

Such linguistic rationalization or standardization can be achieved through different means.[4] One way is merely choosing the language

[3] Rationality and rationalization are main themes of Weber's work. Here we essentially refer to his 1914 essay, published in German in 1922 and translated into English in 1968. See Weber (1968).

[4] See Laitin (2000).

of the majority group—such as French in France, Han Chinese in China, Kuotsugo Japanese in Japan. Another way is to recognize a lingua franca, a language spoken by the majority of the population but that is not the mother tongue of a large group in the country (Swahili in Tanzania, Bahasa in Indonesia, or even English in the United States). Finally, standardization can be achieved by recognizing the language of a minority group. Spanish in South America is such a case; other examples are Amharic in Ethiopia and Afrikaans in South Africa. These policies have been, however, reversed: the current Ethiopian constitution allows teaching in regional languages, whereas South Africa has eleven official languages, all endowed with equal constitutional rights. The last two examples indicate that in some cases a unique language is not sufficient to serve the needs of the entire population, and the concept of rationalization has to be modified to some kind of standardization.

One of the most intriguing and innovative examples of a policy aimed at balancing efficiency, national pride, sensitivity, and the economic well-being of several linguistic groups was undertaken in India some fifty years ago.[5] The so-called three-language formula was introduced as a national policy resolution in response to bitter complaints from southern states, in which Hindi is not widely spoken (mainly by Tamil Nadu). They claimed that the use of Hindi in government services was disadvantaging southern residents, who had to learn two languages, English and Hindi, whereas Hindi speakers had to learn only English. The three-language formula (with some variations across states) implied that children in Hindi-speaking states would study three languages, Hindi, English, and one of the modern, preferably southern, languages, whereas children in non-Hindi-speaking states would be taught Hindi, English, and their regional language. The arrangement generated complaints from the Urdu-speaking minority, who claimed that children of Urdu speakers were forced to learn the regional language instead of their mother tongue. The formula was therefore adjusted to account for the Urdu group grievances, and Urdu became the first language of choice in Andra Pradesh, Gujarat, Maharashtra, Bihar, and Karnataka.[6] This masterful and well-crafted formula, which seemed, in one fell swoop, to achieve group identity,

[5] See Laitin (1989).

[6] There were other complaints of this sort, suggesting that native speakers of minority languages in states where neither Hindi nor English was a state language were forced to study three languages in addition to their native one: Hindi, English, and the state language. Since the Hindi-speaking states require learning two languages, Laitin (1989) labeled the three-language formula the 3 ± 1 arrangement.

preservation of mother tongues and regional languages, national pride and unity (through the spreading of Hindi), and administrative efficiency and technological progress (by means of acquiring English), failed to achieve the success that the formula's creators were hoping for. The reasons were insufficient funding, lack of teachers, inadequate support of the regional administration, and little enthusiasm on the part of students and their families to make the required effort to learn languages spoken in other regions. In Hindi-speaking regions relatively little effort or resources were put into studying English, and even less into learning a third language. In Tamil Nadu, English and Tamil are studied quite extensively, whereas Hindi receives lip service.

A variant of the three-language formula was introduced in another multilingual state, Nigeria, the most populous African country, with 141 million inhabitants who speak 527 languages[7] and are divided into 250 ethnic groups. Nigeria has faced and continues to face tremendous linguistic challenges. In fact, almost every African country turned out to be "a principal victim of God's wrath aimed against those who constructed the Tower of Babel" (Laitin 1994, 623). English is the official language in Nigeria and is used in government and education, but Hausa (spoken by 18.5 million in the north), Igbo (spoken by 18 million in the south east), and Yoruba (spoken by 19 million in the south west) are "official regional" languages. In addition, Edo, Efik, Adamawa Fulfulde, Idoma, and Central Kanuri have "some degree of official status" (Crystal 1999, 231). The three-language formula, based on the use of Hausa, Yoruba, and Igbo, was considered a unifying device for this diverse country. However, its implementation was inhibited by the lack of qualified instruction and the resistance of the linguistic groups identified with one of the languages that were forced to learn another major language.

A similar challenge was faced by Ghana,[8] which, like Nigeria but unlike India, has no indigenous lingua franca that could have served as a unifying language in various administrative and educational aspects of public life. The sole official language of law and administration is English.[9] But as Laitin (1994, 625) writes:

> Most Ghanian citizens are convinced that it is necessary to learn English to get a well-paid job in the modern sector and surmise from this that it is unrealistic to educate their children through the medium of an indigenous language. But most Ghanians have inchoate feelings that

[7] By comparison, India, with over one billion inhabitants, has "only" 452 languages.
[8] The main source for the Ghana discussion is Laitin (1994).
[9] Nevertheless, nine languages are government sponsored.

continued reliance on English is tearing them from their own cultural roots. This reliance is seen as a remnant of colonialism. In terms of linguistic policy, Ghanians are pulled in opposite directions.

Using game-theoretic arguments, Laitin outlines the coordination challenge of Ghana: while Ghanaians would prefer an indigenous language to English, there is no agreement as to which should be chosen. In any case, giving the status of official language to some indigenous languages while denying it to others does not seem to be a viable political strategy. The feeling of disenfranchisement by some linguistic groups and of a distorted linguistic balance affected by such shifts of linguistic policies is difficult to overcome.

In fact, the balanced development of indigenous languages was achieved through the reforms implemented in 1991 by Jerry Rawlings, the military leader of Ghana at that time. During his administration the number of districts with assemblies formed through nonpartisan, local-level elections almost doubled, from 65 to 110. Education, infrastructure development, and health care were all devolved to the districts, which also began to receive annual government subventions. Smaller district sizes and their enhanced linguistic homogeneity, combined with an increased level of local authority, made for intense public debates, often conducted in indigenous languages. One parallel development was the emergence of the speech form that relies on English and Akan languages (with Akim, Brong, Fanti, Nzema, and Twi as the main languages of the group). This form is spoken by about 37 percent of the population and is used for interethnic communication. It is identified neither with the Akan group nor with English, and hence is not considered a threat to indigenous languages. Laitin (1994) called for a three-language formula in which the new speech form and district languages would receive official recognition while English would retain its role in the administrative and legal domains. The search for a balanced linguistic policy that would take into account the wishes of numerous linguistic and ethnic groups continues to be an important challenge for Ghana.

3. SOME PAINFUL ASPECTS OF STANDARDIZATION

It is unavoidable that balanced linguistic policies entail some degree of standardization. However, it could be that delivering benefits in terms of increased trade, enhanced economic cooperation, and reduced social conflict is accompanied by restrictions on the use of native languages. Here we offer two striking examples of the pain caused by the loss of one's native language. The first is the story of Thomas Mowbray, who was exiled by Richard II to Venice, where he died because he could not master Venetian and could not use his native English. The second, much more painful one describes how many Sri Lankans died because some wanted to live their life in Tamil, while others demanded to speak only Sinhalese.

For Thomas Mowbray's plight, we turn to William Shakespeare. In act 1, scene 3 of *Richard II*, the king and his uncle, John of Gaunt, try to convince Henry Bolingbroke, Gaunt's son and the king's first cousin, and Thomas Mowbray, the Duke of Norfolk, to stop quarreling.[10] Henry continues to accuse Thomas of the murder of the king's brother, the Duke of Gloucester.[11] The king is unable to calm the warriors down and allows them to compete in a joust, then stops the joust and delivers punishments to both Thomas and Henry. Mowbray is banished from England forever and Bolingbroke for ten years. Henry does not say much, but Thomas makes two relevant points before leaving the play. First, he correctly predicts that Henry will retaliate and defeat the king.[12] Even more interesting, though, is Thomas's reaction to his banishment. He does not lament the loss of land or status but rather talks about the inability to speak his native language in exile:

> A heavy sentence, my most sovereign liege,
> and all unlook'd for from your Highness' mouth,
> A dearer merit, not so deep a maim
> As to be cast forth in common air,
> Have I deserved at your Highness' hands.
> The language I have learn'd these forty years,
> My native English, now I must forgo;
> And now my tongue's use is to me no more
> Than an unstringed viol or a harp,
> Or like a cunning instrument cas'd up,
> Or, being open, put into his hands
> That knows no touch to tune the harmony:
> Within my mouth you engaol'd my tongue,
> Doubly portcullis'd with my teeth and lips;

[10]We are grateful to Michael Corgan (2004) for refreshing our memory and reminding us about the scene.

[11]The charge was actually false. As a matter of fact, the murder was ordered by the king himself.

[12]Later, Henry Bolingbroke secretly returns to England and usurps the king's power. He then becomes King Henry IV.

And dull, unfeeling, barren ignorance
Is made my gaoler to attend me.

Finally, the complaint of despair and hopelessness, recognizing Thomas's inability to master another language[13] (at the time, he was only forty years old):

I am too old to fawn upon a nurse,
Too far in years to be a pupil now.
What is thy sentence, then but speechless death,
Which robs my tongue from breathing native breath?

Even though the king's decision was not driven by considerations of linguistic policy, Thomas Mowbray's plight is not an isolated episode. Various linguistic policies tend to alienate groups of individuals, whose cultural, societal, and historical values and sensibilities are perceived to be threatened by what we may call linguistic disenfranchisement, as linguistic rights are restricted or even denied.[14]

The long and bloody ethnic conflict in Sri Lanka (formerly Ceylon) shows how emotional, explosive, and dangerous the choice of official or national languages may become. Sri Lanka has two major ethnic and linguistic communities, Sinhalese, predominantly Buddhist, and Tamil, predominantly Hindu,[15] that peacefully coexisted for about two thousand years. After one hundred fifty years under British rule, the island attained self-governance in 1948, which triggered attempts by both groups (the so-called *swabasha* movement) to promote their respective language, replacing English as the official language of (then) Ceylon. Though the swabasha movement had originally unified the two groups, it soon became the Sinhala-Only venture. The reasons for this shift were rooted in economics, nationalism, and religion. A superior system of teaching English in northern Tamil regions allowed Tamils easier access to and numerically disproportionate representation in university education and jobs in the prestigious government sector. According to deVotta (2004, 46–47), in 1946, "Tamils made up 33 percent of the civil service and 40 percent of the judicial service. They also accounted for 31 percent of the students in the university system.

[13]While Thomas leaves the play, history tells us that he died in Venice, about a year after his banishment. He definitely did not have time to acquire Venetian.

[14]The term disenfranchisement for languages was introduced by Ginsburgh and Weber (2005) and Ginsburgh, Ortuño-Ortín, and Weber (2005).

[15]The 2009 *CIA World Fact Book* estimates that the Sinhalese majority and the Tamil minority constitute respectively some 74 and 18 percent of Sri Lanka's population of about 21 million people.

In the medical and engineering fields, Tamils numerically equaled the Sinhalese."

The advancement of a larger number of educated Tamils reduced their support for the swabasha movement, and the desire to receive a larger piece of the national pie drew many Sinhalese into supporting the Sinhala-Only movement. This was led by Buddhist monks, who claimed that not only the Sinhala language but Buddhism itself would be threatened if parity between Sinhala and Tamil were sustained. Another important element in rejecting Tamil was the Sinhalese fear of being dominated by the well-developed Tamil literature and culture. The introduction of the Sinhala-Only Act in 1956 had dramatic consequences, very clearly emphasized by deVotta (2003, 124):

> The Tamil protests that accompanied the passage of the Sinhala-Only Act were unprecedented. When the bill was introduced on June 5, 1956, the Tamil Federal Party organized a satyagraha (peaceful protest) outside the parliament building. The Tamil protest was met by a counter-protest organized by the [activist Sinhalese group] Eksath Bhikku Peramuna. A mob representing the latter attacked the Tamil protesters and was responsible for unleashing riots that killed nearly 150 Tamils. Tamil leaders characterized the Sinhala-Only Act as a form of *apartheid*.

The tension did not subside, and the riots continued: "The passage of the Sinhala-Only Act was a turning point in the Sinhalese-Tamil relations. Tamil grievances subsequently grew, because in Sri Lanka as elsewhere, language policies had wide-ranging implications for educational and economic opportunities" (Brown and Ganguly 2003, 11). By the 1970s, a large part of the Tamil youth had become both radicalized and militarized. The government undertook a range of conciliatory measures toward the Tamil minority. Following the 1977 riots, the government abolished controversial university entrance policies, and the 1978 constitution officially awarded Tamil the status of a *national* but not yet an *official* language.[16] A constitutional amendment in 1988 gave Tamil the status of an official language, but the uncertain meaning and inconsistent implementation of the language-related articles of the constitution only reinforced the obvious: too little too late. A full-fledged civil war was already ravaging the country. Tens of thousands of lives were lost over the course of twenty-six years of fighting, before the conflict recently came to an uneasy halt.

As the case of Sri Lanka makes clear, history shows that a complicated web of linguistic relationships may lead to conflicts whose

[16]The recognition was actually granted earlier, in 1972.

outcome is difficult to predict. Linguistic tensions were and still are crucial in many conflicts all over the globe, and often forcefully overlap with the political agenda. Bernard Spolsky (2004, 10) points to another telling example:

> Often neighboring dialects are close enough to their neighbors to be mutually intelligible. Sometimes political borders divide this chain, so that mutually intelligible dialects might be classified as belonging to two different languages. ... In the same way, political concerns regularly lead to disputes whether a variety is one language or two. Using purely linguistic criteria and mutual intelligibility, linguists claimed that Serbo-Croatian was a single language whereas ... Croatian linguists had no doubt that Serbian and Croatian are as distinct as the Scandinavian languages.

The explosive mix of linguistic issues, nationalism, and civil war was indeed evident during the painful and bloody breakup of Yugoslavia, still fresh in our minds. As Spolsky (2004, 154) notes, "Language played a double role in the disintegration of Yugoslavia, first as an issue used by raising nationalism and secondly as an instrument for developing ethnic hatred." The roots of the conflict are linked to Yugoslavia's linguistic arrangements that existed between World War II and 1991 (the actual breakup of the country was formalized in 1992, with the secession of Slovenia and Croatia). Under President Tito, Yugoslavia had recognized six "nations": Serbs, Croats, Slovenians, Macedonians, Montenegrins, and Muslims. Each had a geographic home in one republic: Serbia, Croatia, Slovenia, Macedonia, Montenegro, and Bosnia-Herzegovina, respectively. In addition, some other linguistic minorities—Albanians, Bulgarians, Czechs, Hungarians, Italians, Roma, Ruthenians, Slovaks, and Turks—were granted various degrees of cultural and linguistic rights, which, however, did not eliminate ethnic and linguistic tensions. In particular, the autonomous regions of Vojvodina and Kosovo witnessed various degrees of ethnic and linguistic conflict long before those tensions boiled over some twenty years ago.

The French linguist Claude Hagège (2000, 2005), who is said to know more than fifty languages, is adamant concerning the importance of French for Europe: "[the] fight for French is a fight of the mind." Though this may be less poetic than Shakespeare, and certainly less dramatic than what happened in Sri Lanka or Yugoslavia, it reflects an opinion that is shared by most European countries that reject the predominance of English as a lingua franca in the EU, an issue discussed further in chapters 7 and 8.

4. How Many Languages: Is More the Merrier, or Is Small Beautiful?

One of the important aspects of the trade-off between standardization and disenfranchisement is the problem of choosing official or working languages in a multilingual society. It is, of course, much easier to standardize in a country where all citizens speak the same language (though they may also speak more than one), as in Portugal. It is already much less so in neighboring Spain, where Spanish is the native language of 73 percent of the population, Catalan is native to 10 percent, Galician to 8 percent, and Basque to 1.5 percent. Catalonia and Galicia lobby hard to have their native languages recognized as official ones in the EU. The actions of some Basque movements for the recognition of their status (not only with regard to their native language) have even taken a more violent form.

On the one hand, the exclusion of one's native language from the set of official languages could have far-reaching economic and emotional consequences. As Pool (1991, 495) points out, "[t]hose whose languages are not official spend years learning others' languages and may still communicate with difficulty, compete unequally for employment and participation, and suffer from minority or peripheral status." On the other hand, opting for a low level of linguistic standardization and too large a number of languages for educational, commercial, and other types of officially sanctioned activities may generate financial costs and communication barriers, which have a negative impact on national unity. The cost of services required to maintain a larger number of official languages could be quite substantial.[17]

In many situations, there is a repeated claim that the extensive use of various languages and excessive multilingualism restrict the ability of citizens to communicate with each other and dilute the sense of national unity and identity. Thus, some degree of linguistic standardization is essential to balance linguistic rights with the requirements of economic efficiency and a proper organization of society.[18]

Pool (1991) expands on the reasons why it is difficult to find a stable and fair resolution of the issue of official languages.[19] The reasons include the divisive, symbolic, and contentious nature of

[17] In chapter 8 we discuss the specific costs of multilingualism in the EU.

[18] One has to be mindful of the warning issued by Grin (1996), who suggests that "[even] researchers need to exercise caution when applying the principles of economic modeling to language issues."

[19] See also Van Parijs (2005).

language conflict; inherent incompatibilities between language communities; reluctance of the majority group to concede linguistic rights to minorities; the power of civil servants to protect their linguistic privileges; and the important and unpredictable material and symbolic consequences of linguistic choices. There is, however, an important difference between the implications for social, economic, and political participation and those that relate to national pride and patriotism. A person whose native language is not accepted as a working language can still get (nearly) all social, economic, and political benefits if she speaks one of the working languages or, to a lesser degree, if the list of these languages includes one that is sufficiently close to her own. But her sense of national pride would nonetheless be adversely affected, even if she were perfectly fluent in one of the working languages.

The trade-off between the economic advantages of standardization and the unwelcome consequences of disenfranchisement is part of a more general problem that often emerges in collective decision making, in which increasing returns to scale have to be weighed against individual or group diversity. Increasing returns to scale and considerations of economic efficiency tend to support greater standardization, whereas group diversity may tip the scale in the opposite direction and dictate a reduction in standardization. This is similar to the political economy question discussed by Alesina and Spolaore (2004)—whether the optimal size of a country is large or small. In general, the benefits of size are neither negligible nor unlimited, and we may see "medium-size" solutions emerging. Indeed, on the one hand, economic considerations lead to the emergence of larger countries, which benefit from the increasing returns to scale of large markets, whereas citizens of smaller countries may have a stronger say in decisions about their economic, political, and cultural life. If one considers a future in politics, joining a larger party could bring greater potential benefits, perks, and prospects. However, membership in a larger group may force an individual to accept decisions and platforms that could be distant from her choices and preferences. On the other hand, "small is beautiful,"[20] and a decision must be made in the individual case as to which of the two opposing forces has a stronger influence on the optimal outcome.

---

[20]This is the title of the 1973 book by the influential and unorthodox German-born English economist F. E. Schumacher. The expression is credited to his teacher and mentor, Leopold Kohr.

5. SUMMARY

Many governments, whether democratic or less so, in the past as well as in the present, have tried to reduce the number of official languages in use in the country of their governance. French, for instance, was imposed in France by Cardinal Richelieu, minister to Louis XIII, in the early seventeenth century to save the unity of the country. Such standardization was never fully accepted, and some four hundred years later, there is still support for local languages in some regions. In fact, several languages—Breton, Corsican, German, Italian, Occitan, Portuguese, and probably Picard—are still each spoken by more than 300,000 French citizens. The notion of "one state, one nation, one language" is nevertheless accepted by most citizens. In other cases, standardization policies have produced long and bloody conflicts, as in Sri Lanka.

In short, the economic advantages of standardization are important, but the threat of survival and the feeling of disenfranchisement by those who face restrictions of their linguistic privileges, deemed to be rights, have to be taken into account. Respecting the will of the people is a necessary condition for any sustainable success of long-range policies in a democratic setting.

The success or failure of linguistic arrangements in a multilingual society mainly depends on the willingness of citizens to buy into the policy and their desire (or lack thereof) to support and implement it. Hebrew succeeded in becoming a lingua franca in Israel, alongside the languages of the various groups of immigrants from North Africa and Eastern Europe. This was partially due to the tremendous efforts by the government and government-related organizations to immerse immigrants in Hebrew schools (*ulpans*) on their arrival. An even more important factor, however, was the willingness of the immigrants to accept the ideas and ideology that led to the creation of the state.

While standardization disenfranchises groups of citizens, it also offers prospects for better communication, enhances administrative efficiency, and strengthens a nation's cohesiveness. Though the trade-off between standardization and disenfranchisement is well documented, the search for an optimal and desirable degree of standardization is a delicate and challenging task.

Chapter 3

LINGUISTIC, GENETIC, AND CULTURAL DISTANCES: HOW FAR IS NOSTRATIC?

> Belladonna, n.: In Italian a beautiful lady;
> in English a deadly poison. A striking example
> of the essential identity of the two tongues.
> —*Ambrose Bierce*

NOSTRATIC IS A HYPOTHETICAL URSPRACHE *that was recon-*
structed by linguists during the nineteenth and twentieth centuries as
the root of five or six important families of languages: Indo-European,
Uralic, Altaic, Dravidian, Kartvelian, and Afro-Asiatic. Like most other
reconstructions, it was criticized by some linguists and enthusiastically
accepted by others. The same happened more recently with the words
that Merritt Ruhlen discovered in what he claims to be the very first lan-
guage.[1] *Two of the more recent scholars of Nostratic, Aron Dolgopolsky*
and Vladislav Illitch-Svitych, even locate the Urheimat of Nostratic in
the Mesolithic Middle East, possibly in Palestine. More disputes to come.

Merritt Ruhlen's (1994a) quest allowed him to reconstruct twenty-
seven words of the very first language, born in Africa 50,000 or 100,000
years ago.[2] Some linguists raised eyebrows about the words themselves, but not so much about the idea that all languages descend from
one or a very small number of languages. This hypothesis is backed
by biology and genetics. If this is so, languages can be represented in
the form of a tree similar to genealogical trees, starting with a root
representing the first language, or ancestor, and followed by branches
and twigs for the descendants. This implies, of course, that languages
are related by their vocabulary, syntax, phonology, and so forth in the
same way that children are genetically related to their parents and

---

[1] Ruhlen is a distinguished linguist who works on the classification of languages and
is professor at Stanford University, where he collaborated for thirty years with Joseph
Greenberg, whose work we will meet many times in this book.

[2] See Ruhlen (1994b).

more distant ancestors. Genetic differences are relatively easy to trace, and DNA analyses have become common to check disputed relations. It is more difficult to count the (dis)similarities between languages, since many characteristics, not only vocabularies, are involved.

The linguistic, genetic, and cultural aspects of a society or a nation are often correlated, since all three are closely linked not only to nature but also to learning and history, that is, nurture. One can therefore wonder when it is appropriate to choose one or the other in representing the proximity of individuals or groups to which they belong. In some cases, one of the measures is obvious. This is so when describing the difficulty of acquiring a foreign language, though even here there may be other types of proximities at work between, say, a Swedish and a Danish speaker than the mere proximity of the two languages. Otherwise there is no obvious answer, and certainly no theory to invoke. The three aspects discussed in this chapter leave this as an open question, but in chapters 4 and 7 we point to several empirical papers where one or the other (or all three) have been used.

1. Languages and Dialects

Before we turn to the problem of measurement, it is useful to know how many languages exist, how many will be left to our heirs, and what distinguishes a language from a dialect. The 2009 edition of *Ethnologue* lists 6,909 languages currently spoken in the world.[3] Whether this number is large or small can be debated, as can the number itself, since it results from a rather subjective count. As *Ethnologue*'s editor, M. Paul Lewis, notes (2009, 9), "every language is characterized by variation within the speech community that uses it. Those varieties are more or less divergent and are often referred to as dialects, which may be distinct enough to be considered separate languages or sufficiently similar" to be called dialects. Moreover, "not all scholars share the same set of criteria for distinguishing a language from a dialect." The criteria used in *Ethnologue* (2009, 9) to arrive at a count of languages and language users "make it clear that the identification of a 'language' is not solely within the realm of linguistics."

---

[3] *Ethnologue: Languages of the World* is a comprehensive catalogue of the world's living languages. The project started in 1951. The 2009 edition, 1,250 pages thick, is a mine of information on languages, where they are spoken, and the number of speakers in each country. If no other source is mentioned, this is the information that is used in our book. *Ethnologue*'s Web site, http://www.ethnologue.com, contains a language family index and language trees.

A couple of examples are useful. *Ethnologue* lists fifty-seven Zapotec languages in Mexico. Some of those, such as Zapotec (San Augustin Mixtepec), count less than one hundred first-language speakers. The largest, Zapotec (Isthmus), has 85,000 speakers. In contrast, *Ethnologue* also lists five dialects in the Flemish part of Belgium (Antwerps, Brabants, Limburgs, Oostvlaams, and Westvlaams) that are certainly all spoken by more than one hundred people and, though they are considered close to Dutch, can probably not be understood by a Netherlander from Amsterdam. Is Québéquois close to French? This is not so obvious, since on French TV, French Canadian series are often subtitled in French.

Little is known about what happened between the birth of the first language and the appearance of the large number of languages that exist today, or about the pace at which some languages were born while others died.[4] Most of what we know was reconstructed by linguists on the basis of languages that exist today or extinct languages for which we have written documents, such as ancient Greek. Obviously, some languages have disappeared or are no longer spoken as first languages. Latin is one such language, but there are certainly many others that we ignore. Hebrew, which was no longer spoken as a first language, has been revitalized and is now Israel's official language.

Slavery and explorations, followed by colonization, had the effect of killing languages at a fast rate. So do, today, mass tourism and globalization. According to Andrew Dalby (2004, ix), "in the present century, 2,500 languages are likely to be lost—which is what happens when the last living speakers turn to another language. A total of 2,500 languages in a hundred years is an average of one language every two weeks," and many people (including linguists) fight against the advancing dominance of English as a world language.

At a time of deforestation, pollution, and global warming and their effects on biodiversity, it is tempting to draw a parallel between the loss of languages and the loss of animal and botanic species, and strive for a maximal level of linguistic diversity. But an equivalence between languages and physical species is not that easy to support. Kibbee (2003, 51), for example, rejects it on the ground that "[a] language is a behaviour, not a physical characteristic. If two languages are in contact, then they influence each other. If a dog lives in the same house as a bird it does not grow wings, nor does the bird sprout paws."

To mitigate the frightening prospect of linguistic and cultural loss, there is good news, as new languages and cultures are also being born.

---

[4]Glottochronology is a science that tries to date when languages diverged from a common source language.

This is certainly what Claude Lévi-Strauss would have thought, he who said in one of his last interviews in 2002:

> On peut se dire, en tout cas c'est un voeu pieux, qu'au moment où nous craignons une uniformisation universelle, en sous-main, sourdement, de nouvelles différences commencent à apparaître que nous ne pouvons même pas percevoir, mais que nos héritiers comprendront et qui, je l'espère, seront exploitées.[5]

Ethnologue (2009, 29) lists seventy-seven creole languages that were created by Dutch, English, French, Portuguese, Russian, or Spanish colonization. These languages resulted from a blending (and from a simplification of the grammar, vocabulary, and style) of the local language and the colonizer's language and have become the mother tongues of many communities. Some examples are Papiamentu (spoken in the Netherlands Antilles), Virgin Islands Creole English (Virgin Islands), Saint Lucian Creole French (Sainte Lucie), Korlai Creole Portuguese (India), and Aleut Mednyj (Russian Federation). In an interesting *Newsweek* article from March 7, 2005, "Not the Queen's English: Non-native Speakers Are Transforming the Global Language," the author distinguishes more than fifty varieties, including British English (BBC English, English English, Scottish English, Scots, Norn, Welsh English, Ulster Scots, Hiberno-English, Irish English), American English (Network Standard, Northern, Midland, Southern, Black English Vernacular, Gullah, Appalachian, Indian English), and Canadian English (Quebec English, Frenglish, Newfoundland English, Athabascan English, Inuit English). Spanglish is not mentioned in *Ethnologue* but is becoming important in the United States, where it is used by a growing community and won acclaim since MIT's creative literature professor Junot Díaz received the 2007 National Book Critics Circle Award for Best Novel and the 2008 Pulitzer Prize for *The Brief Wondrous Life of Oscar Wao*, written in Spanglish.[6]

"Old" languages enrich each other and create exciting new blends that obviously share some or many characteristics with their predecessors.[7] Nobody can claim that newcomers to the linguistic scene, such as the many creoles or Spanglish, are inferior to Rabelais's French, Shakespeare's English or Cervantes' Spanish—none of which can be

---

[5] "We may hope that at the very same time during which globalization is taking place, somehow, in a secret way, new differences are appearing that we cannot perceive but that will be understood by our heirs."

[6] And for which there even exists an *Annotated Oscar Wao: Notes and Translations for the Brief and Wondrous Life of Oscar Wao*. See http://www.annotated-oscar-wao.com.

[7] See the very entertaining book on this issue by McWhorter (2001).

easily understood today by a nonspecialist. The same is true for cultural, ethnic, and religious traits, as is shown by Bisin and Verdier (2000), who describe the theoretical processes that can give birth to what we observe in terms of cultural mixtures. Sushi was exported to the United States, changed there to reflect local tastes, and is now "reimported" as such into Japan.

How can we decide that an idiom (language, dialect, variety) is different from another, and does this matter? Theoretically, one could take into account distances between every two languages, including dialects and the unimaginably large number of varieties, and decide on a threshold that would distinguish "languages" from small variations consisting of a few words, expressions, or ways to pronounce them. This would, however, require a huge effort.[8] Meanwhile, such distances, which play a very important role in our book, can and have been calculated by linguists for a large number of families of languages on all continents. Linguistic and to some extent genetic and cultural distances constitute the backbone of this book.

Given the large number of topics and different facets of linguistic distances and proximity, we divide this chapter into two parts. In section 2 we focus on the distances between languages themselves and on their proximity or dissimilarities. In section 3 we extend our discussion to linguistic distances and proximity between groups of individuals or entire regions and countries in which they live.

2. Distances between Languages

As travelers, we often feel terribly frustrated by our inability to communicate with locals. This desperation is related to the distance between the languages we know and the one spoken in the country we visit. Languages can be distant from each other in many ways. Vocabulary is often thought of as being the main separator, and indeed, though English and German are part of the Indo-European family and belong to the same branch of so-called Germanic languages, the English word *moon* is related to but differs from *Mond* in German. And both differ strongly from the French *lune*, though French is also an Indo-European language but belongs to the branch referred to as Romance languages. *Moon* and *Mond* even have different genders: the first is neuter, the second is masculine, and *lune* is feminine.

---

[8] It is undertaken for German dialects in a recent paper by Falck et al. (2009).

The pronunciation of *moon* is perhaps closer to *Mund* (German for "mouth") than it is to *Mond*, especially if it is poorly pronounced. The final *e* in *lune* is mute, while the *a* in the Italian or Spanish *luna* is not. Diphthongs, sounds composed of two vowels joined to form one sound, as in *sound*, also add to the difficulty of a language. But the French student of English may wonder why the *ou* in *south* is not pronounced like the one in *tour*. Therefore, pronunciation also contributes to the distance between languages. Phonetics and phonology refer to the production of various sounds (phonemes) in each language by means of lips, tongue, teeth, pharynx, and lungs. Both the production and the perception of phonemes differ across languages. Each language has phonemes that may prove difficult for non-native speakers to acquire. It seems easier for a native speaker of a language with a large number of phonemes to learn a language with fewer phonemes, since for her, both the production and the perception of sounds are more developed.[9]

Syntax, the "way in which linguistic elements (as words) are put together to form constituents (as phrases or clauses)"[10] illustrates another difference between languages. *I would like to observe the moon* translates into *Ich möchte (gerne) den Mond beobachten*. While the word *observe* is located in the middle of the English sentence, its translation, *beobachten*, is in terminal position in the German sentence. It is quite difficult to grasp quickly the meaning of *fünfundzwanzig* euros when the German taxi driver tells you how much you ought to pay for the ride; the meaning is "twenty-five," but an English speaker hears it "five and twenty" in German (as well as in other Germanic languages, such as Dutch or Danish).

Grammar is of course another worry. For instance, German has declinations; Dutch does not. None of the declinations that exist in Latin were inherited in contemporary (spoken) French, and a French student who did not have to learn Latin or Greek (or German) at school will hardly know the meaning of the word declination.

These are just a few examples to illustrate that computing the distance between two languages is a stiff challenge, even without getting into the fundamental issue of whether languages have a common structure.[11]

We first describe *lexicostatistical* distances, which are based on one dimension only, the similarity of vocabularies between languages.

---

[9]See Ladefoged and Maddieson (1996) for an extensive discussion.

[10]*Merriam-Webster Dictionary*, http://www.merriam-webster.com/dictionary/syntax.

[11]On the fights that this controversy still generates, see Harris (1993) and Baker (2001).

Biologists construct biological and evolutionary trees using what they call cladistics, a term that comes from the Greek root κλαδος (klados) for branch. To generate a tree, the method starts with a table that lists several animal or vegetal species, as well as characteristics describing the various species supposed to have a common ancestor. Cladograms (trees) are then constructed using the information given by the descriptive characteristics, and the "best" tree is then identified. Implicitly, cladistics also utilizes weights to generate the resulting tree, and therefore shares some of the challenges outlined above.

This idea is now adopted by linguists, who construct language trees on the basis of several linguistic characteristics, including lexical, phonological, and syntactic dimensions.[12]

2.1. Lexicostatistical Distances

Lexicostatistical distances are based on similarities and supposed common roots of words in the vocabularies of various languages. Following Ruhlen (1994a, 12), languages can be related or similar, and these similarities can be explained by three mechanisms only. There may be words that look common for accidental reasons. This is so for onomatopoeic words such as *mama* or *papa*. Languages may also borrow words from other languages belonging to another branch. English, for example, contains many French words. And finally, two languages may have descended from a common, older language.[13] This is the case for French, Italian, Spanish, and Portuguese, which belong to the same branch and have Latin as ancestor. Lexical distances are built on so-called cognate words, occurring in languages with a historical chain linking them via an earlier language, thus ignoring not only borrowings[14] and accidental similarities but also

[12]See Nakhleh et al. (2005) for a description and an example of the construction of the Indo-European language tree.

[13]Dyen, Kruskal, and Black (1992) give the very poetic example of the word *flower*, which is borrowed from the French *fleur*, while quite surprisingly *blossom* and *fleur* descend from the same ancestral word.

[14]Ignoring borrowed words may rule out some factors that influence the closeness of two languages. The case of English and French is a good example. According to Janson (2002, 157–58), "around 90 per cent of the words in an English dictionary are of French, Latin or Greek origin." This, however, does not make English closer to French, since "if one counts words in a text or in a recording of speech [in English], the proportion of Germanic words is much higher, for they are the most frequent ones, while most of the loans that figure in a dictionary are learned, rare items." The French linguist Claude Hagège (2009, 647–70) adds that English is particularly difficult to learn. He probably had in mind French speakers, but his remarks seem to be more general.

syntax and grammar. The reason is that linguists became (and still are) interested in constructing language trees (lexicostatistics), as well as in estimating dates at which one language separated from another (glottochronology).[15]

Since it would be a daunting task to compare long lists of words for each couple of languages, linguists are forced to rely on a small selection of carefully chosen words, a so-called "list of meanings." Morris Swadesh (1952) introduced some rigor (Kessler 2001, 31) into the choice of meanings that one can assume to be basic enough to exist in all languages and cultures (such as animal, bad, bite, black, child, die, eat, eye, hunt, and the digits from one to five), on which deductions can be based.[16] The list we are interested in consists of two hundred basic meanings (which Swadesh later trimmed to one hundred), and is still in use today.

Joseph Greenberg (1956) was probably the first linguist to introduce formally the notion of distances between languages. To produce a uniform quantitative measure of linguistic diversity in different regions of the world, he constructed several diversity indices, discussed here and in chapter 6. His index B, called the *monolingual weighted method*, relies on a language resemblance factor. To formalize the notion, Greenberg (1956, 110) suggested using "an arbitrary but fixed basic vocabulary, e.g., the most recent version of the glottochronology list, [and compute] the proportion of resemblances between each pair of languages to the total list. ... Since we are measuring actual resemblance, not historic relationship, it is suggested that both cognates and loans be included as resemblances." Dyen, Kruskal, and Black (1992) followed up on this idea using Dyen's basic list to classify eighty-four Indo-European speech varieties.[17] They describe the lexicostatistical method as consisting of four phases:

[15]The premises on which glottochronology is based—in particular, that the probability of a word losing its original meaning stays constant over time—are in question, and this area of research fell into some disrepute. See, however, Gray and Atkinson (2003) and Searls (2003) for a recent revival of the concept.

[16]See Kessler (2001, 199–257) for the lists of meanings chosen by Swadesh.

[17]Classifications of languages into families have been produced for several families of languages. See, for example, Dyen (1965) for Austronesian languages and Greenberg (1987) for native American languages. The conjecture that Aryan languages spoken in parts of India and European languages may have a common ancestor was made by William Jones in 1786. See Gamkrelidze and Ivanov (1990), and also Ruhlen (1994a) for a general overview. Though we also deal with more general applications in chapters 4 and 7, here we discuss only Indo-European languages in some detail.

1. Collecting for each of the meanings the words used in each speech variety under consideration (this is what was done by Swadesh, and by others for other language groups).

2. Making cognate decisions on each word in the lists for each pair of speech varieties, that is, deciding whether they have a common ancestral word or not, or whether no clear-cut decision can be made. This phase is performed by linguists who know the language family (here Indo-European).[18]

3. Calculating the lexicostatistical percentages, that is, the percentages of cognates shared by each pair of lists. These percentages lie between 1 (if all words are cognate; actually, the largest number of cognates found by Dyen, Kruskal, and Black was 154, leading to a percentage of 0.770) and 0 (if there is no cognate).

4. Partitioning the word lists into family trees. This is done using one of the many existing clustering algorithms.

The following comments will clarify steps 1 to 4. Table 3.1 gives an example of word lists for the basic meanings of digits one to five (which are part of Swadesh's basic meanings) in twelve languages. This is essentially what is done in step 1, for a much larger list of meanings and languages.

Step 2 is devoted to comparing words for every pair of languages.[19] This is of course made simple here, since the languages are already presented in some convenient order. The words in the first five languages (Danish, Dutch, English, German, Swedish) are all cognates, as the pairwise comparisons show. They constitute the Germanic branch of languages. The same can be verified for the next four languages (French, Italian, Portuguese, Spanish), which belong to the Romance branch. The third group (Cornish, Welsh) also has all five digits cognate. But more important, the first three digits in all three families can be seen to be cognates as well (and indeed, Germanic, Romance, and Celtic language families are part of the larger family of Indo-European languages). Cognation decisions are less obvious and need more linguistic knowledge for the digits four and five. The last language (Swahili) belongs to the Bantu family, and it is clear that the words have little in common with those of the three families of Indo-European languages, but they may nevertheless have a distant

---

[18]See Warnow (1997) for further technical details.

[19]It is not always possible to make a clear distinction between cognate and noncognate; therefore, linguists usually add a third group of "ambiguous decisions."

TABLE 3.1. Words for digits 1 to 5 in some Indo-European
languages and in Swahili

	1	2	3	4	5
Danish	en	to	tre	fire	fem
Dutch	een	twee	drie	vier	vijf
English	one	two	three	four	five
German	eins	zwei	drei	vier	fünf
Swedish	en	två	tre	fyra	fem
French	un	deux	trois	quatre	cinq
Italian	uno	due	tre	quattro	cinque
Portuguese	um	dois	três	quatro	cinco
Spanish	uno	dos	tres	cuatro	cinco
Welsh	un	dau	tri	pedwar	pump
Cornish	un	deu	try	peswar	pymp
Swahili	moja	mbili	tatu	nne	tano

Source: Kessler (2001, 11), except for Italian, Spanish, and Swahili.

ancestor.[20] In general, cognate decisions need trained linguists, as the
following example, borrowed from Warnow (1997, 6586), shows. The
Spanish word *mucho* has the same meaning as the English *much* and is
obviously phonetically very similar. Sound change rules do, however,
indicate that they do not come from a common ancestral word: *mucho*
is derived from the Latin *multum,* meaning "much," while *much* is
derived from the Old English *micel,* meaning "big."

Step 3 is easy once cognate decisions are made. It entails counting
the number of cognates for each pair of languages and dividing that
number by the total number of meanings. If the only meanings to be
compared were our five digits, then the distances between each pair of
the five Germanic languages would all be equal to 1. The same would
be true for the pairwise distances within the two other families. Things
get a little more difficult across the three families, since the words for
digits four and five (compare the English *four* with the French *quatre* or
the Welsh *pedwar*) are certainly farther apart. Assume that as linguists,
we are undecided to classify them as cognate or noncognate. Then the
distance between, say English and French, would be 3/5. Finally, in
our example the distance between any Indo-European language and
Swahili is zero.

---

[20]See Ruhlen (1994a) for a deep but also entertaining exposition. He makes the reader
construct the cognates and guess which languages belong to the same family or branch.
The book reads like a very good crime story in which the detective is not looking for a
criminal but for the very first language.

TABLE 3.2. Distances between selected Indo-European languages
(value × 1,000)

	English	French	German	Italian	Spanish	Polish
Albanian	883	878	870	877	883	871
Bulgarian	772	791	769	769	782	369
Catalan	777	286	764	236	270	784
Czech	759	769	741	753	760	234
Danish	407	759	293	737	750	749
Dutch	392	756	162	740	742	769
English	0	764	422	753	760	761
French	764	0	756	197	291	781
German	422	756	0	735	747	781
Greek	838	843	812	822	833	837
Icelandic	454	772	409	755	763	758
Italian	753	197	735	0	212	764
Latvian	803	793	800	782	794	668
Lithuanian	784	779	776	758	770	639
Norwegian	452	770	367	754	761	762
Polish	761	781	754	764	772	0
Portuguese	760	291	753	227	126	776
Romanian	773	421	751	340	406	784
Russian	758	778	755	761	769	266
Serbo-Croatian	766	772	764	755	768	320
Slovak	750	765	742	749	756	222
Slovene	751	782	733	760	772	367
Spanish	760	291	747	212	0	772
Swedish	411	756	305	741	747	763
Ukrainian	777	781	759	774	782	198

Source: Dyen, Kruskal, and Black (1992, 102–17).

To present these percentages in the form of distances that one is used to, the numbers given in table 3.2 are equal to 1 minus the percentage of cognates. They concern the distances between twenty-five European languages[21] and the six European languages that are most spoken in the EU: two are Germanic (English and German), three are Romance (French, Italian, and Spanish) and the last is Slavic (Polish). It is easy to check that Danish, Dutch, English, German, Icelandic, Norwegian, and Swedish are related. So are the Romance languages Catalan, French, Italian, Portuguese, Romanian, and Spanish, and the Slavic ones, Bulgarian, Czech, Russian, Serbo-Croatian, Slovak, Slovene, Ukrainian, Latvian, and to some extent Lithuanian. Albanian and Greek are distant from any language belonging to the three previous families.

[21] Basque, Estonian, Finnish, Hungarian, and Turkish (spoken in Cyprus) are excluded, since they do not belong to the Indo-European family. The distances from Indo-European languages could be set to 1 as an approximation.

Step 4 needs a clustering algorithm to construct a language tree. Figure 4.1a in chapter 4 shows a tree constructed from the distances calculated by Dyen, Kruskal, and Black for a subgroup of fifteen languages.[22] The reader interested in examples of linguistic trees as well as in detailed trees concerning all existing linguistic families should visit the Web site http://www.ethnologue.com/family_index.asp.

2.2. Cladistic Distances

Lexicostistical distances do not take into account various aspects of languages such as syntax, phonology, and borrowed words, for several reasons. As Laitin (2000, 148) notes:

> First, written forms could be quite different from spoken, and there were no general criteria for judging whether or how far two pronunciations needed to be from one another to be coded as a different word. Second, most languages have many words for each of the items on Swadesh's list, and for any word, [distance] could change based on which word in a set of synonyms was chosen. Third, ... linguistics, especially in the United States, focused almost entirely on structure by the 1960s, and much less on meaning. Therefore languages were coded based on mostly syntactic structures rather than on word relationships.

An alternative way of representing linguistic distances is to utilize linguistic tree diagrams, based on as many characteristics as possible (lexical and other). Fearon and Laitin (1999), Laitin (2000), and Fearon (2003), who suggested this approach, use the distances between linguistic tree branches as a proxy for distances between linguistic groups. In the original Fearon and Laitin (1999) index (LANGFAM), the score takes the level of the first branch at which the languages break off from each other for every pair of languages. The higher the number, the higher the similarity of languages.

We use the Indo-European language tree of table 3.3 to calculate such distances in some examples.[23] Czech and Hungarian come from structurally unrelated linguistic families: Czech is an Indo-European language, while Hungarian belongs to the Uralic family. Therefore,

---

[22]Dyen, Kruskal, and Black's distance matrix is used by Ginsburgh and Noury (2008), Ginsburgh, Ortuño-Ortín, and Weber (2005, 2007), Ginsburgh, Weber, and Weyers (2007), and Ku and Zussman (2008) in various contexts described in chapter 4.

[23]Though Indo-European languages were among the first to be discussed and represented in the form of a tree, this approach is now used for all the world's languages. For other families, see http://www.ethnologue.com/family_index.asp.

TABLE 3.3. Indo-European language tree (general)

```
0. Nostratic
    1. Afroasiatic
    1. Eurasiatic
        2. Eskimo-Aleut
        2. Chukotian
        2. Gilyak
        2. Korean-Japanese-Ainu
        2. Altaic
        2. Uralic-Yukaghirc
        2. Etruscan
        2. Indo-European (449)
            3. Germanic (53)
                4. East (1)
                4. North (11)
                4. West (41)
            3. Italic (48)
                4. Latino-Faliscan (1)
                4. Romance (47)
            3. Slavic (19)
                4. East (4)
                4. South (7)
                4. West (8)
            3. Albanian (4)
                4. Gheg (1)
                4. Tosk (3)
            3. Armenian (1)
            3. Baltic (3)
                4. Eastern (2)
                4. Western (1)
            3. Celtic (7)
                4. Insular (7)
            3. Greek (6)
                4. Attic (5)
                4. Doric (1)
            3. Indo-Iranian (308)
                4. Indo-Arian (219)
                4. Iranian (87)
                4. Unclassified (2)
```

---

the two languages share no common branches and break off at the first branch: their score is 1. Czech and Italian share one common level since both are Indo-European, but separate immediately after that, making their score equal to 2. Czech and Russian share two classifications: they are both Indo-European and Slavic, and break off at the third branch, as Russian belongs to the Eastern branch of the Slavic group, while Czech is in the Western branch. Thus, their score is 3. Czech and Polish share three common levels: in addition to being Indo-European and Slavic, both belong to the Western branch

TABLE 3.3. (cont.) Indo-European language tree (Germanic languages)

---

0. Nostratic
  1. Eurasiatic
    2. Indo-European (449)
      3. Germanic (53)
        4. East (1)
          5. *Gothic* [got] (Ukraine)
        4. North (11)
          5. East Scandinavian (6)
            6. Danish-Swedish (6)
              7. Danish Bokmåll (1)
                8. **Norwegian, Bokmål** [nob] (Norway)
              7. Danish-Riksmal (2)
                8. Danish (2)
                  9. **Danish** [dan] (Denmark)
                  9. *Jutish* [jut] (Denmark)
              7. Swedish (3)
                8. *Dalecarlian* [dlc] (Sweden)
                8. *Scanian* [scy] (Sweden)
                8. **Swedish** [swe] (Sweden)
          5. West Scandinavian (5)
            6. *Faroese* [fao] (Denmark)
            6. **Icelandic** [isl] (Iceland)
            6. *Jamtska* [jmk] (Sweden)
            6. **Norwegian, Nynorsk** [nno] (Norway)
            6. *Norn* [nrn] (United Kingdom)
        4. West (41)
          5. English (3)
            6. **English** [eng] (United Kingdom)
            6. *Scots* [sco] (United Kingdom)
            6. *Yinglish* [yib] (USA)
          5. Frisian (3)
          5. High German (20)
            6. German (18)
              7. *Frankish* [frk] (Germany)
              7. Middle-German (9)
                8. East Middle German (3)
                  9. **German, Standard** [deu] (Germany)
                  9. *Silesian, Lower* [sli] (Poland)
                  9. *Saxon, Upper* [sxu] (Germany)
                8. West Middle German (6)
              7. Upper German (8)
                8. Alemannic (4)
                8. Bavarian-Austrian (4)
            6. Yiddish (2)
          5. Low Saxon-Low Franconian (15)
            6. *Frisian, Eastern* [frs] (Germany)
            6. Low Franconian (4)
              7. **Afrikaans** [afr] (South Africa)
              7. **Dutch** [nld] (Netherlands)
              7. *Vlaams* [vls] (Belgium)
              7. *Zeeuws* [zea] (Netherlands)
            6. Low Saxon (10)

TABLE 3.3. (cont.) Indo-European language tree (Italic languages)

0. Nostratic
  1. Eurasiatic
    2. Indo-European (449)
      3. Italic (48)
        4. Latino-Faliscan (1)
          5. *Latin* [lat] (Vatican)
        4. Romance (47)
          5. Eastern (4)
            6. **Romanian** [ron] (Romania)
            6. *Romanian, Istro* [ruo] (Croatia)
            6. *Romanian, Macedo* [rup] (Greece)
            6. *Romanian* [ruq] (Greece)
          5. Italo-Western (38)
            6. Italo-Dalmatian (6)
              7. *Dalmatian* [dlm] (Croatia)
              7. *Istriot* [ist] (Croatia)
              7. **Italian** [ita] (Italy)
              7. *Judeo-Italian* [itk] (Italy)
              7. *Napoletan-Calabrese* [nap] (Italy)
              7. *Sicilian* ([scn] (Italy)
            6. Western (32)
              7. Gallo-Iberian (30)
                8. Gallo-Romance (14)
                  9. Gallo-Rhaetian (9)
                    10. Oïl (6)
                      11. French (5)
                        12. **French** [fra] (France)
                        12. *French, Cajun* [frc] (USA)
                        12. *Picard* [pcd] (France)
                        12. *Walloon* [wln] (Belgium)
                        12. *Zarphatic* [zrp] (France)
                      11. Southeastern (1)
                    10. Rhaetian (3)
                  8. Ibero-Romance (16)
                  9. East-Iberian (1)
                    10. *Catalan, Valencian, Balear* [cat] (Spain)
                  9. Oc (6)
                  9. West-Iberian (6)
                    10. Asturo-Leonese (2)
                      11. *Asturian* [ast] (Spain)
                      11. *Mirando do Douro* [mwl] (Portugal)
                    10. Castillan (4)
                      11. *Extramaduran* [ext] (Spain)
                      11. *Ladino* [lad] (Israel)
                      11. **Spanish** [spa] (Spain)
                      11. *Spanish, Loreta-Ucayali* [spq] (Peru)
                    10. Portuguese-Galician (3)
                      11. *Fala* [fax] (Spain)
                      11. *Galician* [glg] (Spain)
                      11. **Portuguese** [por] (Portugal)
                8. Pyrenean-Mozarabic (2)
          5. Southern (5)

TABLE 3.3. (cont.) Indo-European language tree (Slavic languages)

---

0. Nostratic
  1. Eurasiatic
    2. Indo-European (449)
      3. Slavic (19)
        4. East (4)
          5. **Belarusan** [bel] (Belarus)
          5. *Rusyn* [rue] (Ukraine)
          5. **Russian** [rus] (Russia, Europe)
          5. **Ukrainian** [ukr] (Ukraine)
        4. South (7)
          5. Eastern (3)
            6. **Bulgarian** [bul] (Bulgaria)
            6. *Slavonic, Old Church* [chu] (Russia, Europe)
            6. **Macedonian** [mkd] (Macedonia)
          5. Western (4)
            6. **Bosnian** [bos] (Bosnia and Herzegovina)
            6. **Croatian** [hrv] (Croatia)
            6. **Slovenian** [slv] (Slovenia)
            6. **Serbian** [srp] (Serbia and Montenegro)
        4. West (8)
          5. Czech-Slovak (3)
            6. **Czech** [ces] (Czech Republic)
            6. *Knaanic* [czk] (Czech Republic)
            6. **Slovak** [slk] (Slovakia)
          5. Lechitic (3)
            6. *Kashubian* [csb] (Poland)
            6. **Polish** [pol] (Poland)
            6. *Polabian* [pox] (Germany)
          5. Sorbian (2)
            6. *Sorbian, Lower* [dsb] (Germany)
            6. *Sorbian, Upper* [hsb] (Germany)

---

of the Slavic group, and their score is 4. Finally, Czech and Slovak belong to the Czech-Slovak sub-branch of the Western branch of the Slavic group, which sets their score at 5. In order to produce linguistic distances, the similarity measure r_{ij} between languages i and j is first normalized to fit the interval $[0, 1]$. For a break at the first branch, $r = 0$; for a break at the second branch, $r = 0.2$; for a break at the third branch, $r = 0.4$; for a break at the fourth branch, $r = 0.6$; for a break at the fifth branch, $r = 0.8$; and for identical languages, $r = 1$ (Laitin 2000, 148). The linguistic distance d is then simply equal to $d = 1 - r$.

Fearon (2003) produces an impressive data set for 822 ethnic groups in 160 countries. However, he points out that an early break between two languages in such a tree generates a higher degree of dissimilarity than later breaks. Therefore, the resemblance function r_{ij} should increase at a lower rate for larger values of distance. To sustain this

TABLE 3.3. (cont.) Indo-European language tree (other languages)

---

0. Nostratic
    1. Eurasiatic
        2. Indo-European (449)
            3. Albanian (4)
                4. Gheg (1)
                    5. *Albanian, Gheg* [aln] (Serbia and Montenegro)
                4. Tosk (3)
                    5. *Albanian, Arbëreshë* [aae] (Italy)
                    5. *Albanian, Arvantika* [aat] (Greece)
                    5. **Albanian, Tosk** [als] (Albania)
            3. Armenian (1)
            3. Baltic (3)
                4. Eastern (2)
                    5. **Latvian** [lav] (Latvia)
                    5. **Lithuanian** [lit] (Lithuania)
                4. Western (1)
                    5. *Prussian* [prg] (Poland)
            3. Celtic (7)
                4. Insular (7)
                    5. Brythonic (3)
                        6. *Breton* [bre] (France)
                        6. *Cornish* [cor] (United Kingdom)
                        6. *Welsh* [cym] (United Kingdom)
                    5. Goidelic (4)
                        6. *Gaelic, Hiberno-Scottish* [ghc] (United Kingdom)
                        6. *Gaelic, Scottish* [gla] (United Kingdom)
                        6. **Gaelic, Irish** [gle] (Ireland)
                        6. *Manx* [glv] (United Kingdom)
            3. Greek (6)
                4. Attic (5)
                    5. *Cappadocian Greek* [cpg] (Greece)
                    5. **Greek** (ell) (Greece)
                    5. *Greek, Ancient* [grc] (Greece)
                    5. *Pontic* [pnt] (Greece)
                    5. *Yevanic* [yej] (Israel)
                4. Doric (1)
                    5. *Tsakonian* [tsd] (Greece)
            3. Indo-Iranian (308)

---

feature, in his derivation Fearon utilizes the square root of linguistic distances rather than the distances themselves.[24]

Cladistic distances are coarser than lexicostatistical distances but are easy to compute for all language families, since linguistic trees (which also take into account lexicostatistical distances, when available) exist for almost all world languages.

---

[24]A variant of Fearon's formalization is used by Desmet, Ortuño-Ortín, and Weber (2009).

TABLE 3.3. (cont.) Indo-European language tree (explanations)

Note: The upper part of the tree in the first part of the table (with the exception of the Nostratic root) is based on Greenberg (2000, 279–81). The tree for Indo-European languages is constructed using *Ethnologue*'s Web site, starting with the root at www.ethnologue.com/show_family.asp?subid=90017, and then following the various branches. We stopped branching when languages became less important, but tried to have all the main official languages in use in Europe and elsewhere if this is the case. Estonian, Finnish, Hungarian, and Maltese are not in this table since they do not belong to the Indo-European family.

The numbers in front of the families and subfamilies represent the branches. For instance, "4. Attic (5)" means that Attic is at level 4 below Nostratic, since it is in the branching starting at "0. Nostratic." It is followed by "1. Eurasiatic," then "2. Indo-European," then "3. Greek," and finally "4. Attic." The (5) means that there are five Attic languages, the details of which can be found in the table under "Other Languages."

Languages are followed by the code of the language used by *Ethnologue* between square brackets and by the name of the country in which they are spoken. They are printed in bold characters if they are the (or a) main official language of a country, and in italics if they are not. For example, "9. **Danish** [dan] (Denmark)" is the official language of Denmark, while "9. *Jutish* [jut] (Denmark)" is not official.

2.3. Distances Based on Learning Scores

Given the difficulty of representing the distance between two languages by a unique encompassing number, Chiswick and Miller (2007, chap. 20) use an alternative measure based on the difficulty speakers of one language face in acquiring another (non-native) language. Such a measure was established by Hart-Gonzalez and Lindemann (1993) using a sample of native Americans who were taught a variety of languages and whose proficiency was measured at different moments of time. The scores (between 1 for difficult—Japanese and Korean—to 3 for easy—Afrikaans, Norwegian, Romanian, and Swedish) are assumed to correlate positively with distance.[25] Table 3.4 lists the full set of scores, some of which look quite surprising. Swahili, a Bantu language essentially used in Eastern Africa, is closer to American English than are German and French. One can, therefore, wonder whether scores are calculated "all other things being equal," and on a sufficient number of observations. To our knowledge, this is the only set of consistent data on learning.

---

[25] This distance is used in two papers by Chiswick and Miller (2007, chap. 1), as well as by Hutchinson (2003) and Ku and Zussman (2008).

TABLE 3.4. Scores of foreign students learning English.

Score	Language of Origin
3.00	Afrikaans, Norwegian, Romanian, Swedish
2.75	Dutch, Malay, Swahili
2.50	French, Italian, Portuguese
2.25	Danish, German, Spanish, Russian
2.00	Amharic, Bulgarian, Cambodian, Czech, Dari, Farsi, Finnish, Hebrew, Hungarian, Indonesian, Mongolian, Polish, Serbo-Croatian, Tagalog, Thai, Turkish
1.75	Bengali, Burmese, Greek, Hindi, Nepali, Sinhala
1.50	Arabic, Lao, Mandarin, Vietnamese
1.25	Cantonese
1.00	Japanese, Korean

Source: Chiswick and Miller (2007, 578).

If such distances were available for a large number of language pairs (and measured according to the same criteria), they would certainly be a very good alternative to lexicostatistical and cladistic distances, since they encompass most of the difficulties encountered in acquiring a language.

2.4. Garbage and Rubbish: Caveats in Using Distances

The distance between English and English is equal to 0, whatever the method used to measure it. This, of course, can raise eyebrows. There is a large (and ever-increasing) number of meanings that are represented by different words in the United States and Great Britain: *garbage* and *rubbish, cell phone* and *mobile, subway* and *tube, faucet* and *tap, janitor* and *caretaker, eraser* and *rubber, truck* and *lorry,* to cite a few. And though the British queen is Canada's head of state, Canadians do not always use similar words as Britons, and identical words can produce different meanings, as noted by Larry Selniker (2001), an American expert on language acquisition:

Take the word *scheme,* for example. On both sides of the Atlantic, *to scheme* suggests nefarious plotting. However, Britons would have no moral objections to going along with *a scheme,* while law-abiding Americans would still be horrified by the word's shady connotations. To *table* a motion in a British boardroom will see it discussed. In America, *tabling* something will see it put firmly on the back burner.

This gets even worse with languages such as "Spanglish" in the United States, "Konglish" (spoken by an older generation in South Korea), or "Globish," spoken everywhere.

This phenomenon is obviously not limited to English. The word cake requires different words in the Spanish-speaking world: *bizcocho* in the Dominican Republic, *torta* in Venezuela, and *tarta* or *pastel* in Spain. There are substantial differences between the German spoken in Germany and in Austria and there even exist Austrian-English dictionaries.[26]

Sue Wright (2007, 158), who spent some time in the European Parliament Babylonian environment, notes that "the high number of Brazilian interpreters was an issue for the Portuguese. Respondents stated that they were irritated by interpretation into a language that they saw as allied to their own, but not their own."

A further caveat in using lexicographic or cladistic distances is symmetry, which implies that the degree of difficulty experienced by a Frenchman in learning Portugese is the same as that experienced by a Portugese in learning French. This is probably true for vocabulary and, to some extent, for grammar. However, insofar as Portugese phonetics is richer than French phonetics, it may be easier for a Portugese speaker to learn French than the other way around. This is picked up by distances based on learning scores.

3. Distances between Groups

In this section we examine various aspects of linguistic, genetic, and cultural distances between *groups* of individuals, regions, or countries.

3.1. Linguistic Communication Distances

The issue raised by the linguistic distance between two countries is different from that of two languages, independent of where they are spoken. The notion of linguistic proximity between two countries has been applied to international trade, which models trade flows between pairs of countries as depending on some variables that measure the dimension of both countries (represented by income, for example) and possible frictions, such as tariff barriers, geographic distances, or the lack of a common language.[27]

[26]Published by Langenscheidt.

[27]Here we just give the essentials of the approach, which is discussed at some length in chapter 4.

A simple approach is to consider the linguistic distance as a dichotomous variable that takes the value 0 if the same language is used "extensively" in both countries (as is the case between Austria and Germany), and 1 otherwise.[28] Melitz (2008), for example, relaxes the notion of "extensive" to "widely spoken" if at least 20 percent of the population knows the language.

A better alternative is to estimate the likelihood that citizens in two countries can speak a common language. For this, one can use Greenberg's (1956) H index of communication or Lieberson's (1964) H_b index.[29] Greenberg's index refers to a multilingual society and is determined by the probability that two members of the population chosen at random will have at least one language in common. Greenberg's original H index is based on the random selection of two individuals from the joint populations of, say, Germany and France and allows for the possibility that either two French or two German citizens are chosen. Lieberson (1964) modified this index to evaluate the degree of communication between two linguistic communities.[30] To calculate H_b in our two-country case (Germany and France), we consider the total populations of both countries and take at random one citizen in each, France (Jean) and Germany (Hans). The probability that these two fellows speak no common language and are unable to communicate is then taken as the communication distance between Germany and France.

Let us consider the example with two languages first, and assume that all French and German citizens speak the language of their country, 20 percent of French citizens speak German, and 25 percent of Germans speak French; no other language is considered. If Jean and Hans are both monolingual, they cannot communicate. Since 80 percent of French citizens and 75 percent of Germans are unilingual, the probability that Jean and Hans are not able to communicate is $0.80 \times 0.75 = 0.60$.

The situation is more complicated if English is introduced, and some Germans and Frenchmen can also communicate in English. We adjust the previous example and assume now that in France, the population consists of four groups: 70 percent are unilingual (group F), 15 percent speak French and German (FG), 10 percent speak French and English (FE), and 5 percent speak all three languages (FGE). The distribution of

---

[28]The tradition in this literature is to set the distance between countries to 1 if they have a common language. This parametrization has no effect on the econometrics.

[29]Both are discussed in more detail in chapter 6.

[30]Lieberson (1969) applies this measure to analyze linguistic diversity in three Canadian cities, Toronto, Montreal, and Ottawa.

linguistic skills in Germany is such that 60 percent are unilingual (G), 15 percent speak German and French (FG), 15 percent speak German and English (GE), and 10 percent speak all three languages (GFE). Let us again pick an individual from each country. Note that for Jean and Hans to be unable to communicate, at least one of them must be unilingual. Indeed, if both speak at least two languages, they will share a common language. If Jean speaks French only (with probability 0.70) but Hans does not, that is, Hans belongs either to group G or GE (with probability $0.60 + 0.15 = 0.75$), Jean and Hans will be unable to communicate. The only case that remains to be covered is that of a unilingual Hans (with probability 0.60) and a bilingual Jean, who belongs to the group FE (with probability 0.10). The total result and the linguistic distance between two countries in this example is $0.70 \times 0.75 + 0.60 \times 0.10 = 0.585$.

Melitz (2008) uses this idea in his notion of "direct communication." He provides data on twenty-nine languages, each of which is spoken by at least 4 percent of the population in 157 countries.[31]

3.2. Genetic Distances

In the *Origin of Species*, Darwin had already understood that languages and genes (Darwin used the word "races") were strongly related. This is what he wrote:[32]

> If we possessed a perfect pedigree of mankind, a genealogical arrangement of the races of man would afford the best classification of the various languages now spoken throughout the world; and if all extinct languages, and all intermediate and slowly changing dialects, were to be included, such an arrangement would be the only possible way.

The real progress was made in the early 1960s, when it became possible to seriously study genetic material.[33] Populations can be distinguished by their genes, which are strictly hereditary.[34] There exist, for instance, several blood types (O, OA, OB, AA, AB, and BB), which are due to large variations of the forms (alleles) A, B, and O of

---

[31] See his appendix table A1, column headed "Spoken Languages." See also Mayer and Zignago (2005).

[32] Quoted by Cavalli-Sforza (2000, 167). See also Sokal (1988).

[33] See Cavalli-Sforza (1997), according to whom the first genetic tree of evolution based on gene frequencies of humans was published in 1963.

[34] The discussion is based on Cavalli-Sforza (2000, 13–25). A more technical approach is given in Cavalli-Sforza, Menozzi, and Piazza (1994).

the gene.[35] The frequencies of the three genes are 27, 8, and 65 percent for Europeans and 1.7, 0.3, and 98 percent for native Americans. The information on frequencies of a single gene, however, is not sufficient to draw firm conclusions on genetic differences (and distances) across populations, since such variations are also present in many other genes. The computation of genetic distances is therefore based on the study of alleles in a large number of different genes in thousands of individuals from different populations. The mathematical formulas used to compute such distances are described in Cavalli-Sforza, Menozzi, and Piazza (1994, 25–30), who suggest they all yield reasonably similar results.

Genetic distances based on living populations are used to construct trees to represent the successive separations and migrations among populations over time, and make it possible to date these separations.[36]

The matrix of genetic distances, reported in table 3.5, is as close as possible to the matrix of linguistic distances in table 3.2, though the genetic distances given in Cavalli-Sforza, Menozzi, and Piazza (1994, 270) do not cover exactly the same populations as those in table 3.2. Moreover, languages and populations are not necessarily in one-to-one correspondence, since the same language may be spoken in various countries.[37]

Some similarities are apparent between the two tables, but there are also striking differences. The distances between English, Danish, Dutch, German, and Norwegian genes are small. But English and German genes are even closer to French genes, though their languages are more distant. German and French genes are closer to each other than French genes are to Italian and Spanish genes. This shows that there exists a positive (and significant) correlation between linguistic and genetic distances, but it is not extremely large. Reasons can be found for these discrepancies. Though, for example, Hungarian (a

[35]Alleles are transmitted by both parents. An individual whose blood is of, say, type AB has inherited A from one parent and B from the other.

[36]This is due to the fact that genes and allele frequencies change over time according to very precise rules. Linguistic and phonetic transformations follow similar patterns, though the precise rules are subject to debate.

[37]Linguistic distances are given for Serbo-Croatian, while genetic distances are given for Yugoslavian. German, for instance, is spoken in Germany and Austria, and Cavalli-Sforza, Menozzi, and Piazza (1994) provide genetic distances for both populations; they also have an entry for the Swiss population in their table, a country and a population in which three languages, German, French, and Italian, are spoken. Research on genetic data and distances is ongoing—see, for example, Piazza et al. (1995)—but we are not aware of any data set as comprehensive as the one used to construct table 3.5.

TABLE 3.5. Genetic distances between selected European populations
(value × 10,000)

	English	French	German	Italian	Spanish	Polish
Czech	60	72	52	77	65	64
Danish	21	43	16	72	80	69
Dutch	17	32	16	64	76	54
English	0	24	22	51	47	70
French	24	0	27	34	39	66
German	22	27	0	38	69	47
Greek	204	131	144	77	162	177
Icelandic	76	146	106	143	163	144
Italian	51	34	38	0	61	64
Norwegian	25	56	21	88	97	58
Polish	70	66	47	64	117	0
Portuguese	46	48	51	44	48	65
Russian	79	59	60	75	122	30
Serbo-Croatian*	160	124	118	119	172	137
Spanish	47	39	69	61	0	117
Swedish	37	78	39	95	99	82
Basque	119	93	169	141	104	146
Finnish	404	350	314	339	452	395
Hungarian	70	70	46	61	118	25
Lapp	404	350	314	339	452	395

Source: Cavalli-Sforza, Menozzi, and Piazza (1994, 270).
*Yugoslavian in Cavalli-Sforza, Menozzi, and Piazza (1994).

non–Indo-European language) replaced a Romance language after the
Magyars invaded the region that is now called Hungary, the number of
Magyars who settled there was too small to impose a radical change on
the genetic stock, which explains the closeness of Hungarian to Polish
and German genes,[38] while their languages are not closely related at
all.

Table 3.5 also illustrates genetic distances for European populations that do not speak Indo-European languages (Basque, Finnish,
Hungarian, and Lapp). Together with Greek, Icelandic, and Serbo-
Croatian, these are outliers for which some objective explanations can
be found.[39]

Genetic distances are used in papers by Guiso, Sapienza, and
Zingales (2009), Giuliano, Spilimbergo, and Tonon (2006), Ashraf and
Galor (2008), Desmet et al. (2009), Spolaore and Wacziarg (2009),

[38] See Cavalli-Sforza (2000, 151ff.) as well as Cavalli-Sforza, Menozzi, and Piazza (1994, 268–72).
[39] See Cavalli-Sforza, Menozzi, and Piazza (1994, 272–77).

and Le Breton, Ortuño-Ortín, and Weber (2009), some of which are discussed in chapters 4 and 7.

3.3. Cultural Distances

Whorf (1956) and Sapir (1970), and more recently Cavalli-Sforza (2000), defend the idea that language and culture are partners, and thus correlated, but that language slows down cultural change. This link makes it useful to describe very briefly how cultural distances can be measured. They have been extensively studied and evaluated by Geert Hofstede (1980, 1991, 2001),[40] whose ideas started with a research project across subsidiaries of the multinational corporation IBM in sixty-four countries. Subsequent research by others covered students in twenty-three countries, elites in nineteen countries, commercial airline pilots in twenty-three countries, up-market consumers in fifteen countries, and civil service managers in fourteen countries. These studies identified and scored the following four dimensions:[41]

1. *Power distance*—A measure of the extent to which the less powerful members of a society accept that power is distributed unequally, it focuses on the degree of equality between individuals.

2. *Individualism*—A measure of the degree to which individuals in a society are integrated into groups, it focuses on the degree to which a society reinforces individual or collective achievement and interpersonal relationships.

3. *Masculinity*—A measure of the distribution of gender roles in a society, it focuses on the degree to which a society reinforces the traditional masculine work role of male achievement, control, and power.

4. *Uncertainty avoidance*—A measure of a society's tolerance for uncertainty or ambiguity, it also refers to man's search for truth.

[40] See also Rask (2004).

[41] The definitions are taken from http://spitswww.uvt.nl/web/iric/hofstede/page3.htm and http://geert-hofstede.international-business-center.com/index.shtml (April 2004), a Web page on which the data can also be found. Hofstede adds a fifth distance (long-term orientation) that originates in research conducted in twenty-three countries only. See Hofstede and Bond (1988).

Ginsburgh and Noury (2008) examined the correlation between lex-icostatistical distances and the aforementioned four measures for the average of twenty-two (mostly European) countries that participated in the annual Eurovision Song Contest between 1975 and 2003. The correlations are equal to 0.205, 0.254, −0.092, and 0.319, respectively, for power, individualism, masculinity, and uncertainty avoidance.

Shalom Schwartz revisited the topic starting in the early 1990s. He has written several papers on his research, including a very recent survey,[42] on which the following short description of his work—carried out between 1988 and 2002 in sixty-eight countries located on all continents, with a total number of 67,145 individual surveyed—is based.

His cultural dimensions are based on a priori theorizing. The cultures are arrayed along the dimensions between polar orientations. They prescribe how institutions and people should behave in order to deal optimally with the key problems that societies face. The following "poles" are considered:

1. *Autonomy vs. embeddedness.* To what extent should people be treated as autonomous (intellectually and affectively), or embed-ded in their groups?

2. *Egalitarianism vs. hierarchy.* How can human independencies be managed in a way that elicits coordinated, productive activity rather than disruptive behavior or withholding of effort?

3. *Harmony vs. mastery.* To what extent should individuals and groups control and change their social and natural environment or leave it undisturbed and unchanged?

Other researchers have measured cultural distances in a variety of ways. Desmet et al. (2009) suggest constructing cultural distances between nations using answers to the 430 questions related to per-ception of life, family, and religion and morals from the four waves of the World Values Survey.[43] Felbermayr and Toubal (2007) construct cultural distances between European countries using the scores given by expert or popular juries in the Eurovision Song Contest held every year since 1956, in which countries grade other countries' perform-ers.[44] The advantage is that distances are not necessarily symmetric,

---

[42]Schwartz (2010), which includes an important bibliography.

[43]These are currently available online at http://www.worldvaluessurvey.org/.

[44]Since 1998, citizens have been allowed to cast their votes by telephone or email. See more on the competition in section 5 of chapter 4.

since country A may have a different feeling for country B than B has for A. Such feelings may also change over time, and so may distances.

4. SUMMARY

In this chapter, we have offered a short, nontechnical overview of the types of distances (linguistic, genetic, and cultural) that will be used in the remainder of the book. It is worth stressing the conceptual difference between linguistic distances related to pairs of languages and genetic or cultural distances related to populations within a country or between countries. It may, of course, be the case that the three types of distances are strongly correlated within a fractionalized country, but other configurations are also possible. The same language, German, is spoken in both Austria and Germany, though the populations have different genetic structures and the cultures are not identical.

Chapter 4, as well as chapters 6, 7, and 8, illustrates how such notions are used, and how important they can be to explain economic outcomes.

Chapter 4

DISTANCES MATTER

> [We] have really everything in common with
> America nowadays, except, of course, language.[1]
> —*Oscar Wilde, The Canterville Ghost*

NEWTON'S APPLES. *Newton has two reasons to be invoked here. First, he is said to have made his discovery under a tree from which a few apples fell on his head. Apples were already there when the world started in the Garden of Eden. Why did it take so long for a scientist to think of gravity? Almost as long as it took for economists to think that distances were responsible for many economic phenomena, though they were there even before God created the Garden of Eden. Second, it so happens that Newton's gravity model is now used in economics.*

The linguistic, genetic, and cultural distances that we discussed in the previous chapter have important applications, and many economists have shown that they matter greatly. This chapter focuses on inter-country differences and their impact on trade, migration, translations, and certain aspects of voting behavior. Within-country differences and fractionalization aspects of linguistic diversity are examined in chapter 6.

Most applications of intercountry linguistic differences are based on what is now known as the gravity model, whose name comes from its analogy with Newton's 1687 law of universal gravitation. Newton's reasoning was that any two objects in the universe exert gravitational attraction on each other with a force, denoted f_{AB}, that is proportional to the product of their masses, m_A and m_B, and inversely proportional to the square of the distance d_{AB} that separates the two objects. Distance thus has a negative effect on the attraction force.

Jan Tinbergen, the very first 1969 Nobel Prize winner in Economics (jointly with Ragnar Frisch) and who had studied physics, suggested

---

[1]A similar saying is attributed to George Bernard Shaw: "England and America are two countries divided by a common language," and Bertrand Russell expressed the same feeling in the *Saturday Evening Post* in 1944: "It is a misfortune for Anglo-American friendship that the two countries are supposed to have a common language."

that the law of gravitation could be applied to study international trade flows between countries.[2] Now, the force f_{AB} represents the volume of exports from country A to country B, m_A and m_B are measures of wealth or income (population, gross domestic product), and d_{AB} is the geographic distance between, say, the capitals of the two countries A and B.

The gravitational analogy had been utilized even earlier by Torsten Hägerstrand et al. (1957), who applied it to migrational flows in Sweden.[3] The difference with Tinbergen's idea is that here, f_{AB} represents a flow of migrants between two cities or regions A and B. In both cases distances can be more generally thought of as costs and impediments to trade and migration. Though the gravitational equation had no theoretical economic underpinnings for many years, it became very popular, and fitted the data very well.

Section 1 is devoted to the best-known and most frequent application: international trade flows. Section 2 discusses migrational flows. The last two sections examine various aspects of mass culture. Section 3 analyzes the number of translations of literary works into and from various languages, whereas section 4 is devoted to a description of countries' voting patterns in the annual international Eurovision Song Contest.[4]

1. INTERNATIONAL TRADE

> [Wenn] Sie verkaufen und ich kaufe, sprechen wir Deutsch.
> Aber [wenn] Sie kaufen und ich verkaufe, dann sprechen wir
> Ihre Sprache.[5]
> —*Attributed to Willi Brandt*

1.1. Newton's Trade Equation

The basic gravitational trade equation can be written:

$$\exp_{AB} = \gamma + \alpha \times \text{GDP}_A + \beta \times \text{GDP}_B + \delta \times \text{dist}_{AB},$$

[2] Tinbergen (1962).

[3] According to Kerswill (2006, 4), who in turn cites it from a 1984 book by Gareth Lewis.

[4] The gravitational equation is used in other fields, for example to explain the flows of money laundering (Walker 2000). Other papers use linguistic distances without applying the gravity model. See, for example, Hix, Noury, and Roland (2007), who examine voting patterns in the European Parliament.

[5] "When you're selling and I'm buying, we speak German. But when you're buying and I'm selling, then we speak your language."

where γ, α, β, and δ are parameters whose values have to be assessed, $\exp_{AB}$ represents exports from A to B, GDP_A and GDP_B represent the economic power of both countries (often measured by their gross domestic products), and $dist_{AB}$ is the distance between A and B. The expected signs of α and β are positive: the richer a country, the larger its propensity to export or import; the expected sign of δ is negative, since an increase in distance should reduce the trade flow $\exp_{AB}$.

Note that in the trade equation, all variables are logarithms of the original variables. This simplifies somewhat the presentation, since we can interpret the parameters as elasticities. Take, for example, δ, which multiplies the distance term $dist_{AB}$, and assume $\delta = -0.80$. What this says is that if the distance between A and B is 10 percent larger than the distance between another pair of countries C and D, all other things (here GDP_A and GDP_B) being equal, exports from A to B will be 8 percent smaller than exports from C to D. Distance has an effect on trade, and a larger distance reduces trade.

The first applications were based on this simple model, but economists rapidly realized the importance of alternatives to simple geographic distances. The $dist_{AB}$ term was soon supplemented by other types of costs (or benefits), such as the transaction costs caused by the search for trading partners, bilateral tariffs, nontariff barriers (prohibiting imports of wines containing sulfites), countries' geography (adjacency, islandness, landlockedness, the presence of a common sea), former colonial links, immigration stocks (which could foster trade between countries through the building of social and commercial networks), as well as cultural, genetic, and linguistic distances.[6] Therefore, the simple $dist_{AB}$ term is replaced by several terms that contain the various frictions and distances.

A second issue that attracted economists' attention was the observation that the simple gravity model had a very loose connection with trade theory. James Anderson (1979) was the first to examine this issue, and many contributions have followed since.[7] Without going into a detailed discussion, we simply state that the introduction of trade-theoretical arguments led to a somewhat more complicated gravity-like equation that reads:

$$(\exp_{AB,t} + \exp_{BA,t}) = \gamma + \alpha \times (GDP_{A,t} + GDP_{B,t}) + \delta \times dist_{AB}$$
$$+ \text{ other variables.}$$

[6]Some researchers have added variables that represent common markets or common currency zones.

[7]Anderson and van Wincoop (2004) give an overview of today's state of the art in this line of research.

Note that in this new form, there is an additional index t, which represents time (years): $\exp_{AB,t} + \exp_{BA,t}$ is a bilateral trade flow (exports of A to B plus exports from B to A) in year t. The right-hand side of the equation contains the terms $GDP_{A,t}$, $GDP_{B,t}$, and $dist_{AB}$ of the simple equation, except that now $GDP_{A,t}$ and $GDP_{B,t}$ are also added, and theory tells us that the parameter α should not be significantly different from 1. Finally, the term $\delta \times dist_{AB}$ (which could also be taken as changing over time) is replaced by several terms that measure frictions of different kinds, such as geographic distance, the presence of a common border, former colonial ties, common languages, and so on.

1.2. The Curse of Distance: Some Empirics

Since we are mainly interested in the effect of language on trade, we chose to discuss at some length the recent results obtained by Jacques Melitz (2008), who has tested several possible ways of introducing the language dimension to explain trade flows. We also cover some applications that use genetic or cultural distances.

Melitz uses two measures of linguistic distances. The first, "open-circuit communication" (OCC), demands that the language be either official or widely spoken (at least 20 percent of the population knows the language). Spanish, for instance, is an OCC between Bolivia (where 44 percent of the population knows Spanish) and Mexico (88 percent). Likewise, Arabic is an OCC between Mauritania (38 percent) and Iraq (58 percent). Melitz identifies fifteen such languages. If two countries are linked through an OCC, the OCC distance is equal to 0. If they are not, the distance is 1.

The second measure is "direct communication" (DC). Here, Melitz takes any language common to a pair of countries (the language is "common" as long as it is spoken by at least 4 percent of the population in each country). He then computes the probability that two randomly chosen citizens, one in each country, can communicate in this language.[8] If several languages meet the 4 percent criterion, Melitz takes the sum of the probabilities over all common languages. This procedure approximates the probability that two citizens from two different countries can communicate with each other. The linguistic distance between the two countries is then defined as 1 minus that

---

[8]This probability is the product of the share of citizens who speak that language in each country.

TABLE 4.1. List of open-circuit communication (OCC) and
direct communication (DC) languages

OCC Languages	DC Languages
Arabic	Albanian
Chinese	Fang
Danish	Fulfulde
Dutch	Hausa
English	Hungarian
French	Italian
German	Javanese
Greek	Lingala
Hindi	Nepali
Malay	Pashto
Farsi	Quechua
Portuguese	Swahili
Spanish	Tamil
Swedish	Urdu
Turkish	

Source: Melitz (2008, 671).

probability.[9] The full set of direct communication languages, listed in table 4.1, consists of twenty-nine languages: fifteen OCCs and fourteen DCs.

The rationale for introducing the second measure is based on Melitz's claim that any linguistic distance measure works, but not all of them tell the same story.[10] He suggests distinguishing channels through which the effect takes place, and therefore separates OCCs, which depend on translation (which can be produced as long as there are enough people who can provide it in both countries), and DCs, which make possible direct communication between traders. The estimation results of Melitz, reproduced in table 4.2, point to four groups of significant effects: (1) wealth effects, (2) geographic distances, (3) political and economic links, and (4) linguistic effects:

1. *Joint GDPs:* The effect is positive and not significantly different from 1, as predicted by theory.

[9]This definition of linguistic distances is closely related to Lieberson's (1964) inter-communication index H_b, based on Greenberg's (1956) H. See chapter 6.

[10]Conversation with the author. Melitz (2007b) argues that the same is true for geographic distances, which are supposed to reflect frictions between trading partners. An alternative interpretation is that north-south geographic distances represent instead differences in endowments, "and therefore more opportunity for profitable trade" (Melitz 2007b, 986).

2. *Geographic distances:* Distance has a large negative effect, since a 10 percent increase in distance leads to a 12.4 percent decrease in trade.[11] Adjacency leads to a substantial increase in trade.[12]

3. *Former or current political or economic links:* All of them have significant positive effects on trade, with the exception of political unions.

4. *Linguistic distances:* The specifications are different across columns of the table. DC obviously has the deepest effect. A 10 percent increase in the probability that two citizens, one in A, the other in B, speak the same language increases their trades by 10 percent. Next comes the OCC languages variable, when languages are restricted to European ones. Arabic, Chinese, Hindi, Malay, Farsi, and Turkish have no effect on trade. English is not more effective than other European languages in promoting trade, as can be seen from column 3 of table 4.2, where English is separated from other languages. The coefficient is not significantly different from 0 and is positive, whereas it should be negative. The two lessons to be learned are that close languages in the importing and exporting country have an effect that is quite large, but also that English is not a better communication language than other ones. In the last result, the OC Communication European and Direct Communication variables are combined (using an average of both).

There is a short but growing list of papers that introduce genetic distances in economic analyses. Guiso, Sapienza, and Zingales (2009) use genetic distances between various European populations as a proxy (in fact, as an instrument) for trust. More trust induces more trade, but since trust is negatively correlated with genetic distances, larger distances again have a negative effect on trade. Giuliano, Spilimbergo, and Tonon (2006) experiment with the impact of genetic distances (as proxies for cultural distances) on trade. They argue that geographic barriers (mountains, common seas, altitude) alter both genetic distances and modern transportation costs. Therefore, when they are introduced simultaneously in the model, the effect of genetic distance becomes negligible.

---

[11]All the effects are measured ceteris paribus.

[12]The increase in trade between adjacent countries with respect to nonadjacent countries is equal to $e^{0.44} = 55$ percent.

TABLE 4.2. Trade flow equations

	(1)	(2)	(3)	(4)
Sum of real GDPs	1.04**	1.04**	1.04**	1.04**
Geographic distance	−1.24**	−1.24**	−1.24**	−1.25**
Adjacency	0.44**	0.44**	0.43**	0.44**
Ex-colonial relationship	1.69**	1.63**	1.63**	1.61**
Ex-common colonizer	0.71**	0.65**	0.66**	0.58**
Currency union	0.92**	0.91**	0.89**	0.91**
Political union	0.50	0.52	0.51	0.62
Free-trade area	0.28*	0.29*	0.30*	0.33*
Open-circuit communication	−0.09			
OC communication European		−0.27**	−0.34**	
OC communication English			0.14	
Direct communication	−1.00**	−0.83**	−0.83**	
Combining OC European and DC				−0.95**
R^2	0.73	0.73	0.73	0.73
No. of observations	31,010	31,010	31,010	31,010

Source: Melitz (2008, 680).

Note: $*p \leqslant .01$, $**p \leqslant .001$, significantly different from zero. Other values not significantly different from zero at conventional levels of probability.

Ku and Zussman (2008) detect two shortcomings in the existing literature. First, it fails to take into account the possibility that potential trade partners may communicate via a non-native language, such as English, but this is partly resolved in Melitz (2008). Second, measures of linguistic distances are often static, while the number of speakers of a lingua franca may change through learning, which is obviously the case for English. To measure English proficiency, they construct a data set based on TOEFL (Test of English as a Foreign Language) results, submitted by all foreigners who wish to study in an English-speaking country. They then estimate trade equations that contain a variable measuring linguistic distance between two countries (equal to 0 if they share the same language, and to 1 otherwise), as well as the TOEFL distance of a certain number of languages to English. Ku and Zussman (2008) are able to show that the effect of English largely overshadows the effect of a common language. Moreover, the effect is of the same order of magnitude in countries that share a common language as in countries that do not. They conclude that their results "demonstrate that acquired proficiency in English can assist countries in overcoming historically determined language barriers."

2. MIGRATIONS

> A man travels the world in search
> of what he needs, and returns home to find it.
> —*George Moore*

The standard approach in analyzing the trade-offs of a decision to migrate is based on evaluating costs and benefits. The prospects of higher wages or other benefits[13] are compared with the monetary and psychological costs, adjustment to a new culture, and possible uprooting of the family. The cultural and linguistic frictions in a new country, based on earlier immigrants' experience, can profoundly influence individual decisions. The degree of labor adjustment and complementarity to existing technological processes are also crucial to well-being and the adaptation process.

To illustrate this point, we can compare Chinese immigration to the United States and to Japan.[14] In general, Chinese immigrants find it difficult to integrate into Japanese production processes, which require a high degree of cultural homogeneity and an intensive level of interaction and communication within the labor force. The situation is different in the United States, which is more open to immigrants than Japan and where, after some initial period, Chinese immigrants exhibit a reasonably high degree of labor complementarity. In addition, there are linguistic and historical challenges for Chinese immigrants in Japan. Though Chinese characters are used to some extent in Japanese writing, their pronunciation is completely different from the Chinese. More important, the Chinese and English language structures are very similar, while both are quite different from Japanese. Finally, lingering memories of painful historical events and relationships between the two countries generate a higher degree of cultural friction in Japan than in the United Sates.

The difference in immigration targets is even more profound in the case of immigration from India to the United States and Japan. In 1990, Japan implemented profound changes to its restrictive immigration policy (Immigration-Control Refugee-Recognition Act, or ICRRA) and made it easier for highly educated engineers and computer specialists from abroad, including India, to immigrate. However, the cultural and

---

[13] In migrations between developing countries, risk containment rather than income maximization seems to be of relevance in the decision to migrate. See Guilmoto and Sandron (2001).

[14] See Fujita and Weber (2009).

technological adjustment for Indians in Japan has proved quite challenging. As a result, their satisfaction with working conditions is quite
low compared with that of immigrants from other Asian countries.[15]
Moreover, given the Indian colonial past, a large number of educated
people speak English, which mitigates the degree of cultural friction
faced by Indians in the United States.

The form of the typical immigration equation is very close to the
trade equation, but its theoretical underpinnings are different. Massey
et al. (1993) and Carrington, Detragiache, and Vishwanath (1996) relate
it to existing migrant networks that create positive externalities for
those who migrate later, since they decrease immigrants' costs and
facilitate their assimilation.[16]

As in the previous section, we concentrate on a representative and
recent paper by Beine, Docquier, and Özden (2009), who studied the
determinants of migration flows between 1990 and 2000 from 195
countries to thirty OECD countries. Since the incentives to migrate
may be different, they also distinguish flows of low-skilled workers
(with less than upper secondary education) and high-skilled workers
(with post-secondary education), looking at how migrants sort themselves across destinations. Instead of estimating an equation for each
skill level, they estimate, as many others do in this literature, how the
ratio of high-skilled to low-skilled emigrants is affected by a certain
number of determinants. The basic results are illustrated in table 4.3.

The most important determinant of total flows is the size of the
diaspora (population older than twenty-five years, born in the country
of origin). Wages in the destination country and the generosity of
immigration policies (represented by the share of refugees in the total
number of migrants) also have a positive impact, but larger social
expenditures (as a share of GDP) have no effect on the total number
of skilled and unskilled migrants. The Schengen Agreement, signed
by several member countries of the EU, abolishes border barriers:
immigrants in one of the Schengen countries can circulate freely in
other countries. This too has a positive effect, as might be expected.
Finally, a common language between a pair of countries has a strong
influence on the migratory flow.

The second equation (skill ratios) is concerned with the education
level of migrants. A positive sign of the coefficient of a variable shows
that the ratio of skilled to unskilled migrants increases if the value of the
variable increases. Larger population, higher wages, greater distance,

---

[15]Ota (2008).
[16]See also Grogger and Hanson (2007) and Beine, Docquier, and Özden (2009).

TABLE 4.3. Migration flow equations

	Total Flows	Skill Ratios
Characteristics in destination country		
Size of diaspora	0.831**	−0.132**
Population	0.109*	0.082**
Wages	0.040**	0.045**
Immigration policy	0.035**	−0.015**
Social expenditures	0.175	−1.253**
Other characteristics		
Geographic distance	−0.095	0.263**
Ex-colonial relationship	−0.051	−0.410*
Schengen area	0.599*	0.303**
Common language	1.056**	0.721**
No. of observations	4,992	4,992

Source: Beine, Docquier, and Özden (2009), table 2, column 4, and table 4, column 4.
Note: Econometric method used: two-step Heckman estimator. $^*p \leqslant .01$, $^{**}p \leqslant .001$, significantly different from zero. Other values not significantly different from zero $p \geqslant .05$.

or a common language favor the immigration of skilled workers. On the contrary, laxer immigration policies, generous social expenditures and large diasporas decrease the ratio, and thus attract more low-skilled migrants.[17]

But migrations are not only international and intercontinental, they also happen within a continent and across regions within a country. Falck et al. (2009) examine the effect of various factors, including linguistic data, on the variation of phonological and grammatical attributes across regions in Germany. They find that these have a significant effect on regional migrations, beyond what geographic distance only would suggest. They interpret the closeness of dialects as explaining cultural identity.

3. LITERARY TRANSLATIONS

> Translation is not a matter of words only.
> It is a matter of making intelligible a whole culture.
> —*Anthony Burgess (1984)*

The literature on cultural exchanges essentially deals with the media industries, and especially with movies and television programs.[18]

---

[17] See also Docquier, Lohest, and Marfouk (2007).
[18] See Hoskins, McFadyen, and Finn (1997) and the list of references therein.

Much less is written on music, which does not need translation, dubbing, or subtitles. But as pointed out by Simon Frith (1996, 157) well before the explosion of the Internet, MP3, and iTunes, "the point is not that a new technology enabled—determined—a new music international, but, rather, that the music's own essential mobility enabled the new technology to flourish, and shaped the way it worked."

People do not only watch television, go to the movies, or listen to music, they also read. As of May 2006, sixty million copies of Dan Brown's *Da Vinci Code*, published in early 2003, were in print or sold.[19] Books are an important factor of transmission, but in most cases they need to be translated. In fact, *The Da Vinci Code* was translated into forty-four languages, and by October 2004 it had generated some sixteen titles supporting or debunking its premise.

Though television and broadcasting have considerably changed the way culture is transmitted, books (and more generally written material, including the Web) remain essential. As Susan Sontag pointed out on receiving the Peace Prize at the Frankfurt Book Trade Fair in 2003:

> [W]hat saved me as a schoolchild in Arizona, waiting to grow up, waiting to escape into larger reality, was reading books, books in translation as well as those written in English. To have access to literature, world literature, was to escape the prison of national vanity, of philistinism, of compulsory provincialism, of inane schooling, of imperfect destinies and bad luck. Literature was the passport to enter a larger life; that is, the zone of freedom.[20]

On some occasions, books translated from a foreign language even become part of national literary heritage. The beautiful novel *Ali and Nino: A Love Story*, which became a national emblem in Azerbaijan, was written in German by Baku-born author Lev Nussimbaum under the pseudonym Kurban Said.[21]

However, translations are sometimes accused of leading to a form of cultural domination by some languages. According to Melitz (2007a), "if one language is sufficiently larger than others in the sales of original-language works, it will tend to crowd out the rest in translations [and] those writing in the dominant language are privileged." A similar opinion was recently expressed in one of the important French literary bimonthly magazines, *La Quinzaine Littéraire* (2006), claiming

---

[19] See http://en.wikipedia.org/wiki/The_Da_Vinci_Code (accessed June 12, 2009).
[20] See www.boersenverein.de/sixcms/media.php/806/2003_sontag.pdf for Sontag's most beautiful acceptance speech.
[21] It was first published in German in Vienna in 1937. See Reiss (2005).

that translations from English into French dominate in France.[22] The title of the article is unequivocal: "Fiction Is American." Valérie Ganne and Marc Minon (1992) show that France, Italy, Spain, and Germany translate much more (18, 25, 26, and 15 percent) than the United Kingdom (3.3 percent). They attribute this fact to the "abundance of books that originate in the United States" and need no translation for British readers. They also show that English is the language that generates the largest number of translations in France, Italy, Spain, and Germany. Johan Heilbron (1999) describes the system as accounting for uneven flows between language groups: on the European continent, 50 to 70 percent of published translations are from English.

This is hardly surprising, since the population speaking English as a first language is, with the exception of Mandarin, the largest in the world. It is therefore somewhat expected that English produces more fiction (and much more scientific literature, as scientists from all countries write in English with increasing frequency) than any other language. However, as will be argued, if factors such as production in the original language and distances between cultures are taken into account, translations from English are in fact dominated by translations from other languages, including Scandinavian ones and French.

To simplify the discussion, let us make the following two rough and all-other-things-equal (such as literacy rates) assumptions: (1) the number of books written in a language is proportional to the population that speaks it and (2) every reader reads the same number of books. Then it will be the case that (1) more books, available for translation, will be written in large-population countries or in languages that are native to many speakers and (2) large-population countries will need fewer translations than small ones, because more books are available in their own language. If this were true, then the English domination hypothesis simply arises from the facts that English is the mother tongue of some 400 million people (Crystal 1999), produces more fiction (and science) than any other European language, and has more books put into translation from English. Table 4.4, which tabulates (per 1,000 speakers, in the source and the destination language) the number of literary works translated from some European languages, shows that this is roughly the case. Indeed, even though a large number of books are translated from English

---

[22]This is reminiscent of the literature on the "American hegemony" following the popularity of the television series *Dallas* in Europe in the seventies and eighties (Biltereyst 1991). The filming location of the series, Southfork Ranch, is very close to the residence of one of the authors of this book.

TABLE 4.4. Number of translations, 1979–2002 (per 1,000 speakers)

Language	From	To
Bulgarian	0.158	1.182
Czech	0.333	1.702
Danish	1.329	5.730
Dutch	0.276	2.159
English	0.950	0.043
Estonian	—	5.480
Finnish	0.312	3.330
French	0.884	1.069
German	0.451	1.220
Greek	—	0.500
Hungarian	0.201	0.667
Icelandic	—	14.300
Italian	0.270	0.204
Latvian	—	1.652
Lithuanian	—	1.083
Norwegian	1.319	5.586
Polish	0.113	0.482
Portuguese	0.023	0.139
Romanian	0.073	0.279
Russian	0.133	0.156
Serbo-Croatian	0.038	0.291
Slovak	0.237	1.248
Slovene	—	2.180
Spanish	0.054	0.277
Swedish	1.759	1.500
Ukrainian	—	0.041

Source: Calculations based on UNESCO data.

(0.95 per 1,000 speakers) and very few are translated into English (0.043), there are almost as many that are translated from French (0.88), and many more from Danish (1.33), Norwegian (1.32), and Swedish (1.76). Likewise, "small" languages such as Danish, Estonian, Finnish, Icelandic, Norwegian, and Slovene generate a large number of translations, while languages spoken by large populations, such as English, yield as few as 0.043 translated books per thousand readers.

These simple arguments support the claim that the number of translations from English is indeed "overall dominating and disproportionately" large, but they show that this situation is essentially due to the large population of English speakers and thus of writers who use English. In fact, some authors even claim that the share of English in printed and electronic media is declining. Melitz (2007a, table 1, 212) provides data suggesting that the role of English in literary works has declined over the past thirty years, while Pfanner (2007) indicates that only 36 percent of all blog postings on the Internet are in English, 37 percent are in Japanese, and the share of Chinese and Spanish blogs is rapidly increasing.

There is another important factor that should be taken into account in comparing the number of translations: the role of cultural proximities. Except for the sake of exoticism, a thriller that features New York is more likely to be translated from English into French than a Chinese or an Estonian thriller that unfolds in Shanghai or Tallinn. Just think how hard it is to read Dostoevsky or Tolstoy, before trying to get accustomed to Chinese or Estonian names of characters and streets. Our theoretical and empirical investigations are in line with the view that, since more novels are produced in English, which is culturally closer to other European languages than is Mandarin, Arabic, or Hindi, more works should be translated from English than from other languages, even though these languages have large numbers of native speakers (Mandarin Chinese is spoken by 1.2 billion people; Crystal 1999). This argument is reinforced by the cost aspect of translation. De Swaan (1993, 45) estimates this cost at 30 percent of the price of a three-hundred-page book of which two thousand copies ("certainly not a too conservative estimate," according to De Swaan) are circulated. Publishers seldom translate books that have a low probability of being read.[23] The role of cultural distances makes it necessary to take into account bilateral translations (both to and from), rather than the totals presented in table 4.4.

The economic literature on translations, including Melitz's (2007a) pioneering paper, is quite small. The word "translation" appears nowhere in *Books* (Coser, Kadushin, and Powell 1982) or in the very comprehensive survey on the book industry by Canoy, van der Ploeg, and van Ours (2006). Caves (2000) discusses books at great length without dwelling on translations. The closest to what we discuss is Hjorth-Andersen's (2001) work. He estimates a three-equation model of the translation industry in which the first equation identifies the total number of titles in a given country, the second determines the aggregate propensity to translate, and the third disaggregates this total into single languages.

[23]According to an article by Sonia Kolesnikov-Jessop, "Sold in Translation," that appeared in *Newsweek* on January 11, 2010, 275,000 titles were published in China in 2008, and 6.9 billion books were printed, but only a few dozen of those will likely ever be translated. This is changing also. At the 2009 Frankfurt Book Fair, to which China was invited as the guest of honor, foreign publishers snapped up the rights to about 1,300 Chinese books.

Ginsburgh, Weber, and Weyers (2007) develop a microeconomic model that leads to an equation in which the number of titles translated from a source language A to a destination language B is determined by the following variables: (1) the sizes of the populations that speak A and B as first languages, (2) the distance between the two languages, and (3) the literacy rate and the average income of the population speaking the language into which the title is translated. The effects of all the variables, with the exception of distance, should be positive. For example, if the population that speaks language A is larger, then the number of books translated into B will be larger, since more will be written in A. Likewise, if population B is larger, readers will look for more variety and demand more translations. The literacy level and income of population B are expected to have a positive influence, since more books will be read, including more books translated from other languages, in more literate and richer regions. The effects of distance go in the other direction, since if the cultural distance between A and B is larger, fewer titles will be translated. The resulting model and the direction of the effects are again similar to the Newton gravity equation described in the introduction to this chapter.

The data on distances between languages are those calculated by Dyen, Kruskal, and Black (1992) described in chapter 3. In this context, they are not meant to measure the difficulty of translating from A to B, which is more complex than just the relative proximities of vocabularies.[24] Nida (1975, 98) is very explicit about the two questions translation is confronted with: "The first concerns translation as an art rather than a science and the second raises the issue as to whether translation is even possible." The Italian motto "*traduttore, traditore*" (translator, traitor) is well known. The German poet Heinrich Heine claimed that his poems, when translated into French, were just "moonlight stuffed with straw," and Nabokov, who used to write in both English and Russian, notes (in "On translating Eugeny Onegin", a Pushkin poem) that translation is "[o]n a platter a poet's pale and glaring head, a parrot's screech, a monkey's chatter, and profanation of the dead." In ancient times, the translation of God's words was blasphemy. The Roll of Fasting (first century A.D.) "records the belief that three days of utter darkness fell on the world when the Law was translated into Greek."[25] We

[24]See, for example, Catford (1967) and Nida and Taber (1969).
[25]See Steiner (1992, 251–52).

rather follow Cavalli-Sforza (2000) and assume that linguistic distances are a proxy for cultural distances.[26] Data on the number of translations are collected by UNESCO and produced in their *Index Translationum*.

Estimation results for literary translations from 1979 to 2002 appear in table 4.5. They are calculated for nineteen source and twenty-six destination countries.[27]

All estimated parameters are significantly different from 0 at the 1 percent level and carry the expected signs. Since they can be interpreted as elasticities, they show that a 1 percent increase in population speaking the source language increases the number of translations by 0.76 percent. The elasticity with respect to the destination language is much smaller (0.42). This is because more books are written in languages that are spoken by many. Therefore, populations that speak these languages are more self-sufficient and less affected by translations from other languages. On the other hand, fewer titles are translated into languages spoken by smaller and more homogeneous populations. Returns to scale are strongly decreasing in the population of destination. The elasticity of the number of translations with respect to distance is −1. This is the expected sign, since a larger linguistic-cultural distance between two languages should decrease the number of translations. The effect is large: an increase in the linguistic distance of 10 percent decreases the number of translations by 10 percent. The elasticity with respect to the literacy rate is quite important (3.65), while wealth in the destination country plays only a marginal role.

In the second equation, each of the nineteen source languages is represented by a dummy variable (which takes the value of 1 if a book is translated from that specific language, and 0 otherwise). Each dichotomous variable is multiplied by (the logarithm of) the population that speaks the language. This transformation changes neither the specification nor the values of the other parameters, but

[26]Though cultural distances are available, Ginsburgh, Weber, and Weyers (2007) use linguistic distances. The reason is twofold: cultural distances are available for countries, not for languages, while UNESCO data on translations are for languages, and cultural distances exist only for a small number of countries, and certainly not for all those that are accounted for in the sample of translations between languages.

[27]This leads to 475 = 19 × 26 − 19 translation flows. Four observations are ignored (translations from Finnish to Hungarian and Estonian, and from Hungarian to Finnish and Estonian), since Dyen, Kruskal, and Black (1992) do not provide distances for non–Indo-European languages. This leads to 471 observations. Some languages (Estonian, Greek, Icelandic, Latvian, Lithuanian, Slovene, and Ukrainian) are included as destination languages only, since the number of titles translated from these languages is very small.

TABLE 4.5. Translation flow equations

	Equation 1	Equation 2
Source-language population	0.76***	
Destination-language population	0.42***	0.43***
Distance between languages	−1.00***	−1.05***
Destination-language literacy rate	3.65**	3.93***
Destination-language income (GNI/head)	0.45***	0.52***
Intercept	3.13*	3.17***
Source language × population		
Norwegian		1.40 (0.20)
Danish		1.38 (0.17)
Swedish		1.29 (0.13)
French		1.13 (0.07)
English		1.09 (0.05)
German		0.99 (0.06)
Finnish		0.84 (0.16)
Italian		0.79 (0.07)
Czech		0.78 (0.11)
Russian		0.74 (0.05)
Hungarian		0.74 (0.11)
Spanish		0.57 (0.05)
Polish		0.55 (0.07)
Dutch		0.54 (0.09)
Portuguese		0.31 (0.05)
Romanian		0.27 (0.09)
Bulgarian		0.23 (0.13)
Serbo-Croatian		0.17 (0.08)
Slovene		0.00 (—)
No. of observations	471	471
Adjusted R^2	0.440	0.774

Source: Ginsburgh, Weber, and Weyers (2007).

Note: In equation 2, Slovene is the omitted variable. $*p \leqslant .05$, $**p \leqslant .01$, $p \leqslant .001$ (coefficient is significantly different from 0). Next to each language coefficient in equation 2 we give the standard error in parentheses, so that the reader can see that, for instance, Norwegian and Danish have statistically equal coefficients. The same is true for French and English.

it frees the parameter picked up by the dummy from the size of the population that speaks the language and makes the values of the parameters directly comparable. The interesting point here is that it allows ranking of source languages, and as can be seen, English is far from the first, being preceded by Norwegian, Danish, Swedish, and even French. If all languages had the same number of speakers, there would, for example, be $1.40/1.09 = 1.28$ times more books

TABLE 4.6. Translations: ranking source languages (1979–2002)

	1979–2002	1979–1987	1988–1997	1998–2002
Norwegian	1	5	5	1
Danish	2	1	2	2
Swedish	3	3	1	3
French	4	2	3	4.5
English	5	4	4	4.5
German	6	6	6	6
Finnish	7	10	10	8
Italian	8	11	7.5	7
Czech	9	9	7.5	10
Russian	10	7	9	11
Hungarian	11	8	11	12
Spanish	12	13	12	13
Polish	13	12	13	14
Dutch	14	14	14	9
Portuguese	15	18	16	15
Romanian	16	16	17	17
Bulgarian	17	15	18	19
Serbo-Croatian	18	17	15	16
Slovene	19	19	19	18

Source: Ginsburgh, Weber, and Weyers (2007).

Note: During the period 1988–1997, Italian and Czech tie for eighth place; during the period 1998–2002, French and English tie for fifth place.

translated from Norwegian than from English. There are also relatively more books translated from French than from English (although the difference between the two parameter values is small). This mitigates the claim of a predominance of translations from English. Though Russian, Spanish, and Portuguese are spoken by large populations, their role is often dwarfed by languages spoken in smaller countries, such as Finnish, Czech, and Hungarian. The model, however, offers no explanation for this effect.

A second question considered here is whether the situation changed during the twenty-three years under review. Three subperiods are examined: 1979–1987, 1988–1997, and 1998–2002, using the same analysis as above on each subperiod. The results that appear in table 4.6 are rankings based on the parameters of the dummy variables representing source languages. The first column ranks the nineteen source languages according to increasing order of rank over the whole period, while the three following columns give the rank in each of the subperiods. As an example, French is ranked fourth over the whole period, and this ranking hardly changes over time (4, 4, and 4.5 in each of the subperiods). Roughly speaking, there are no changes: the six first languages (Norwegian, Danish, Swedish, French, English, and German) during the early 1980s are still the first six in the early twenty-first century. Finnish, Italian, and Dutch seem to have slightly gained, while Eastern European languages, including Russian, have lost some ground.

That being said, it is true that English has a privileged (rather than a dominant) position in the market for novels. Much is translated from English, and very little is translated into English. Authors who write in English thus benefit from two advantages. They have a large market in their own language, and they have access to other large markets through translations. This is also reflected in the number of British (and probably American) high school students who learn foreign languages. A recent survey shows that while some 98 to 99 percent of children in the EU study at least one foreign language, that figure is 81 percent in Ireland and 48 percent in the United Kingdom.[28] Some, it seems, benefit from a free lunch....

4. The Eurovision Song Contest: Is Voting Political or Cultural?

> Wagner's music is better than it sounds.
> —*George Bernard Shaw*

In this section we analyze the voting behavior and ratings of judges in a popular song contest, the Eurovision Song Contest, and relate the bilateral votes to cultural and linguistic factors.

This annual contest has been held in Europe since 1955. Although only seven countries took part in the first competition, the number of participants increased to sixteen in 1961. Some non-European countries also take part: Israel and Morocco are now regular participants. In the Moscow contest in 2009, twenty-five countries out of forty-one participating were selected to take part in the final round of the competition, the live broadcast of which was watched by several hundred million people around the world.

Since 1975—the first year in the data set—the eleven (sixteen between 1988 and 1997) jury members in each country (often a popular jury, not consisting of experts) can rate on a scale of 1 to 12. Televoting was introduced in 1998, so that every citizen can participate, and according to Haan, Dijkstra, and Dijkstra (2005), in

---

[28] *Eurostat Newsrelease* 137/2009, September 24, 2009. Details can be found in table 7.4.

many countries the number of people calling in to register their vote is in the hundreds of thousands.[29]

Ratings are normalized so that the favorite song gets twelve points, the next one ten, and then eight, seven, six, five, four, three, two, and one. This allows each voting country to give positive ratings to ten other countries. Participating countries are not allowed to vote for their nationals.

The data set makes it possible to analyze the determinants of success in the competition. Though the votes cast may appear to result from political consideration and vote trading, Ginsburgh and Noury (2008) show that they are rather driven by the "quality" of singers, as well as by linguistic and cultural proximities between singers and voting countries. Therefore, and contrary to what is often suggested, there seems to be no reason to take the result of the contest as mimicking political conflicts or friendships.

Such exchanges seem indeed to happen. In the 2004 contest the winning country, Ukraine, benefited from the votes of all its former political "neighbors." Its average marks were 8.1, but it received 12 (the highest marks) from Estonia, Latvia, Lithuania, Poland, and Russia, and 10 (the next highest, since 11 does not exist) from Belarus and Serbia. Another example involves two other countries which, though they were far from winning, could be thought to have colluded: the Netherlands, with an average rating of 2.3, received five points from Belgium, which in turn received six from the Dutch judges, though its average rating was only 3.7. It is therefore reasonable to suspect that voting agreements are implicitly or explicitly struck, or that countries' votes are based on political rather than on "artistic" considerations, even though there is no political issue at stake.

The issue was taken up by the *Economist*,[30] following the publication of a paper by Fenn et al. (2005):

What makes a song good? Lyrics, melody and rhythm have their place, of course, but for entrants of the Eurovision Song Contest on May 21st [2005], geopolitics may be the decisive factor. The data [analyzed by Fenn and colleagues] confirm what many already suspected: that the contest

[29]In some countries, voting can become a contentious issue. For example, the BBC reported on September 18, 2009, that a number of people in Azerbaijan were questioned by the police after voting for a song by neighboring Armenia in the 2009 contest. The Azerbaijani authorities responded that people had merely been invited to explain why they voted for Armenia. To recall, Armenia and Azerbaijan have been in a state of war since the two states fought over the disputed Nagorno-Karabakh region in the 1990s.

[30]May 21, 2005, 93.

is not always about the quality of the songs. The research published has shown the contest also has a deeper meaning, and reveals how "European" each country is. Despite its Euro sceptic image, for instance, the data suggest that Britain is very much in tune with the rest of Europe. Supposedly Europhile France, by contrast, is actually out of kilter with many of its European cousins.

The collusive voting behavior in the Eurovision Song Contest has been studied by an increasing number of scholars from various backgrounds, including computer sciences, economics, and sociology. Yair (1995) finds three bloc areas, namely Western, Mediterranean, and Northern Europe. Gatherer (2004) analyzes the period 1975–2002 and identifies two large blocs, which he calls respectively the "Viking Empire," including the Scandinavian and Baltic countries, and the "Warsaw Pact," comprising Russia, Romania, and the former Yugoslavia.[31] Gatherer (2004, 2006) uses Monte Carlo simulation methods to study voting patterns of countries over the period 1975–2005. He emphasizes the emergence of large geographic blocs in the mid-1990s. Fenn et al. (2005) investigate the relations between European countries represented in the contest in terms of a dynamical network and conclude that there exist "unofficial cliques of countries" and vote patterns. They highlight this result using several network techniques, as well as cluster analysis, including a dendrogram, which seems to support the existence of cliques.

Some additional issues in the context of the Eurovision are analyzed by Haan, Dijkstra, and Dijkstra (2005) and Bruine de Bruin (2005), who mainly focus on the effect of performance order on the voting outcome and the difference between televoting and votes cast by a jury.

4.1. Exchange of Votes: Political Reasons?

The order in which candidates perform is randomly drawn before the competition starts. After the performance ends, countries are asked to cast their votes. Results are announced country by country, in the order in which countries performed. Participants are ranked according to their aggregate score.

Ginsburgh and Noury's purpose is to examine the score cast by the judges of a country A in evaluating the performer of a country B. If both countries exchanged their votes without taking into account any other

---

[31]The name is misleading, since Yugoslavia refused to join the bloc of the Warsaw Pact countries created in 1955.

dimension, the voting equation would simply relate the vote received by B to the one cast by A. But other factors may also determine the vote. They include the quality of the song, the characteristics of performer B and voter A, and the cultural and linguistic distances between A and B.

In an ideal world the most important determinant of voting would be the quality of the performance. Quality, however, is not observed and must be constructed. One way of doing this is to take the ex-post average rating of a musician of country B by the judges of all other participating countries, with the exception of the votes cast by countries that are said to belong to the same bloc as B, as identified by Gatherer (2006), since including their vote would possibly overestimate quality. Thus excluded are the votes cast in 2001–3 by Poland and the Russian Federation for Ukraine, the votes cast from 1996 to 2000 by Cyprus for Greece, and so on.[32] "Quality" is thus not affected by the presence of voting blocs.

In addition to quality, individual characteristics of the performer(s) may also affect the number of votes received. These characteristics include (1) an indicator for the performer who represents the country that hosts the competition, (2) the language in which the artist sings (English, French, other), (3) the gender of the artist, and (4) whether the artist sings alone, in a duet, or in a larger group.[33]

The order in which musicians appear in a competition seems to have an effect on the outcome. Flôres and Ginsburgh (1996) and Glejser and Heyndels (2001) observe that in one of the top-ranked international piano competitions, the Queen Elisabeth competition, those who perform first are less likely to receive high ratings.[34] Order of appearance is thus included as a determinant.

Voters' characteristics are also important. Since these are more difficult to describe,[35] Ginsburgh and Noury (2008) include linguistic (Dyen, Kruskal, and Black 1992) and cultural distances (Hofstede 1980, 1988, 1991) between performers and voters. Note that languages are not used as a measure of the distance between the language spoken

---

[32] For more details concerning blocs, see figures 1 and 2 in Gatherer (2006).

[33] Gender of the singer or composition of the group (male, female, duet) were constructed from the records' covers, which, in most cases, include pictures. In some cases, however, neither name nor photograph was sufficient to determine gender. Sometimes the cover of the record was not available at all. All those cases were dropped from the data set.

[34] See also Haan, Dijkstra, and Dijkstra (2005) and Bruine de Bruin (2005) for the Eurovision contest.

[35] They could be by country dummies, but this can be shown to create problems.

by voters and the one in which the song is performed—most today are performed in English. They represent cultural proximities between populations.

4.2. No. Votes Are Exchanged for Linguistic and Cultural Reasons

Data on contests cover twenty-nine years (1975–2003), with an average of twenty-two participating countries. Though the competition started in 1956, the analysis starts in 1975, since the current rating system was adopted in 1975. In 2004, new rules were again adopted for the voting system: semifinals started to be organized, in which some countries are eliminated but can still vote in the finals. Therefore, Ginsburgh and Noury chose to examine the voting patterns prior to the change. This produced 462 votes (22 times 21) for each competition. Given that values of several variables are missing—in particular, cultural and linguistic distances—and since, for econometric reasons that we do not discuss here, lagged votes instead of contemporaneous ones have to be used, a total of 4,074 voting observations are left.

The voting equation is estimated by linear methods, but since votes (in fact, ratings) are integers that take values between 0 and 12 (with the exclusion of 9 and 11), and since only ten performers out of an average of twenty-two get positive ratings, other, more sophisticated estimation methods were also used. They lead to qualitatively comparable results, which are not reported here. One may also think that quality as measured here is not exogenous. The results show that instrumenting quality by previous year's quality does not change the results either.

Columns 1 to 3 of table 4.7 contain the results of a linear (ordinary least squares) estimation of the voting equation. It is apparent that quality always plays a large role, which can be interpreted as showing large agreement between judges on the rating of candidates. Vote trading is significant only in equation 1, from which linguistic and cultural distances are absent. It ceases to be so in equations 2 and 3 once linguistic and cultural distances are also accounted for. Although the coefficient on vote trading is significantly different from zero in the first equation, its value is very small and therefore unlikely to affect the final rating. Though not all distance coefficients are significantly different from zero at the 5 percent probability level, they all have negative signs: the larger the distance, the lower the rating.

The results make it clear that some variables have statistically significant effects on votes. However, since they are measured in different units, it is not easy to see which ones have meaningful effects. The last column of table 4.7 compares the coefficients in specification

TABLE 4.7. Vote trading equations in the Eurovision song contest

	Equation 1	Equation 2	Equation 3	Standardized Coeff. of Equation 3
Quality	0.966**	0.968**	0.960**	0.532
Lagged vote	0.026*	0.023	0.014	0.014
Host country	0.255	0.269	0.253	0.016
Sung in English	0.110	0.149	0.104	0.011
Sung in French	0.233	0.226	0.219	0.018
Male singer	0.157	0.163	0.167	0.018
Duet	0.135	0.065	0.091	0.007
Group	0.076	0.057	0.053	0.006
Order of performance	0.003	0.003	0.004	0.006
Language		−0.955**	−0.577**	−0.041
Power			−0.010*	−0.038
Individualism			−0.002	−0.008
Masculinity			−0.004	−0.024
Uncertainty avoidance			−0.008*	−0.044
Intercept	0.081	0.633**	1.105**	
R^2	0.30	0.30	0.30	
No. of observations	4,074	4,074	4,074	

Source: Ginsburgh and Noury (2008).
Note: $^*p \leqslant .05$, $^{**}p \leqslant .01$.

3 with standardized coefficients, which eliminate the differences in the values in which variables are measured.[36] The results show that the quality of the singer (or group) is the most important variable, and that the effect of vote trading is dwarfed by the effect of linguistic and cultural distances.

All results, including those not reported here but that can be found in Ginsburgh and Noury (2008), point in the same direction. Quality is the main determinant of the vote; linguistic and other cultural factors are present, but they are not at the forefront. Political vote trading is not an issue once cultural factors are taken into account. This does not imply that there is no vote trading but rather that it can be explained by cultural and linguistic factors.

The results of Fenn et al. (2005) may be biased or misleading, since quality is absent from their calculations. But even if their results were taken for granted, most of them point to linguistic affinities, as is

[36]These can be obtained after multiplication of the coefficients of column 3 by s_j/s_y, where s_j and s_y represent the standard deviations of regressor j and of the dependent variable y. See Goldberger (1964, 197–98).

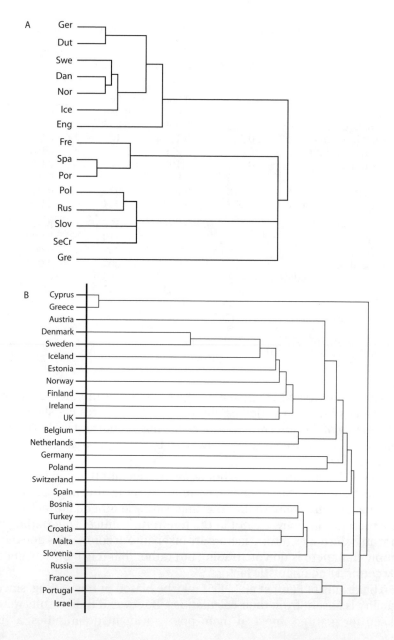

FIGURE 4.1. (A) Language dendrogram (*Source:* Own calculation based on Dyen, Kruskal, and Black 1992). (B) ESC countries dendrogram (*Source:* Fenn et al. 2005).

clear from their dendrogram, reproduced here as figure 4.1B, next to a dendrogram based on distances between Indo-European languages obtained from Dyen, Kruskal, and Black (1992), which uses a clustering algorithm (figure 4.1A). We discuss clusters of countries starting with those that are close in terms of the distance appearing on the vertical axis of the Fenn at al. (2005) dendrogram.

1. Greece and Cyprus appear very close. Greek is, of course, spoken in Greece, and by some 75 percent of the Cypriot population.[37]

2. Denmark and Sweden come next, but their languages are very close, as can be seen from the language dendrogram.

3. Next come Iceland and the group of Nordic countries. Though Estonian and Finnish do not belong to the same group of Nordic languages, the countries are probably close in terms of other dimensions.

4. At approximately the same distance, one finds Ireland and the United Kingdom, which should hardly come as a surprise.

5. The same applies to the Netherlands and Belgium, where 60 percent of the population speaks Dutch.

6. Likewise, at a rescaled distance of 1, there is a cluster formed by Bosnia, Turkey, Croatia, Malta, and Slovenia. Three of these countries share Slavic languages, but still, this is a rather strange group, which probably shares a feeling of being in the "marches" of Europe.

7. Finally, there are two countries (France and Portugal, where Romance languages are spoken) that are far from the rest of Europe. But so are Germany and Poland, Switzerland, Spain, and Russia.

Though in clusters 1 to 6 there are indeed factors that can be explained by geopolitics, they can also be cast in terms of sharing cultural traits and languages. It is true that on some occasions France and Portugal, and to some extent Germany, Poland, Switzerland, Spain, and Russia, cast votes in a way that can hardly be explained. But this still does not fully support the claim made by the *Economist* that "Britain is in tune with the rest of Europe, [while] France is out of kilter with many of its European cousins."

[37] See www.ethnologue.com.

5. Summary

In the four applications described in this chapter, both distances between languages and cultural distances were shown to have an important impact on economic outcomes.

The trade theory–adjusted gravity model has often been used to explain bilateral trade flows. The variables used are of two types: push-pull variables (such as GDP in both countries) and variables representing frictions (geographic distances, common border, political or economic associations, including former colonial relationships, currency unions, free-trade areas) and linguistic distances. The latter are represented under several forms: common native or acquired languages, the probability that two randomly chosen individuals from two countries speak the same language, and others. In all cases, empirical results make it clear that linguistic distances matter, and affect bilateral trade flows.

Immigration decisions are essentially based on the existence of networks of former immigrants in the country of destination, but the choice is also influenced by a common language between the source and the destination country. Moreover, a common language is more likely to attract high-skilled than low-skilled workers.

Ginsburgh, Weber, and Weyers (2007) constructed and estimated a model that offers some insight into determinants of literary translations. Though the resulting demand equation for translations is very close to the gravity model, its theoretical roots are derived from microeconomic assumptions (not discussed here). The model fits well the data and shows that the supposed English (American) language hegemony in literature is based on an incomplete reasoning: the number of books that are translated from language A to other languages is not necessarily an accurate indicator of the "power" of language A. Account has to be taken of the number of books written in the source language, as well as the cultural distances between languages. It is obvious that the more titles that are written in a language, the more will be translated into other languages, as long as cultural traits are reasonably similar (the smaller the distance, the larger the number of translations). Once the number of titles translated takes the two factors into account, the apparent English-language hegemony hypothesis has to be revisited.

The analysis of the Eurovision Song Contest shows no evidence of vote trading beyond the one that can be explained by linguistic or cultural traits or proximities. The data at hand here make it possible to isolate the effect, since judges cast votes for individuals and the rating system is finer than the usual "yes, no, abstain" voting system. It may well be that cultural proximities are also at work in international political bodies, such as the European Parliament, and that what appears as vote trading may rather be the consequence of cultural factors. The effect of vote trading, if there is one, is small: the largest coefficient obtained in the equations whose results are shown in table 4.7 is equal to 0.03, while the "average" value of the vote cast by a country is equal to 5.8.[38] Though the effect is significantly different from zero, it disappears once account is taken of culture and language. But even so, ratings that should be based on quality only incorporate other factors, such as linguistic and cultural proximities.

One wonders whether televoting, in which every citizen in a country can vote through the Internet or by telephone, will not be even more distortive, though experts are by no means very good judges.[39] Televoting may also have unexpected consequences in today's global world. Migrants, who often long for their home country, are obviously likely to support their nationals, and probably more inclined than the country's nationals to take part in popular polls such as the Eurovision Song Contest, therefore biasing the result in favor of their home country. The 2009 decision to retreat from popular voting and restore expert voting is therefore a move in the right direction.

[38]Derived from $(1 + 2 + \cdots + 8 + 10 + 12)/10$.
[39]See, for example, Ginsburgh and van Ours (2003).

Chapter 5

INDIVIDUAL COMMUNICATIVE BENEFITS

Wer fremde Sprachen nicht kennt,
weiss nichts von seiner eigenen.[1]
—*Johann Wolfgang Goethe*

VITO CORLEONE'S ENGLISH. *Vito Corleone was born in the small Sicilian town of Corleone. He migrated to New York City in 1887. According to his father, Mario Puzo, he was unable to fully hide his Sicilian accent, but was fluent in American English. Communicative skills obviously helped him become the head of the most powerful Mafia family.*

In this chapter we shift our focus to considerations and decisions made by individuals and try to offer some insight into incentives to acquire languages in addition to one's mother tongue. We have already touched on related issues in the previous chapter. For example, it may be beneficial for an individual to acquire one or several languages spoken by important trade partners of her own country. If there existed a lingua franca spoken by everybody, it would be easy for traders to communicate. According to some authors (Crystal 2003; Graddol 2006), English may already be or become such a language. English speakers would then have no incentive to learn Chinese and would communicate in English with their Chinese trading partners. But China's population is much larger than that of all English-speaking countries combined, and one may wonder why a Chinese would learn English, since at home he has more than a billion countrymen to communicate and trade with. Obviously, it may also be in the best interest of an American, Englishman, or Australian to learn Chinese. To resolve this dilemma, an English speaker will ponder the costs and benefits of learning Chinese, and so will the Chinese speaker who contemplates learning English. Both individuals will evaluate their learning costs, direct and indirect, including the tuition fees charged

---

[1] "The one who knows no foreign languages knows nothing about his mother tongue."

by schools and the time commitment to classes and homework, and balance these with the benefits. This is also true for domestic languages in multilingual societies such as Belgium (Flemish and French), Canada (English and French), South Africa (English and Afrikaans), Switzerland (German, French, and Italian), and the United States (English and Spanish), among others.

Proficiency in languages has important consequences for earnings. Job opportunities are more and more often open to applicants who speak several languages, though not all languages are identical in that respect. Grenier (1985), for example, finds that in Quebec, Canada, there is a 6 percent wage differential for a French-speaking Canadian who learns English, but the reverse is not true. Now that the EU is almost a single market, and workers are somewhat free to move across country borders, the same conclusions hold. Ginsburgh and Prieto's (2010) results show that a second language (in most cases, English) raises wages in the range of 5 to 15 percent in Austria, Finland, France, Germany, Greece, Italy, Portugal, and Spain; much less so in Denmark and the Netherlands, where English is known by 70 to 75 percent of the population; and has no effect in the United Kingdom, where no second language is in high demand.[2]

Immigration became one of the most important aspects of worldwide globalization. In chapter 4 we briefly discussed reasons that drive migration decisions. Proximity between the language of the migrant and that of the destination country is one of the factors to be taken into account. Once in the new country, the migrant will have to learn or at least polish knowledge of the local language to get a job, and thus will be faced with a learning decision comparable to the one alluded to above. This aspect gave birth to an important research literature that was initiated by Chiswick and Miller in the mid-1970s. The importance of linguistic skills for migrants' labor markets is confirmed by the literature on patterns of language acquisition by immigrants in traditional immigration targets such as Australia, Canada, Germany, Israel, the United Kingdom, and the United States.

Such benefits are related to expanded employment opportunities and higher monetary returns, but there are also some mundane rewards that drive people to acquire languages. Being immersed in a different culture and gaining unfiltered access to its history, arts, and especially its literature in the original language are considered essential by some.

---

[2]See also Chiswick and Miller (2007, chaps. 14–16), MacManus, Gould, and Welsh (1978), and Vaillancourt and Lacroix (1985), and a longer discussion of some results in section 3.

1. Modeling Language Learning

In their pioneering 1991 paper, the 1994 Nobel Prize winner in Economics, Reinhard Selten, already mentioned in this book in the context of his Esperanto links, and political scientist Jonathan Pool, another Esperanto enthusiast, consider a general approach to the benefits of language learning that subsumes both private monetary rewards and the "pure communicative" benefits of exposure and access to different cultures.[3] An important aspect of this approach is that the gross communicative benefits of every individual are positively correlated with the number of others with whom he or she can communicate through sharing at least one common language.[4] The more people we can speak with, the more advantageous the learning of other languages may seem. We have to proceed with some caution here. Some cultures and languages are more difficult to learn than others. It would be reasonably easy for a person who speaks German, English, or French to acquire Italian, Spanish, or Dutch. However, the decision to learn Mandarin, Japanese, or Korean may be much more demanding in terms of patience, time, effort, and financial commitment. As we pointed out in chapter 3, the similarity or dissimilarity of various languages affects the cost of learning and has an important impact on individual choices. In short, while contemplating learning Mandarin, this individual would weigh the substantial cost of his undertaking against the exciting prospects of getting access to the ancient Asian culture and, sometimes more important, its modern industrial juggernaut. The proximity of the Italian, Spanish, or Dutch cultures and languages to German, English, or French could make the benefits quite limited. But so would be the costs, and again, in both cases one should weigh the net communicative benefits before embarking on the learning process.

Inspired by the linguistic fabric of Canada, and especially of Quebec, Church and King (1993) adapted the Selten and Pool (1991) approach to a bilingual society in which the strategic choice of each citizen is driven by the net communicative benefit of learning the other language. This benefit is simply represented by the number of people an individual can communicate with. The linguistic links between the

---

[3]See also earlier contributions by Breton (1978) and Vaillancourt(1980).

[4]One can also consider the benefit of using a prestigious language or protecting an endangered one, a dimension we do not examine here. See, for instance, the game-theoretic model of Iriberri and Uriarte (2008).

two groups create a network externality,[5] since the decision of English-speaking Canadians to learn French will expand their communication range and increase their communicative benefits. This decision will reduce the incentives of French-speaking Canadians to learn English as, in general, the incentive of an individual to learn the language of the other group declines if others are willing to learn her own language.

Indeed, consider a country with two linguistic groups, speaking their native languages e and f. Individuals in each group may decide to learn the language of the other group. The population sizes are E and F. Assume that e is the larger group, so that $E > F$. As indicated above, the sizes of the groups may influence decisions, and the smaller group would, in general, be more inclined to learn the larger group's language. In fact, the incentive for an e-citizen to learn f is likely to be quite low, since she can communicate with enough citizens in her own group, while a large value of E may also attract members of the f-group. As Lazear (1999a, 124) points out, "the incentives are greater for any individual to learn the majority language when only a few persons in the country speak his or her native language." Every individual is endowed with a benefit function B that increases with the number of others with whom she shares a common language, and since it was assumed that e is a larger group, $B(E) > B(F)$. Note that if learning costs are the same for all citizens of a group, then once an individual decides to acquire the other language, all members of the group should reach the same conclusion. Therefore, there exists only a so-called corner solution in which all the members of the same group make the same decision to invest (or not) in acquiring the other language.

We illustrate the range and benefits of the individual decisions of Joan, who belongs to the e-group. If she decides to learn f, incurring cost c, she will be able to communicate with the entire country, and her net benefit will be $B(E + F) - c$. If Joan decides against learning f, her benefit will depend on the decision made by group f. If they decide to learn Joan's language, they will be able to communicate with Joan (and vice versa), so that her gross (and net) communicative benefit is $B(E + F)$. But if group f refrains from learning e, Joan's benefit is reduced to $B(E)$, as she will be able to communicate with her fellow e-speakers only.

The range of potential outcomes for Jacques, who belongs to group f, is quite similar. If he learns e he invests c, but he will be able to communicate with all members of group e, and his net benefit will be $B(E + F) - c$. If he (and therefore the whole group f) does not learn e, his benefit will be $B(F)$ only. But if group e decides to learn, then Jacques will be able to communicate with both groups, and his net communicative benefit will be $B(E + F)$. Note that formulating the benefit as $B(E + F)$ implies that once they know both languages, individuals are indifferent between the two languages and benefit equally from both: the two languages are perfect substitutes.[6]

The outcome of the linguistic dilemma described here obviously depends on the value of the learning costs. If these are large, even members of the smaller group f may find it prohibitively expensive to invest in learning the other language. This will happen if

$$B(E + F) - c < B(F) \quad \text{or} \quad c > B(E + F) - B(F).$$

Since the net benefits of language acquisition are even lower for the e group because $B(F) < B(E)$, no language learning takes place. However, the no-learning outcome could be inefficient, and it may well be that learning e by group f could be better from the overall societal point of view. However, the decision of some to forgo learning the other language is based on their individual considerations without taking into account the network effect, or the externality, on the other group. Why is there such an externality? Just because the decision made by members of group f to learn e also benefits e-members, who are then able to communicate with f-citizens, thus raising their communicative benefit.

Conversely, small learning costs create incentives for both groups to acquire the other language. This is likely to happen if

$$B(E + F) - c > B(E) \quad \text{or} \quad c < B(E + F) - B(E),$$

which, since e is a larger group, entails $B(E + F) - c > B(F)$. However, the coordination nature of the problem rules out a situation in which each group acquires the other language. The decision by members of one group to acquire the other group's language eliminates the incentive of the other group to engage in learning. If all English-speaking Canadians learn French, French-speaking Canadians would have no incentive to learn English. Simply put, French-speaking Canadians would be wasting their time or money (the cost c) trying to

---

[6]It is easy to alter this assumption to accommodate situations such as "Joan prefers to speak and hear her own language than to speak and hear f." This merely needs some additional properties for the net communicative benefit function B, but would not change the qualitative results.

TABLE 5.1. Joan's and Jacques's communicative benefits

Joan's communicative benefits

Learning strategies	Jacques learns e	Jacques does not learn e
Joan learns f	$B(E + F) - c$	$B(E + F) - c$
Joan does not learn f	$B(E + F)$	$B(E)$

Jacques's communicative benefits

Learning strategies	Jacques learns e	Jacques does not learn e
Joan learns f	$B(E + F) - c$	$B(E + F)$
Joan does not learn f	$B(E + F) - c$	$B(F)$

communicate with their English counterparts, who would, in that case, know French. The case of both groups learning the other language can thus be excluded. Note that from the gross communicative benefits angle, the situation is identical, as both cases guarantee that every citizen communicates with everybody else in the country, leading to a gross benefit of $B(E + F)$. However, the total learning costs differ. If group e learns f, the total cost is cE, whereas if group f learns e, the cost is cF. Thus, from a welfare point of view, it is better for the country that the smaller linguistic group engage in learning. Here small is beautiful, but is also efficient and cost-saving.

In the middle range of the learning costs, that is, if

$$B(E + F) - B(E) < c < B(E + F) - B(F),$$

the small group f invests in second-language acquisition, while the large group does not. Regardless of group f's learning decision, the communicative benefit to the large group e from language acquisition does not outweigh the learning costs. Thus the only outcome is learning by group f and no-learning by group e.[7] The various configurations that emerge from this reasoning for Joan and Jacques (and thus for all members of their respective groups) are shown in table 5.1.

The all-or-nothing decision is due to the assumption that learning costs are homogeneous, in which case once learning is beneficial for

[7]Belleflamme and Thisse (2003) extended some of these results to three languages. See also Athanasiou, Dey, and Valetta (2007) for an axiomatic approach to the theory of communicative benefits in the multilingual case.

one, it is beneficial for all other members of that group. However, not all individuals are born equal, and the differences in linguistic aptitudes could be quite substantial for those with distinct educational and social backgrounds. Some can learn a language effortlessly (in their sleep) and achieve the same degree of command that for others would be an uphill battle. Piron (1994, 65–71) suggests that an individual needs 12,000 hours of active study of a foreign language in order to claim he knows the language, but this is an average over individuals.

The motivation to acquire another language varies across individuals and is usually strengthened by migration or educational opportunities. In line with this argument, Gabszewicz, Ginsburgh, and Weber (2011) examine a society where individuals in both linguistic groups have heterogeneous levels of linguistic aptitude and consequently incur personalized second-language learning costs. This assumption allows a departure from the corner solutions of Church and King (1993) and for different language acquisition decisions within a group. Given the number of learners of language f in group e, some members of group f may decide to learn e, while others may refrain from doing so. Naturally, it is more likely that the decision to learn e will be made by individuals who incur a relatively low learning cost. In other words, there could be a threshold learning cost such that all individuals in group f with learning costs below the threshold will learn e, while others will forgo the option. The same is true in group e, where there also exists a cost threshold that separates learners from nonlearners of f. The learning costs are not necessarily identical in both groups. For example, it is often claimed that it is more difficult for native Spanish speakers to learn Portuguese than it is for native Portuguese speakers to learn Spanish. Though the lexicostatistical distance between Spanish and Portuguese is quite small (and symmetric), Portuguese is phonetically closer to Catalan or French, and the complex phonology of Portuguese compared with Spanish explains why it is easier for a Portuguese speaker to understand Spanish than the other way around.

In comparing the two groups, an important role is played by the *cost-adjusted communicative benefit*, the ratio of the population of one linguistic group and the unit cost of studying its language. It turns out that the fraction of learners of the other language is higher in the group with higher cost-adjusted communicative benefits. To test empirical evidence here, one cannot ignore political, geographic and cultural realities. Belgium, with its two major linguistic groups, is a good example. Dutch (actually Flemish, which is considered a little different) is the native language of 60 percent of the population, while 40 percent speak French as their native language. Therefore, one should expect the share of French speakers in Belgium who learn Dutch to be larger than the share of Flemish speakers who learn French. Reality, however, is quite different, probably because Belgium is located between the Netherlands and France. Since there are more Frenchmen than Dutchmen, this reverses the ratio between the populations of the two relevant linguistic communities and increases the potential benefits for Flemish speakers in Belgium to learn French, while it decreases the incentive of French-speaking Belgians to learn Flemish. Indeed, as the INRA (2001) Eurobarometer survey shows, 40 percent of the Dutch-speaking Belgian population claim to know French, while only 12 percent of those who speak French know Dutch. A similar situation prevails in Canada, where, according to Bond (2001), only 10 percent of Anglophones know French, whereas according to the 2001 census results 41 percent of Francophones know English. Naturally, the roles of English and French are reversed in Quebec, where, again according to the 2001 census, some 43 percent of residents whose mother tongue is English are able to communicate in French.

The communication benefits generated by language acquisition in the context of migrations are examined by John and Yi (1997). In their setting with two languages, say, English and Spanish, and two locations, an individual can decide to learn the other language (or not) and migrate to the other location (or not). Depending on the various parameters of the model, including the size of both linguistic groups, John and Yi obtain corner solutions, which they call "full assimilation": all members of one linguistic group learn the other language and both groups are located in the same place. Two types of interior solutions with "partial assimilation" and without full economic integration are also possible: (1) all individuals locate together, but there are monolingual individuals in each group who are unable to communicate with the other group and to overcome the linguistic barrier; and (2) there is a monolingual group, say, Spanish speakers, at one location who do not learn English and do not migrate, and who are therefore geographically separated from the rest of the society.

Nettle (1999) ran computer simulations with several groups of individuals speaking different languages and located in different places. Individuals in each group have some probability of migrating to another group and learning its language. The purpose is to study under which conditions (probability of migrating, various types of social structures, and various types of linguistic forms, some easier to learn than others) diversity persists or disappears. A similar method is used by Schulze and Stauffer (2006) to study language death. Other approaches, ones based not on explicit individual behavior but on aggregate dynamic (differential) equations, are used by physicists to study language death (Abrams and Strogatz 2003) or language competition (Castelló, Eguíluz, and San Miguel 2006).

It should be noted that network effects may lead to insufficient learning that takes place in equilibrium.[8] This raises the possibility of governments intervening and trying to implement more efficient outcomes by subsidizing their citizens' acquisition of the other language.

Another avenue is to open the market to language schools, which would enrich the self-learning options. Gabszewicz et al. (2009) introduce language schools (such as the Berlitz School of Languages, which is active in many European countries) and show that schools will generate additional learning at least in one of the regions or countries. In attempting to maximize its overall profit, the school sets tuition fees, which partly replace self-learning costs by making learning somewhat easier. In fact, the school emerges as a two-sided intermediary or platform embarking citizens belonging to the two linguistic groups that constitute two markets interlinked by the existence of the platform. This platform is essential in coordinating the decisions between the two sides (schools and students) of the market. The setting falls into the framework of two-sided markets introduced by Rochet and Tirole (2003). Interestingly, the various applications of this model to several industries, such as credit cards[9] or media,[10] generate *positive* cross-network externalities. Indeed, a larger number of shops and customers accepting and using a credit card increases the mutual benefits and attractiveness of the card's membership; a larger number of advertisers and readers of a newspaper increases its potential benefits (as long as readers are not too advertising averse). In the language school context, individuals are faced with *negative* cross-network externalities since the net benefit to e-citizens of learning language f declines if members of the linguistic group f are engaged in acquiring language e.

The observation that individuals may decide to learn other languages indicates that the distribution of linguistic skills within a society can be remarkably dynamic and change over time. As an example, table 5.2 exhibits the stunning cross-generational advancement of English in the EU. While only 26 percent of the elderly (sixty years and

---

[8]It is interesting to note that this situation can be described in terms of Greenberg's (1956) and Lieberson's (1964) communication indices, discussed briefly in chapter 4 and examined in more detail in chapter 6.

[9]Wright (2003).

[10]Gabszewicz, Laussel, and Sonnac (2004), Anderson and Coate (2005), Anderson and Gabszewicz (2006).

TABLE 5.2. Knowledge of main languages by
age groups (years) in the European Union (%)

	15–29	30–44	45–60	>60
English	56.8	42.7	33.4	25.7
German	27.4	26.0	25.7	26.0
French	22.9	20.2	20.4	19.5
Italian	13.7	14.1	14.3	13.7
Spanish	13.6	11.6	10.8	11.2
Polish	9.0	9.0	8.8	8.8
Dutch	5.3	5.2	5.2	5.1

Source: Fidrmuc, Ginsburgh, and Weber (2007).

older) know the language, 57 percent of the young generation (aged
fifteen to twenty-nine years) claim they know it. This does not hold,
however, for the other main European languages (German, French,
Italian, Spanish, Polish, and Dutch), for which there is almost no
change.[11] The patterns of language learning may have far-reaching
policy implications. It is therefore important to lay out a theoretical
framework of language acquisition and use it to estimate demand
functions for languages.

2. DEMAND FUNCTIONS FOR LANGUAGES

The demand functions estimated by Ginsburgh, Ortuño-Ortín, and
Weber (2007) are based on a simple extension of the models discussed
earlier. The substitution between languages, however, is imperfect,
and they assume that the benefits of communication are larger when
two (or more) people speak their own language than when they
communicate through another language. The delicacy, success, and
pitfalls of communication often hinge on whether a multiparticipant
meeting (or simple discussion) is conducted in the native languages
of all parties or whether some or all of them speak an acquired lingua
franca. As Piron (1994, 65–71) points out, non-native speakers of a
language often do not use the right idiomatic expressions, mistrans-
late, misinterpret the real meaning of words or sentences, and cannot,
for example, tell the difference between "might" used to mean power
and "might" as the past tense of "may." One can also add that a
frequent visitor to the headquarters of the European Commission in

[11] See more on this in chapter 7, section 2.

Brussels may observe that the English spoken by the majority of the commission's civil servants is quite different from the language used in deliberations in the British Parliament in London or the U.S. Senate in Washington, DC.[12]

In the estimated demand functions, the gross communicative benefit of an individual is a function of three variables: the number of those who speak his native language, the number of individuals who speak the language he wants to learn, and the lexicostatistical distance[13] between native and acquired languages, which represents the cost of learning. Some simple algebra leads to a demand function, which can be written:

$$N_{ef} = h(E, F, D_{ef})$$

where N_{ef} is the fraction of individuals whose native language is e and who learn f, E and F are the world populations of individuals who speak languages e and f, and D_{ef} is the distance between languages e and f. It is easy to see that N_{ef} should be decreasing in the number of speakers of e and in D_{ef}, since the larger the number of those who know the native language, the smaller the need to learn the other language, and the larger the distance, the more reluctant learners will be; N_{ef} should be increasing in the number of speakers of f, since the larger the number of speakers of the foreign language, the larger the benefits if one speaks their language, so the larger the number of learners.

Ginsburgh, Ortuño-Ortín, and Weber (2007) estimate such functions for English, French, German, and Spanish learning by citizens of the EU whose native languages are none of these. The estimates are based on data from the INRA (2001) survey organized at the time the EU was composed of fifteen countries, thus before the last two enlargements to Eastern Europe.

Table 5.3 gives a general overview of the six languages most extensively used by native speakers in the EU. It also shows to what extent each language is spoken elsewhere than in its country of origin. Column 1 shows the number of native speakers—in fact the population in each country.[14] Column 2 displays estimates of the worldwide use of each language as a mother tongue. The last column gives estimates of worldwide knowledge of each language as a mother tongue and otherwise.

---

[12]See also chapter 8.

[13]Lexicostatistical distances are defined in chapter 3.

[14]To simplify, we assume that immigrants speak the language of the country to which they migrated.

TABLE 5.3. Main languages used in the European Union (millions)

	Native Speakers in the EU (1)	Mother Tongue (2)	Worldwide Use (3)
English	62.3	341	1,800
French	64.5	77	169
German	90.1	100	126
Spanish	39.4	340	450
Italian	57.6	62	63
Dutch	21.9	20	20

Note: Column 1: English is the native language in Great Britain and Ireland. French is the native language in France and is spoken by 40 percent of Belgians. German is the native language in Germany and Austria. Spanish and Italian are the native languages in Spain and Italy, respectively. Finally, Dutch is the native language in the Netherlands and is spoken by 60 percent of Belgians. Note that for Dutch, there is a discrepancy between speakers in the EU and the estimates in columns 2 and 3.

Column 2: Number of first-language speakers as given by www.ethnologue.com. For Spanish, the number is the average between the two estimates according to *Ethnologue* (www.ethnologue.com).

Column 3: See Dalby (2002, 31) for English and Spanish. The French diplomatic service (www.france.diplomatie.fr/francophonie/francais/carte.html) provided the estimation of 169 million people who use French. For Italian and Dutch, see Crystal (2003).

Though Italy has a larger population than Spain, and the number of native speakers is larger, unlike Spanish, Italian is hardly spoken anywhere else.[15] Dutch is spoken only in the Netherlands and Belgium. Therefore, in table 5.4 we restrict our attention to four acquired languages (English, French, German, and Spanish) in thirteen EU countries.[16] Column 2 lists the world population that speaks the language of the country listed in column 1 as a first language.[17] Columns 3 to 6 give for each EU country the share of the total population that claims to know English, French, German, and Spanish. Lexicostatistical distances can be retrieved from chapter 3, table 3.2.[18]

[15] Italian is known by 9 percent of the population in Austria, 6 percent in Belgium and Greece, 5 percent in France, and 1 percent in other countries of the EU.

[16] Austria, Denmark, Finland, France, Germany, Greece, Italy, Ireland, the Netherlands, Portugal, Spain, Sweden, and the United Kingdom. Belgium and Luxembourg are omitted because they are both bilingual and would be more difficult to treat (and Luxembourg's population is extremely small).

[17] Following *Ethnologue.*

[18] The distance between Finnish and other Indo-European languages is set to 1, since Finnish does not belong to the Indo-European family.

TABLE 5.4. Knowledge of languages in the European Union (millions, %)

Country and Native Language (1)	Native Language Known By (millions) (2)	Percentage Who Know			
		English (3)	French (4)	German (5)	Spanish (6)
Austria (German)	100.0	46	11	100	1
Denmark (Danish)	5.3	75	5	37	1
Finland (Finnish)	6.0	61	1	7	1
France (French)	77.3	42	100	8	15
Germany (German)	100.0	54	16	100	2
Greece (Greek)	12.0	47	12	12	5
Italy (Italian)	62.0	39	29	4	3
Ireland (English)	341.0	100	23	6	2
Netherlands (Dutch)	20.0	70	19	59	1
Portugal (Portuguese)	176.0	35	28	2	4
Spain (Spanish)	340.0	36	19	2	100
Sweden (Swedish)	9.0	79	7	31	4
United Kingdom (English)	341.0	100	22	9	5

Note: The numbers in column 2 are from *Ethnologue* (www.ethnologue.com). The percentages of people who know English, French, German, and Spanish in each country are from Ginsburgh and Weber (2005).

A separate demand function is estimated for each of the four acquired languages. The results are reproduced in table 5.5. Distance always picks up a negative sign: the larger the distance between two languages (origin and acquired), the smaller the proportion of foreigners who will learn it. The sign of the coefficient for the "population speaking native language" variable should be negative: the larger this population, the less it needs to learn a foreign language. This is so for English and German as foreign languages, but for French and Spanish, the sign is not the one that is expected. The sign of the coefficient for the "population speaking acquired language" variable is positive in all cases (but not significantly different from zero for French and Spanish).[19] The demand functions for English and German are the only ones that are consistent with theory; they also fit well the data (large R^2). Finally, note that English has a larger attraction power (0.733) than German (0.586), French (0.193), or Spanish (0.091), though Spanish is widely spoken in the rest of the world.

[19]This variable is in fact a constant for each language, since in each of these four regressions, the destination language is the same. We chose this normalization (instead of a simple intercept) to be able to compare the individual coefficients for the four languages.

TABLE 5.5. Language demand functions

	Language(s) Acquired			
	English (1)	French (2)	German (3)	Spanish (4)
Distance between native and acquired language	−0.408*	−0.512	−1.362*	−0.560
Population speaking native language	−0.153*	0.355*	−0.361*	0.032
Population speaking acquired language	0.733*	0.193	0.586*	0.091
R^2	0.919	0.599	0.910	0.232
No. of observations	11	12	11	12

Source: Ginsburgh, Ortuño-Ortín, and Weber (2007).

Note: The number of observations is equal to 12 for French and Spanish, since both are an acquired language by citizens in 12 of the 13 countries. This number is 11 for English (spoken in the United Kingdom and Ireland) and German (spoken in Germany and Austria). $*p \leqslant .05$.

The results show that the attraction power differs significantly for the four foreign languages, and that other determinants, mostly historical, must be at play. Spanish, for instance, should attract Europeans much more than it does, but with the exception of France, there is no country in which more than 5 percent of the population knows it. The isolation of Spain until 1975 partly explains this result, but the large population of native Spanish speakers (essentially in Mexico and Latin America, and increasingly so in the United States) does not seem to generate large incentives to learn the tongue. France, on the other hand, is quite restrictive in the use of foreign languages in the public domain. It issued, for instance, regulations that make it difficult for certain categories of civil servants to use languages other than French in national and even international meetings. Dynamics, past as well as current cultural relations, common borders (Germany and the Netherlands), and noncentrality of a country (Spain and to some extent France) can be represented by trade shares. This does not improve the estimation results in any significant way. Therefore the questions of why English is becoming the lingua franca in Europe (and probably in the world) and why Spanish is relatively less spoken in Europe remain unexplained by the model.

3. PRIVATE RETURNS ON LANGUAGES

Globalization, increasing international trade flows, the establishment of new free-trade areas, and the efficient performance of international common markets result from improvements in transportation, but also and probably even more so from the ability of economic agents to communicate. Given new communication technologies, the only restrictions left are those created by language. Although English has become the current lingua franca, understood by about 1.5 billion citizens, countries in which the official tongues are not English represent a large share of the world's GDP, and their inhabitants may substantially improve their human capital if they know languages other than their own mother tongue. In section 2.1 of chapter 4, Melitz's (2008) conclusion that English is not more effective than other European languages in promoting trade was stressed. Obviously, however, not all languages will be equally rewarded by the labor market as a consequence of both supply and demand factors. From a more individualistic point of view, since it is expensive in terms of time and effort to acquire a second or third language, it is useful to know what the market value of such learning is worth.

Though languages are important in international transactions, the domestic relevance of language skills—for example, the importance for immigrants to know the language spoken in the country to which they move—is the topic of many papers. Not surprisingly, therefore, most papers on the returns on language proficiency deal with the skills of immigrants in traditional immigration countries such as Australia,[20] Canada,[21] Germany,[22] Israel,[23] the United Kingdom,[24] and the United States.[25] As expected, all these studies show that proficiency in the language of the immigration country has a positive and sometimes large effect on earnings.

This line of research is coupled with a second one concerned with the determinants of language acquisition by immigrants.[26] Language

[20]Chiswick and Miller (2007, chaps. 7, 9, 11).

[21]Abbott and Beach (1992), Aydemir and Skuterud (2005), Chiswick and Miller (2007, chaps. 1, 3, 4, 11).

[22]Dustmann and Van Soest (2002).

[23]Berman, Lang, and Siniver (2003), Chiswick and Miller (2007, chaps. 10, 11, 13).

[24]Leslie and Lindley (2001).

[25]Bleakey and Chin (2004), Bratsberg, Ragan, and Nasir (2002), Chiswick and Miller (2007, chaps. 2, 4, 6, 8, 11, 12), Hellerstein and Neumark (2003); see also the survey by Grin and Vaillancourt (1997).

[26]Chiswick and Miller (2007, chaps. 1–4), Dustmann (1994), Dustmann and Van Soest (2001), among others.

proficiency is assumed to depend on three sets of factors: economic incentives linked to expected returns, individual efficiency in language acquisition, and exposure to the language prior to and after immigration. Chiswick and Miller's (2007, xxii) general conclusions are as follow: (1) destination language proficiency increases with duration in the destination country, education acquired before immigration and in the destination country, immigration from a country that is more distant both geographically and linguistically from the destination country, and younger age at immigration; and (2) destination language proficiency is higher among immigrants from previous colonies, and lower among refugees.

Only a few studies consider the case of natives in multilingual societies, such as Bolivia,[27] Canada,[28] Hungary,[29] Luxembourg,[30] Switzerland,[31] Ukraine,[32] the United States,[33] and the EU before its two last enlargements.[34]

Estimating the financial returns on languages poses a problem similar to the one encountered in estimating returns on education. In both cases, returns indeed depend on the languages that an individual knows or on the number of years of study. However, returns are also affected by an unobservable characteristic, namely, the individual's intrinsic talent or aptitude, and ignoring this in the model generates several econometric issues that end up biasing the parameter of interest picked up by the variable representing either language proficiency or the number of years of education. There are several econometric tools that can be used to bypass this so-called "endogeneity" problem, but the discussion is beyond the scope of our presentation.[35]

We concentrate on the returns on multilingualism in a certain number of countries of the EU, thus following on three studies that considered the same issue. Galasi (2003) uses two Hungarian surveys of young career beginners who graduated from public higher education as full-time students in 1998 and 1999. He finds that speaking English or German increases wages by some 6 and 4 percent, respectively,

[27]Chiswick and Miller (2007, chap. 16).
[28]Shapiro and Stelcner (1997), Chiswick and Miller (2007, chap. 15).
[29]Galasi (2003).
[30]Klein (2003).
[31]Cattaneo and Winkelmann (2005).
[32]Constant, Kahanec, and Zimmermann (2006).
[33]Chiswick and Miller (2007, chap. 14), Fry and Lowell (2003).
[34]Williams (2006).
[35]Those who are interested in the technical aspects of the problem are referred to an excellent discussion by Angrist and Krueger (2001).

although the results are not very robust to alternative specifications. In some cases he even obtains negative, though insignificant, returns.

In his paper on the returns on languages in Luxembourg, Klein (2003) concludes there is little advantage to being proficient in any of the official languages (French, German, and Luxembourgish) but that it pays to know English, the only truly foreign language.

Williams (2006) uses data from the European Community Household Panel Survey (ECHP) between 1994 and 1999. The information comes from answers to the following question included in the survey: "Does your work involve the use of a language other than [the official language of the country]?" Williams ignores the endogeneity problem alluded to above, and simply runs ordinary least squares regressions where the explanatory variables include a broad array of socioeconomic indicators. To capture the effect of language knowledge, a dichotomous 0–1 variable is introduced for each of the following languages if cited as the first foreign language used in the workplace: English, French, German, Spanish, Italian, and "all other." In an alternative specification, all languages are pooled, and only one parameter is estimated. Equations are run for each of the EU fifteen member states (with the exception of Sweden) in 1996. The results indicate that in Austria, Finland, Italy, Spain, and the Netherlands, English is the only language that yields a significant return. However, substantial returns are also found for French in Denmark, Luxembourg, Greece, and Portugal. German generates positive and significant returns in Belgium, Luxembourg, and France; Spanish does so in France; Italian in Luxembourg, and Portuguese in Belgium. In the United Kingdom, no second language is rewarded. Languages add 5 to 20 percent to earnings, depending on the country and the language considered.

Ginsburgh and Prieto (2010) estimate returns on languages in nine European countries in 2001, a more recent year of the same panel survey as the one used by Williams. They differ, however, in three respects from Williams. First, they try to take into account the endogeneity issue between earnings and the use of foreign languages on the job. Second, instead of representing proficiency in languages by dichotomous variables or by the level of efficiency of the individual, they use disenfranchisement rates.[36] This provides a link with the usefulness of the language and the frequency with which it is spoken in a given country (actually, the supply scarcity of the language). For individuals who use only the language of the country (French

---

[36]Calculated by Ginsburgh and Weber (2005). Disenfranchisement rates measure the percentage of a population that does *not* know a certain language. See section 2 of chapter 7 for more details.

in France, for example), this share is 0 or close to 0 if the country hosts immigrants who do not speak the official language, while for a language that nobody knows but is useful in the workplace, the share is equal to 1. The parameter associated with the variable allows retrieving returns on languages for which one knows the disenfranchisement rate, and as long as the estimated parameter is positive, the implied returns will be larger for languages that are less common.[37] Third, they also estimate (instrumental variable) quantile regressions that illustrate how returns on languages vary at different points of the distribution of earnings.[38]

The survey describes the socioeconomic characteristics of individuals older than 16, grouped by households, including personal characteristics, family structure, current employment, education and training, labor status, wages, family income from sources other than wages and salaries, region of residence, and languages used on their main job. Though the survey includes fifteen countries, the questions on languages failed to be included for Sweden, the United Kingdom, and the Netherlands. Luxembourg and Belgium are left out because of their multilingual setting. Ireland was also dropped since the survey included a very small number of respondents who needed a foreign language at work. Immigrants and women are excluded as well.

Table 5.6 contains information on the number of individuals included in the survey in each country and the number of those who report needing one or several important European languages (English, French, German, Italian, and Spanish), including the official language of the country. The model is as close as possible to the Mincerian model used in the literature on returns on education. The dependent variable is the natural logarithm of the wage rate. The right-hand side contains the following variables: two dichotomous variables that represent higher (college or university) and secondary level education, respectively; the number of years of job tenure and its square; the number of years of potential experience and its square. Language effects are represented by the country's disenfranchisement rate for the main language used by the individual at his or her place of work. For some countries, the square of this variable had also to be introduced, since the relation between returns and disenfranchisement is not necessarily linear.

---

[37] However, Ginsburgh and Prieto also include results for other specifications of language proficiency, in particular English used at work, as well as foreign language knowledge, whether used at work or not.

[38] We return below to an intuitive explanation of what quantile regression is about.

TABLE 5.6. Overview of the data (no. of individuals)

	Austria	Denmark	Finland	France	Germany
Total	1,166	1,029	928	1,649	2,383
Speakers of:					
English	204	532	454	350	411
French	2	3	0	1,649	3
German	1,166	107	9	44	2,383
Italian	1	0	1	7	6
Spanish	0	2	0	14	4

	Greece	Italy	Portugal	Spain
Total	1,304	2,214	2,242	2,401
Speakers of:				
English	222	230	287	256
French	16	44	80	87
German	4	53	7	19
Italian	3	2,214	1	8
Spanish	0	4	28	2,401

Source: Ginsburgh and Prieto (2010).

Table 5.7 shows estimates of the parameters of interest picked up by the disenfranchisement variable(s) (corrected for the possible endogeneity bias). As is evident from the first two lines, the relation between returns and disenfranchisement is linear for France, Greece, Italy, Portugal, and Spain and is quadratic for Austria, Denmark, Finland, and Germany. The estimated parameters are significantly different from 0 in all cases. In the linear case, returns increase with disenfranchisement: the less a foreign language is known in a country, the higher the reward for knowing it and using it at work. In the quadratic case, returns increase with disenfranchisement up to a certain point and decrease thereafter (the parameter picked up by the linear term is positive, while the other is negative).

The two groups of countries thus differ in their behavior. In Northern Europe, English is used in the workplace by some 20 to 50 percent of workers, and benefits from larger (log) returns than other languages with higher rates of disenfranchisement but less often used in the workplace. English can thus be considered the dominant lingua franca in Northern Europe, with little competition from other languages.

The Danish case is worth a couple of remarks. German is rather common in Denmark, where it is used in 10 percent of cases, but its returns are much lower than those of English. This may be due to the fact that almost 40 percent of the Danish population knows German, while only 10 percent seem to be needed by firms, thus driving the return on knowing German to almost 0. A similar though weaker force is at work for English, which is known by 75 percent of the Danish population and used by some 50 percent of the firms.

In Southern European countries, the relation between returns on knowing languages and disenfranchisement can be considered linear, so that languages for which the rate of disenfranchisement is larger than the one for English may also yield higher rewards. And this is indeed the case for German in France, French in Greece, French and German in Italy, French and Spanish in Portugal, and French in Spain. Four countries on this list (France, Italy, Portugal, and Spain) share Romance languages. Though English is also the language most used by firms, any other Romance language, especially French, is an alternative to English. There are no alternatives to English in Northern Europe. This dichotomy between the two parts of Europe is consistent with Melitz's (2008) empirical conclusion that English is not more effective than other European languages in promoting trade.

Greece is again a special case since Greek is not a Romance language. Therefore, Greeks may be indifferent between the cost of learning any Romance or Germanic language, but the expected benefit of learning French is higher.

In the bottom part of Table 5.7, these coefficients are transformed into returns on languages for the five most widely used languages in Europe. Since the dependent variable (wage rate) is defined in logarithms, the parameters can be interpreted as reflecting the percentage increase in the wage rate for a language that is known by the individual and used at his job. Returns will be large if either the estimated country parameter or if the disenfranchisement rate for the language is large in the specific country, since returns are obtained as the product of the parameter and the disenfranchisement rate.

Quantile estimation, the results of which are represented in figure 5.1, can be understood as "completing the regression picture."[39] The usual regression model used by most economists gives, as mentioned by Mosteller and Tukey (1977, 266),[40] "a grand summary for the averages of the distribution corresponding to the set of [right-hand-side variables]. We could go further and compute several different regression curves corresponding to the various percentage points of the distributions and thus get a more complete picture of the set."

[39] Koenker and Hallock (2001).
[40] Quoted by Koenker and Hallock (2001, 154).

TABLE 5.7. Returns on languages in a selection of
European countries: estimation results

	Austria	Denmark	Finland	France	Germany
Disenfranchisement rate parameters					
Linear term	0.940	1.482	0.914	0.505	1.160
Squared term	−1.377	−2.639	−0.858	—	−1.288
Inferred returns					
English	0.11	0.21	0.23	0.29	0.26
French	—	—	—	0.00	—
German	0.00	−0.11	—	0.46	0.00
Italian	—	—	—	—	—
Spanish	—	—	—	—	—

	Greece	Italy	Portugal	Spain
Disenfranchisement rate parameters				
Linear term	0.275	0.292	0.471	0.608
Squared term	—	—	—	—
Inferred returns				
English	0.15	0.18	0.31	0.39
French	0.24	0.21	0.34	0.49
German	—	0.28	—	—
Italian	—	0.00	—	—
Spanish	—	—	0.45	0.00

Source: Ginsburgh and Prieto (2010).
Note: Returns are obtained by multiplying the regression coefficient(s) on disenfranchisement (first row and second row) by the disenfranchisement rates and their squares. Since there are no immigrants in the samples, the return of the domestic language is always set to 0. Returns for which the number of speakers is smaller than 1 percent of the country's sample are not displayed. All estimated parameters are significantly different from 0 at the 1% probability level.

This is what quantile regression does in a more sophisticated way than estimating a regression for each quantile.

The results of this technique show that there is a significant degree of heterogeneity within countries. The effects are larger in the upper deciles of the wage distribution for half the countries in the study (Austria, Denmark, Italy, Portugal, and Spain). This is not very surprising, since foreign languages are more useful for white-collar workers, whose incomes are likely to be in the upper part of the wage distribution. But even in those countries where the picture is flatter, the return on languages is proportional to the wage rate, since wages are measured in logarithms. In Germany, for example, the parameter picked by the disenfranchisement variable is flat in relative terms. According to the results in table 5.7, this makes for a return of some 30 percent for an individual who uses English at work. Thirty percent at the bottom of the wage scale of, say, 1,500 euros per month translates into a premium of $1,500 \times 0.30 = 450$ euros, whereas at the top of the wage scale of, say, 4,000 euros, the premium amounts to 1,200 euros (figure 5.1).

The returns on languages identified by Ginsburgh and Prieto are much larger than in most studies of immigrants who acquire the language of the country to which they move. This is not unexpected, since immigrants usually form small communities in countries where most citizens are fluent in the native language and there is less market pressure to pay higher wages to immigrants who learn and speak the national language than to those who do not learn it. Nevertheless, private returns end up decreasing as disenfranchisement decreases, an interesting (and expected) feature that points out that more language education may eventually crowd out private returns.

The paper by Constant, Kahanec, and Zimmermann (2006) on Ukraine leads to similar conclusions. Ukraine is populated by three times more ethnic Ukrainians than ethnic Russians, and Ukrainian, the official language, is spoken by roughly three times more citizens than Russian (Crystal 1999, 350). One should thus expect that Russian speakers earn more than others, and this is indeed what shows up in the econometric results. The authors observe, however, that this premium is decreasing over time. This may be due to the increasingly pro-Western economic and political orientation of Ukraine.

In an interesting study, Grinblatt and Keloharju (2001) show that language and cultural issues may hinder the value of individual investments. They use a Finnish database on investment behavior by Finnish investors and companies by examining the daily trades over two years. They also take into account the language spoken by each investor (Finnish or Swedish),[41] the language in which the annual report is published (Finnish, Swedish, or multilingual, including English),[42] and

[41] Both are official languages. According to Grinblatt and Keloharju, Finnish is spoken by some 93 percent of the population, Swedish by 6 percent only (note that these shares do not correspond with those of the Special Eurobarometer 255 [2006] survey). Swedish speakers seem to be more active in trading and hold 23 percent of household share-owner wealth.

[42] Of the ninety-seven firms whose stocks are traded, twelve report in Finnish only, two report in Swedish only, and eighty-three reports are multilingual.

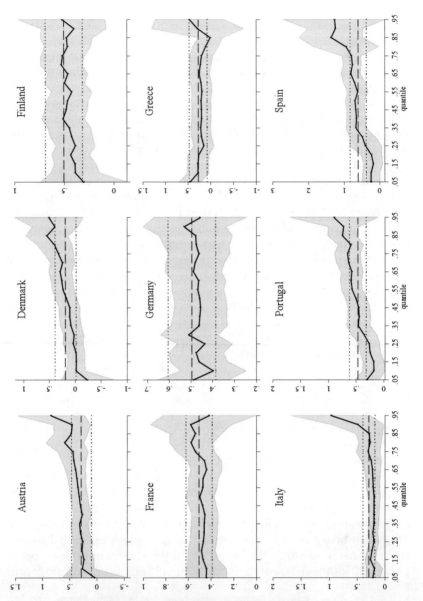

FIGURE 5.1. Quantile regression results.
Disenfranchisement coefficients and their confidence intervals.

Note: The shaded regions represent the 95 percent confidence intervals around the IV quantile regression estimates of the effect of the disenfranchisement rate on wages (plain curves). The horizontal discontinuous lines represent GMM mean coefficients and the dotted straight lines delimit their 95 percent confidence intervals.

the so-called culture of the firm, Finnish or Swedish, based on the name and native language of the CEO.[43]

Their results indicate that both language and culture impact the investment behavior of households: Swedish (respectively, Finnish) speakers invest more in Swedish (Finnish) firms that publish their annual report in Swedish (Finnish). Moreover, Swedish-speaking (Finnish-speaking) households prefer (Finns are reluctant) to hold and trade the shares of companies whose CEO is of Swedish origin. Some additional results make these findings even more remarkable. They estimate the parameters of a model in which they explain the fraction of Swedish-speaking shareholders in a given firm by the language in which the annual report of the firm is published, the culture of the firm, as well as some other variables. For households, they find that the effect of an annual report in Finnish (respectively, Swedish) is strongly negative (positive): a report in Swedish increases the fraction of Swedish shareholders by 8 percent, with respect to Finnish shareholders. The effect of a Swedish CEO also exerts a significantly positive though rather small influence. The results are not as clear-cut for trading institutions (which are probably more interested in returns than in languages), though they point in a similar direction.

4. SUMMARY

The chapter started with a discussion of the incentives to learn foreign languages. These go from the most obvious one, an expected increase in earnings, to the pleasure it can provide through immersion in a different culture and having the ability to speak, read, or at least understand the language. Theoretical models of learning a language different from the native one were covered in section 1, while section 2 gave an example of estimating the resulting demand equations for foreign languages. Section 3 was devoted to the private monetary benefits that result from the use of the native language of a country to which one immigrates, or the use of foreign languages for those citizens who know the language of their native country. Most econometric results point to relatively large returns on knowing non-native languages in firms that employ these workers.

---

[43] Eighty-three firms are of Finnish culture, fourteen of Swedish culture.

Chapter 6

DIVERSITY AND DISENFRANCHISEMENT INDICES

> An angel is more valuable than a stone. It does not
> follow, however, that two angels are more valuable
> than the one angel and one stone.
> —*Thomas Aquinas, Summa Contra Gentiles* [1]

IT IS PROBABLY EASY TO RECOGNIZE *the difference between an angel and a stone (when one is blessed to see the former). Also, the difference between Chinese and Italian languages is quite obvious. But it is less so for Italian and Venetian, or Czech and Slovak. Sometimes it is much more challenging to notice and even recognize differences between people. The great Russian writer Ivan Turgenev once wrote, "Most people can't understand how others can blow their noses differently than they do." But the fact is that people are different and even speak different languages. As an American proverb says, "Variety is the spice of life," and we are going to measure how hot the spice is.*

This chapter is concerned with the measurement of *diversity*, which has recently become a very popular concept in a wide range of contexts. There is an ever-growing number of diversity consultants, officers, and advisers whose role and function are to preserve and enhance diversity in the workplace or in student bodies. While all of us have an intuitive understanding of the concept, its precise meaning is not always clear, which makes it important to link diversity with a numerical measure, such as an index.

The first known effort to quantify diversity was undertaken in 1912 by the Italian statistician Corrado Gini in his article, "Variabilità e mutabilità," where he introduced the concept of *mutability* or *otherness* in a study of economic inequality. More than thirty years later, scholars across various disciplines almost simultaneously (and independently) addressed the issue of measuring diversity in their

---

[1] The quotation is cited in Nehring and Puppe (2002).

own field of research. In 1949 Edward Simpson wrote a one-page article that produced what is now known as the Gini-Simpson index of biodiversity. A seminal contribution by Claude Shannon (1948) also describes a diversity index, the entropy index, which influenced a large volume of research in information theory and statistics.[2]

A seminal contribution to the measurement of linguistic diversity was made by the prominent American linguist Joseph Greenberg, whose 1956 paper is often cited in this book.[3] His aim was to draw a quantitative distinction between regions or countries of great linguistic diversity and others of relative uniformity. Though this is obvious in some extreme cases, such as diverse Papua New Guinea, with 830 languages, and a practically monolingual North Korea, it is less so for intermediate cases. Greenberg's (1956, 109) goal was to develop quantitative measures of linguistic diversity and to allow "comparing disparate geographical areas, and eventually to correlate varying degrees of linguistic diversity with political, economic, geographic, historic, and other non-linguistic factors."

In our analysis of diversity we distinguish two main types of indices: *fractionalization indices* and *disenfranchisement indices.*

Fractionalization indices, based on Greenberg's approach, capture the ethnolinguistic mosaic of existing societies. They allow conducting cross-country or cross-regional comparisons and examining differences in various economic and political systems, institutions and outcomes influenced by the diversity of societies. We also discuss *polarization indices*, since the concept of polarization, formalized by Esteban and Ray (1994), is based on the same fundamentals. In our context, polarization, as well as fractionalization, entails several groups with similar or identical members whose linguistic or ethnic characteristics are substantially different from those in other groups. However, in addition to exogenous ethnolinguistic distances between groups, polarization also introduces the idea of *identification* and *alienation*. Individuals feel a sense of identification with members of their own group. This sense may, in principle, depend on the size of their group and the characteristics or attributes of its members. But Esteban and Ray also take into account alienation from other groups,

---

[2] Shannon's entropy index is sometimes mistakenly called the Shannon–Wiener index. While Norbert Wiener's pioneering work (1948) on cybernetics influenced developments in information theory, Wiener himself had no direct involvement in constructing the entropy index.

[3] Greenberg's work was further expanded by Stanley Lieberson (1964, 1969, 1981) and Laitin (2000).

which again may depend on size and distances between groups, and possibly on other characteristics of its members. The insertion of identification-alienation considerations into the measurement of diversity obviously affects the functional form of polarization indices. But it goes beyond that, since, as we shall see later, the two concepts may yield different conclusions: diversity and polarization do not necessarily go together.

Disenfranchisement indices are related to the notion of linguistic disenfranchisement caused by government policies. Societies sometimes have to choose a set of official languages that will be used for administrative, legal, and educational purposes (recall the cases of India, Sri Lanka, Nigeria, and Ghana, discussed in chapters 1 and 2). To analyze in a rigorous way the potential impact of such policies that unavoidably create "disenfranchised communities," requires a quantitative evaluation of disenfranchisement.

We also discuss the links between fractionalization, disenfranchisement, and communication indices, which were introduced in chapter 3. Applications are described in chapter 7.

1. Fractionalization and Polarization Indices

In evaluating linguistic (and almost every other aspect of) diversity, one has to recognize that there are distinctive *attributes* (languages) that identify members of a given society. The presence of different attributes generates a partition of this society into *groups* distinguished by their linguistic repertoire: speakers of English, of French, of English and French, of Chinese, and so forth. The two aspects of linguistic diversity, languages and the number of their speakers, give rise to three types of diversity indices:

1. *Attributes only.* This type of measurement is based on the ranking of *the sets of attributes* to determine the degree of societal diversity. The approach is common in studies of biodiversity in biology, zoology, and botany, as well as in the social choice literature concerned with choices over opportunity sets available to decision makers.[4] The questions treated in this literature are presented as follows by Bossert, Pattanaik, and Xu (2003, 405):

[4]See Weitzman (1992, 1993, 1998), Pattanaik and Xu (2000), Bossert, Pattanaik, and Xu (2003), Nehring and Puppe (2002, 2003), and Weikard (2002).

> Does the newly created, left-wing party increase the diversity of political opinions available to the voters in a country? ... Would the extinction of giant pandas reduce the diversity of species on the planet? How does the preservation of a native American language add to the diversity of world cultures?

Diversity, based only on the range of existing attributes, had already been addressed by Noah when he chose representatives of each existing species (without bothering with the size of the populations from which they came) to save them from the flood.[5] In the language setting, this could imply computing diversity between two groups as the ratio of the number of common languages to the total number of languages spoken by both groups.[6] Because this approach ignores the number of speakers, the measure has limited economic interest and is not covered in this book.

2. *Sizes only.* This family of indices is concerned only with the number of groups in the society and their sizes. The role of attributes is reduced to group identification, which determines the partitioning into groups. In most cases the value of the index is determined by the probability that two randomly chosen individuals of the society belong to different groups.

3. *Sizes and attributes.* The most general family of indices accounts for both group sizes and distances (or similarity) between attributes identifying various groups. In many cases the numerical value taken by these diversity indices amounts to an average (dissimilarity) distance between two randomly chosen members of the society. In fact, an index of type 2 can be considered a special case of type 3. Indeed, by setting the distance between every pair of distinct groups equal to 1, the probability of two randomly chosen individuals being members of different groups amounts to the average distance between the two groups.

Most of the empirical research, some of which is described in chapter 7, uses size-based fractionalization indices. Defining the set of distinct attributes, and hence linguistic groups, is a difficult challenge. Do speakers of Venetian and Italian belong to different groups? And if the answer is affirmative, it is difficult to argue that the linguistic distinctiveness of Venetian and Italian

---

[5]Weitzman's (1998) paper on diversity is elegantly titled "The Noah's Ark Problem".
[6]See Jaccard's (1901) similarity coefficient and Sorensen's (1948) index.

speakers is the same as the one separating Greeks and Turks. Indeed, the relationship between the two pairs is drastically different. Venetian is a dialect of Italian, whereas Greek and Turkish stem from two entirely different families: Greek is an Indo-European language, whereas Turkish belongs to the Altaic family of languages. When using a size-based index, one might decide that Venetian and Italian are in fact the same language, and assign their speakers to the same group. An index that accounts for both group sizes and attributes yields a clear advantage: by shifting from a dichotomous 0–1 measure of distance to a continuous measure, both indices avoid ad hoc group identification problems. Venetian and Italian are considered two different languages, but the distance that separates them is small, which is not the case for Greek and Turkish.[7]

Laitin (2000, 143) points out that "people have multiple ethnic heritages, and they can call upon different elements of those heritages at different times. Similarly, many people throughout the world have complex linguistic repertoires, and can communicate quite effectively across a range of apparently diverse cultural zones." But languages are not the only aspect of dissimilarity across groups. Measuring linguistic diversity could be viewed as a proxy for the broader notion of ethnolinguistic or cultural diversity, but linguistic and ethnic divisions do not always coincide. Rwanda, for example, is linguistically homogeneous (Kinyarwanda is spoken by almost every citizen in Rwanda), but the country is nevertheless ethnically very sharply divided between Tutsis and Hutus, which led the two groups to almost endless fighting and killing. Identifying groups in a society is therefore a delicate problem. For instance, one of the most widely used, comprehensive world classification studies, the *Atlas Narodov Mira* (1964), discussed in section 1.4, treats Tutsis and Hutus as members of the same ethnolinguistic group.

Three ingredients are needed to construct fractionalization or polarization indices:

1. the functional form that determines their meaning and properties;

2. the database of linguistic or ethnolinguistic groups created by using a group identification methodology;

[7]See Desmet, Ortuño-Ortín, and Weber (2009).

3. the set of attributes (languages), often represented by bilateral linguistic distances.

We now describe the various functional forms that such indices can take, and the databases used for their construction.

1.1. Size-Based Indices

Greenberg's (1956) size-based index, also called the *monolingual nonweighted index*, is referred to as the *A* index. It is usually defined for a multilingual society, where members of a group speak the same language, which serves as their unique identification device, and no account is taken if members of a group know languages of other groups. More precisely, the value of the *A* index is determined by the probability that two randomly chosen members of the society belong to *different* linguistic groups. Obviously, this probability, and thus the value of the *A* index is equal to 0 in a monolingual society.

Assume that there exist K distinct groups with population shares $s_1, s_2, \ldots, s_K$, summing to 1. Let us first calculate the probability that two randomly chosen members of the society belong to the *same* linguistic group. The probability that both individuals are chosen from, say, group 1 is equal to the square of that group's share. Since there are K groups, the probability that two randomly chosen members of the population belong to the *same* group is equal to the sum of the squares of all population shares. For example, if a society consists of three groups of respectively 50, 30, and 20 percent, then the value of the index is $0.50 \times 0.50 + 0.30 \times 0.30 + 0.20 \times 0.20 = 0.38$.

Note that this expression is the same as that of the celebrated Hirschmann-Herfindahl index HHI defined for an industry with K firms, where s_k stands for the market share of firm k. HHI is often viewed as an indicator of the industry's degree of monopolization and is widely applied in competition and antitrust law.[8] If the industry consists of one large firm (monopoly), HHI reaches its absolute maximum of 1. In the case of two firms with market shares s and $1 - s$, $HHI = s^2 + (1 - s)^2 = 1 - 2s + 2s^2$, whose minimum obtains at $s = 0.5$. An industry with two firms (duopoly) is the most competitive if the two firms are of equal size. Thus, equality of firms' size increases the intensity of competition. So does a larger number of firms. For example, in an industry with ten equal-sized firms, $HHI = 0.10$.

---

[8]In industries with many firms, only market shares of the fifty largest firms are considered in computing HHI.

Obviously, the probability that randomly chosen individuals belong to two *different* groups is equal to the sum of the squares, subtracted from 1, which yields the formal representation of the A index:

$$A = 1 - (s_1^2 + s_2^2 + \cdots + s_K^2).$$

This functional specification of diversity already appears in seminal contributions by Gini (1912), who calls it the *mutuality index*, and Simpson (1949). The index has been used in a wide range of applications in political science, linguistics, sociology, economics, genetics, biology and other disciplines. Specific examples are given in section 1 of chapter 7.

It is important to point out that the A index satisfies two fundamental requirements of diversity formulated by Shannon (1948), who developed a different functional form of size-based diversity indices:

Size uniformity: For a given number of groups, the index reaches its maximum when all groups are of the same size,

Richness: If all groups are of equal size, the diversity index of a society with a larger number of groups will be larger.

To illustrate that the size uniformity property holds, consider two societies, S and S', with two linguistic groups in each. S consists of two equal-size groups; in S' the two groups contain 60 and 40 percent of the population, respectively. Society S turns out to be linguistically more diverse since its A index is equal to $1 - 2 \times 0.5^2 = 0.5$, while for $S', A = 1 - 0.6^2 - 0.4^2 = 0.48$. If the size inequality of the two groups in S' increases, say, to 80 and 20 percent, the value of the diversity index will decline even further, to $1 - 0.8^2 - 0.2^2 = 0.32$. If the smaller group vanishes, we reach a homogeneous one-group society that exhibits no diversity, so that $A = 0$. A similar pattern emerges for societies with a larger number of linguistic groups. For example, the configuration with three equal-size groups $(1/3, 1/3, 1/3)$, whose A index is $2/3$, is more diverse than a society with unequal group sizes, say $(0.5, 0.3, 0.2)$, for which $A = 0.62$.

Comparisons between societies with different numbers of groups are more complicated. However, the pattern is quite clear in the case of equal-size groups. Compare the two-group and the three-group societies with profiles $(0.5, 0.5)$ and $(1/3, 1/3, 1/3)$. The latter is more diverse, as its A index of $2/3$ is larger than that of the two-group society, 0.5. Moreover, in compliance with the richness property of Shannon, the value of A increases with an increasing number of groups: for the four-group society $(0.25, 0.25, 0.25, 0.25)$ it is equal to 0.75.

Even though the A index is the most often used size-based diversity index in empirical studies, it is by no means exclusive. In addition to various generalizations of the Shannon index and the A index, Gunnemark (1991) has constructed several additional indices. One is based on the share of the population in each linguistic group for which the language spoken at home is not the official language of the country. As Easterly and Levine (1997) point out, this measure exceeds 90 percent in most African countries. Another Gunnemark measure is the number of individuals in every group who do not speak the official language or the country's most widely used language.

1.2. Indices Based on Group Sizes and Distances

Before proceeding with the formulation of indices, based both on the sizes of groups and their linguistic distinctiveness, let us consider the example of two West European countries, Andorra and Belgium, discussed in Desmet, Ortuño-Ortín, and Weber (2009). In tiny Andorra, roughly half the population speaks Catalan and the other half speaks Spanish (two relatively similar Romance languages), whereas in Belgium, about 60 percent speak Dutch, a Germanic language, and the other 40 percent speak French, a Romance language. Given the linguistic proximity of Spanish and Catalan as opposed to French and Dutch, one would expect Belgium to be linguistically more diverse than Andorra, though the A index is larger for Andorra. To overcome this sometimes unwelcome property of size-based indices, Greenberg (1956, 110) proposed a *monolingual weighted index* that accounts for distinctiveness between groups:[9]

> For each pair of languages (i, j) the probability of choosing successively a speaker of i and a speaker of j is the product $s_i \times s_j$, where s_i and s_j respectively designate the proportion of i speakers and j speakers to the total population. Each such product is weighed by multiplication with a number between 0 and 1, here called the resemblance factor r_{ij} between languages i and j. Then the sum of such weighted products $s_i \times s_j \times r_{ij}$ for all pairs i, j subtracted from 1 will give the monolingual weighted index. In fact the A index can be considered a special case of [this one], in which by all-or-none decision each product is multiplied by 1 when i and j are the same, and by 0 when they are different.

---

[9]The quotation is from Greenberg (1956). Notations are in conformity with those used in the rest of this book.

116   CHAPTER 6

Note that the distance between every pair of languages is equal to their resemblance factor subtracted from 1. This index can thus be rewritten as 1 minus the sum of $s_i \times s_j \times (1 - d_{ij})$ terms, where d_{ij} is the linguistic distance between groups i and j. Its functional form is

$$1 - \sum_{i=1}^{K} \sum_{j=1}^{K} s_i \times s_j \times (1 - d_{ij}).$$

To verify that the A index is indeed a special case, note that for every term that includes different groups i and j, the A index sets the distance d_{ij} equal to 1, so that the term vanishes. If i and j are identical, $d_{ij} = 0$, so that the term boils down to $s_i \times s_i$. Therefore, the A index collects only $s_i \times s_i$ terms; all the others will be equal to 0.

By using some simple algebra, it is easy to transform this index into a more useful form,[10] which consists of the sum of the terms $s_i \times s_j \times d_{ij}$:

$$B = \frac{1}{2} \sum_{i=1}^{K} \sum_{j=1}^{K} s_i \times s_j \times d_{ij}.$$

The factor 1/2 is introduced to avoid double counting, since otherwise the term related to any two groups i and j would be counted twice, once as $s_i \times s_j \times d_{ij}$, and a second time as $s_j \times s_i \times d_{ji}$. This, of course, makes no difference when comparing values for different countries. Note that B has a nice intuitive interpretation. It measures the average linguistic distance between all pairs of members of the society.

Index B has an important advantage over A since it satisfies a continuity property: if the distance between two groups is close to 0, the diversity of the society with two similar groups (such as Andorra) is close to the extreme case of a homogeneous society in which both groups merge into a single one. Ceteris paribus, one would expect such an index to have superior explanatory power in applications. This assertion is confirmed by Desmet, Ortuño-Ortín, and Weber (2009) in their study of the linkage between societal diversity and the scope of redistribution in 218 countries.

Desmet, Ortuño-Ortín, and Weber (2005) propose a variant of the B index in the setting with a dominant group, called *center*, as in Spain, Russia, Kyrgyzstan, Laos, Thailand, Iran, Saudi Arabia, and

---

[10]See Nei and Li (1979), Rao (1982a), Ricotta and Szeidl (2006), Desmet, Ortuño-Ortín, and Weber (2005), Bossert, D'Ambrosio, and La Ferrara (2006), and Desmet et al. (2009).

Kuwait, among others.[11] In viewing linguistic distances as proxies for the alienation of groups from one another, the diversity index proposed by Desmet, Ortuño-Ortín, and Weber (2005) takes into account only the distances between the center and the peripheral groups, not between the peripheral groups themselves. The functional form of the peripheral index PI is similar to B, except that the distance between every pair of peripheral groups is 0. Thus, in a society with a central group whose population share is s_c, the PI index contains only $s_i \times s_c \times d_{ic}$ terms, where d_{ic} is the distance between language i and the language of the central group.

One of the drawbacks of the B and PI indices is that they fail to satisfy Shannon's size uniformity and richness conditions. In the context of biodiversity, Botta-Dukát (2005) argues that whereas inserting a new group of individuals will contribute to the richness of the set of attributes, it may reduce the average distance between individuals. There could thus be situations in which the distance shift outweighs the size effect. Indeed, consider a society S_3, consisting of three equal-size groups with a linguistic distance of 0.3 between every pair of groups, and society S_2, which is equally split between two groups, whose linguistic distance is 0.8. The B index for S_3 is $3 \times (1/9) \times 0.3 = 0.1$. The B index for S_2 is $(1/4) \times 0.8 = 0.2$. Thus, the index violates Shannon's richness condition, according to which B should be larger when the number of equal-size groups is larger. Furthermore, let us now modify society S_2 by adding a tiny number of members as a third group, thus turning S_2 into a three-group society. It would not change the fact that the newly created three-group society (with unequal group size) is still more diverse than S_3. This conclusion violates Shannon's size uniformity condition, according to which the maximal diversity among a given number of groups obtains if all groups are of equal size.

Note that the values of A are larger than those of B. The reason is that in A, the distance between two different groups is always 1, whereas in B, it is replaced by a number between 0 and 1. Moreover, when compared to B, PI discounts bilateral terms related to the links between all pairs of peripheral groups. Thus, PI is smaller than B (except in the case of two groups only). We therefore have the following

[11]Dominance is not always correlated with the relative size of the group. For example, Tutsis, who account for only 14 percent in Rwanda, represent a dominant minority group in a country where almost everybody else is of Hutu ethnic origin. Laitin (2000) also points to several cases of minority groups imposing their language on the majority, such as Spanish in South America, Amharic in Ethiopia, and Afrikaans in South Africa.

TABLE 6.1. Values of A, B, and PI indices for
examples with two and three groups

Society's Profile	Distances	A Index	B Index	PI Index
Two groups $(0.5, 0.5)$	0.5	0.5	0.125	0.125
Two groups $(0.6, 0.4)$	0.5	0.48	0.12	0.12
Two groups $(0.6, 0.4)$	0.75	0.48	0.18	0.18
Two groups $(0.8, 0.2)$	0.5	0.32	0.08	0.08
Two groups $(0.8, 0.2)$	0.75	0.32	0.12	0.12
Three groups $(0.333, 0.333, 0.333)$	0.5	0.667	0.167	0.111
Three groups $(0.333, 0.333, 0.333)$	$(0.6, 0.6, 0.2)$	0.667	0.156	0.089
Three groups $(0.5, 0.25, 0.25)$	0.5	0.625	0.156	0.125
Three groups $(0.5, 0.25, 0.25)$	$(0.6, 0.6, 0.2)$	0.625	0.162	0.1
Three groups $(0.7, 0.2, 0.1)$	0.5	0.46	0.115	0.105
Three groups $(0.7, 0.2, 0.1)$	$(0.6, 0.6, 0.2)$	0.46	0.13	0.098
Three groups $(0.8, 0.1, 0.1)$	0.5	0.34	0.085	0.08
Three groups $(0.8, 0.1, 0.1)$	$(0.6, 0.6, 0.2)$	0.34	0.098	0.064
Four groups $(0.25, 0.25, 0.25, 0.25)$	0.5	0.75	0.188	0.094

Note: The first column shows the population shares of various groups.

The second column shows the linguistic distances between the groups that constitute a society. This is a unique number in a two-group society and/or in a society with equal-size groups. In the three-group society X, Y, Z with distinct group sizes, distances are presented in the following order: distance between X and Y, then X and Z, and finally, Y and Z.

In calculating the PI index the largest group is assumed to be dominant. In the case of equal-size groups, the first is considered to be the dominant group.

relationship between the three indices:

$$A \geqslant B \geqslant PI.$$

Examples of calculations for all four indices for two- and three-group societies are given in table 6.1.

Distances vary widely in the real world. This is illustrated in table 6.2 which lists the values of A, B, and PI for 218 countries (Desmet, Ortuño-Ortín, and Weber 2009). These data will be used in section 1 of chapter 7.

1.3. Polarization Indices

The measurement of polarization developed by Esteban and Ray (1994)[12] is based on what they call a general index of *social effective*

---

[12]See also Wolfson (1994).

antagonism in an environment where groups are determined by their incomes. Desmet, Ortuño-Ortín, and Weber (2009) apply this approach to multilingual societies.

An individual in a specific group identifies with other individuals in the group because of the common language spoken by its members. The degree of identification depends on the size of the group, s_k, and is given by the value s_k^α, where the exponent $\alpha \geqslant 1$ captures the notion that if $\alpha > 1$, identification is stronger in larger groups.

An individual who belongs to group k also feels alienation toward an individual of another group l. The degree of alienation is positively correlated with the linguistic distance between groups.[13] The degree of alienation is given by $s_k \times d_{kl}$, where d_{kl} represents the linguistic distance between the groups.

The two features, identification with own group and alienation toward others, create societal antagonism. Given the population shares of two groups, s_k and s_l, the combined effective antagonism of group k toward group l is equal to $s_k^\alpha \times (s_k \times d_{kl}) \times s_l$ or $s_k^{1+\alpha} \times s_l \times d_{kl}$.

The societal level of social effective antagonism is the sum of the effective antagonisms between all pairs of groups:

$$ER = \sum_{k=1}^{K} \sum_{l=1}^{K} s_k^{1+\alpha} s_l d_{kl},$$

where from the formal point of view, the only difference between ER and B is the exponent α. The axioms introduced by Esteban and Ray allow them to narrow the range of α to the interval between 1 and 1.6.

The polarization index ER can be considered the counterpart of the B fractionalization index. One can also consider a version A of their index by ignoring distances, that is, by setting all the d_{kl} terms equal to 1 in the expression of ER. Reynal-Querol (2002) constructed a special case of such an index by setting α equal to 1. By some algebraic rearrangement, her index can be written:

$$RQ = \sum_{k=1}^{K} s_k^2 (1 - s_k).$$

Montalvo and Reynal-Querol (2005) justify this functional form by showing that α has to be equal to 1 for a size-based index to satisfy the polarization properties. They focus on what they call *relevant* groups,

---

[13]It may also happen that the sense of identification of an individual with her own group may affect her alienation toward another group.

TABLE 6.2. Indices for 218 countries (Africa)

Number	Country	A Index	B Index	PI Index
North Africa				
31	Sudan	0.587	0.457	0.393
140	Morocco	0.466	0.062	0.057
152	Egypt	0.509	0.048	0.038
155	Algeria	0.313	0.046	0.043
164	Libya	0.362	0.038	0.033
206	Tunisia	0.012	0.005	0.005
Sub-Saharan Africa				
6	Chad	0.950	0.591	0.177
11	Niger	0.646	0.540	0.420
17	Congo	0.820	0.511	0.465
21	Namibia	0.808	0.488	0.239
24	Kenya	0.901	0.472	0.135
27	Nigeria	0.870	0.463	0.137
28	Uganda	0.928	0.461	0.119
37	South Africa	0.869	0.394	0.118
39	Central African Republic	0.960	0.385	0.183
40	Dem. Rep. of Congo	0.948	0.376	0.077
53	Sao Tome e Principe	0.389	0.311	0.282
57	Mali	0.876	0.303	0.113
60	Guinea-Bissau	0.853	0.278	0.090
68	Cameroon	0.942	0.248	0.062
69	Sierra Leone	0.817	0.245	0.101
80	Eritrea	0.749	0.178	0.088
81	Mauritania	0.172	0.170	0.167
85	Tanzania	0.965	0.149	0.022
88	Liberia	0.912	0.142	0.043
92	Gabon	0.919	0.137	0.032

thus avoiding the issue of distances by implicitly using a dichotomous 0–1 distance measure between groups. The axiomatic support for the choice of $\alpha = 1$ is suggested by Geng (2009).

1.4. Identification of Groups and Data

The most widely used data set of worldwide ethnolinguistic fractionalization was constructed by a group of about seventy Soviet ethnographers from the Miklukho-Maklai Research Institute in Moscow, which was part of the Department of Geodesy and Cartography at the USSR State Geological Committee. Their country-by-country construction, widely known as ELF (ethnolingistic fractionalization), is based mainly on the linguistic and historic origins of various groups. The findings

TABLE 6.2. (cont.) Indices for 218 countries (Africa)

Number	Country	A Index	B Index	PI Index
	Sub-Saharan Africa			
100	Equatorial Guinea	0.453	0.112	0.086
103	Ethiopia	0.843	0.109	0.057
105	Djibouti	0.592	0.099	0.064
111	Gambia	0.748	0.094	0.064
113	Burkina Faso	0.773	0.091	0.051
119	Cote d'Ivoire	0.917	0.085	0.029
123	Guinea	0.748	0.078	0.058
126	Botswana	0.444	0.076	0.059
128	Senegal	0.772	0.076	0.039
129	Benin	0.901	0.075	0.029
131	Cape Verde Islands	0.070	0.070	0.070
134	Malawi	0.519	0.067	0.048
141	Zimbabwe	0.526	0.060	0.043
142	Togo	0.897	0.060	0.023
149	Madagascar	0.656	0.051	0.035
150	Ghana	0.805	0.050	0.029
163	Angola	0.785	0.038	0.019
167	Zambia	0.855	0.035	0.015
172	Mozambique	0.929	0.029	0.008
178	Somalia	0.179	0.025	0.023
202	Lesotho	0.260	0.007	0.006
207	Swaziland	0.228	0.005	0.005
212	Burundi	0.004	0.001	0.001
213	Rwanda	0.004	0.001	0.001

Source: Desmet, Ortuño-Ortín, and Weber (2009).

Note: The number appearing in the first column is the order in which countries are ranked according to the *B* index, starting with the largest value of the index.

of this remarkable and impressive project were published in the *Atlas Narodov Mira* (*Atlas of Peoples of the World*) in 1964 and introduced into the Western literature by Rustow (1967) and Taylor and Hudson (1972). There is a consensus among scholars that, to a large extent, ELF is not contaminated by political motives, even though some delicate political cases at the time, such as South and North Vietnam, South and North Korea, and Taiwan, are omitted from the survey. Taylor and Hudson argue that the Soviet data contain no systematic differences between countries from the Western and Eastern blocs. Moreover, there is a strong degree of similarity between ELF and other data sets, such as those of Roberts (1962) and Muller (1964).

Roberts focuses on the challenges of linguistic communication created by industrial development in Asia, Africa, and Latin America.

TABLE 6.2. (cont.) Indices for 218 countries (America)

Number	Country	A Index	B Index	PI Index
North America				
94	Canada	0.549	0.129	0.097
96	Mexico	0.135	0.127	0.123
112	USA	0.353	0.092	0.078
Central America				
2	Belize	0.693	0.624	0.433
14	Guatemala	0.691	0.518	0.500
51	Panama	0.324	0.322	0.303
120	Nicaragua	0.081	0.081	0.081
151	Costa Rica	0.050	0.049	0.049
154	Honduras	0.056	0.046	0.046
208	El Salvador	0.004	0.004	0.004
Antilles-Caribbean				
18	Cayman Islands	0.547	0.505	0.499
22	Trinidad and Tobago	0.696	0.487	0.338
43	Aruba	0.387	0.359	0.355
52	U.S. Virgin Islands	0.339	0.319	0.316
54	Dominica	0.313	0.308	0.306
59	Bahamas	0.386	0.295	0.272
82	British Virgin Islands	0.167	0.167	0.167
86	Turks and Caicos Islands	0.145	0.145	0.145
89	Anguilla	0.140	0.140	0.140
107	Netherlands Antilles	0.266	0.097	0.088
115	Barbados	0.091	0.091	0.091
143	Antigua and Barbuda	0.057	0.057	0.056
147	Dominican Republic	0.053	0.051	0.051
158	Martinique	0.043	0.043	0.043
165	Guadeloupe	0.084	0.038	0.037
177	Montserrat	0.026	0.026	0.026
181	Grenada	0.064	0.022	0.022
186	Saint Lucia	0.020	0.020	0.020
193	Jamaica	0.011	0.011	0.011
196	Saint Kitts and Nevis	0.010	0.010	0.010
198	St. Vincent and Grenadines	0.009	0.009	0.009
203	Puerto Rico	0.049	0.006	0.006
216	Haiti	0.000	0.000	0.000
217	Cuba	0.001	0.000	0.000
218	Bermuda	0.000	0.000	0.000

Her relatively small data set[14] includes sixty-six Asian and African countries and summary statistics for Latin America. Muller's more extensive data set (and its elegant description) covers 144 languages with at least one million speakers each (at that time), and fifty-six

[14]That includes South and North Vietnam, South and North Korea, and Taiwan, all missing from ELF.

TABLE 6.2. (cont.) Indices for 218 countries (America)

Number	Country	A Index	B Index	PI Index
South America				
1	Bolivia	0.680	0.650	0.463
5	Suriname	0.788	0.595	0.301
44	Peru	0.376	0.350	0.336
50	Paraguay	0.347	0.322	0.314
56	French Guiana	0.480	0.304	0.244
70	Ecuador	0.264	0.243	0.238
95	Argentina	0.213	0.127	0.118
124	Guyana	0.078	0.077	0.076
171	Chile	0.034	0.030	0.030
176	Colombia	0.030	0.026	0.026
179	Venezuela	0.026	0.024	0.024
194	Brazil	0.032	0.011	0.011
201	Uruguay	0.092	0.007	0.007

Source: Desmet, Ortuño-Ortín, and Weber (2009).

Note: The number appearing in the first column is the order in which countries are ranked according to the *B* index, starting with the largest value of the index.

additional languages of some political, anthropological, or cultural importance. The size of both data sets is small in comparison with ELF, which covers about 1,600 languages and almost all countries in the world.

The ELF project was expanded by Alesina et al. (2003), who disentangle the linguistic and ethnic aspects of fractionalization and construct separate data sets determined by linguistic, ethnic, and religious affiliation. While the linguistic variable is calculated entirely on the basis of data from the 2001 *Encyclopaedia Britannica*, the construction of the ethnic data set necessitated using additional data from the 2000 *CIA World Fact Book*, as well as Levinsohn (1998) and the Minority Rights Group International (1998). In summary, the impressive Alesina et al. data sets cover some two hundred countries, 1,055 major linguistic groups, and 650 ethnic groups. Although these data sets are based on countries, Alesina and Zhuravskaya (2008) went a step farther and, using census data, extended the previous data sets to cover about one hundred countries on a subnational (regional) level.

Desmet, Ortuño-Ortín, and Weber (2009) construct an alternative data-set using distances based on *Ethnologue*'s much richer[15] lin-

---

[15] For example, *Ethnologue* lists 291 living languages in Mexico, while *Britannica* lists only twenty-one.

TABLE 6.2. (cont.) Indices for 218 countries (Asia)

Number	Country	A Index	B Index	PI Index
Middle East				
3	United Arab Emirates	0.777	0.623	0.382
8	Qatar	0.608	0.545	0.500
16	Iran	0.797	0.512	0.403
25	Bahrain	0.663	0.467	0.314
32	Georgia	0.576	0.453	0.366
36	Israel	0.665	0.407	0.296
45	Azerbaijan	0.373	0.349	0.332
48	Iraq	0.666	0.328	0.205
61	Oman	0.693	0.269	0.149
64	Turkey	0.289	0.258	0.245
75	Syria	0.503	0.203	0.157
77	Saudi Arabia	0.609	0.191	0.111
87	Lebanon	0.161	0.144	0.142
108	Armenia	0.174	0.096	0.091
138	Yemen	0.579	0.065	0.044
148	Jordan	0.484	0.051	0.040
170	Kuwait	0.556	0.031	0.026
190	West Bank and Gaza	0.208	0.015	0.015
Central Asia				
13	Kazakhstan	0.701	0.521	0.369
23	Kyrgyzstan	0.670	0.481	0.349
33	Bhutan	0.846	0.442	0.335
35	India	0.930	0.427	0.111
42	Tajikistan	0.482	0.360	0.320
47	Nepal	0.742	0.333	0.201
49	Afghanistan	0.732	0.325	0.186
55	Sri Lanka	0.313	0.306	0.303
63	Uzbekistan	0.428	0.263	0.228
73	Turkmenistan	0.386	0.221	0.194
114	Pakistan	0.762	0.091	0.051
168	Bangladesh	0.332	0.034	0.030

guistic trees, discussed in chapter 3.[16] One may argue that highly detailed data lead to group identification problems if the A index is used. As argued above, the introduction of linguistic distances largely solves these problems and it is no longer necessary to make ad hoc choices about whether Venetian and Italian belong to the same group or not. By using distances, Venetian and Italian are two distinct groups,

[16]Trees are also used by Fearon (2003) and Alesina et al. (2003). Desmet, Ortuño-Ortín, and Wacziarg (2009) use such data to point out the important role played by varying (exogenously chosen) levels of linguistic aggregation.

TABLE 6.2. (cont.) Indices for 218 countries (Asia)

Number	Country	A Index	B Index	PI Index
Far East				
12	Malaysia	0.758	0.525	0.341
15	Singapore	0.748	0.515	0.298
26	Laos	0.678	0.466	0.336
62	Brunei	0.456	0.265	0.221
65	Thailand	0.753	0.254	0.111
66	Myanmar	0.521	0.254	0.196
83	Viet Nam	0.234	0.161	0.150
90	Indonesia	0.846	0.138	0.064
104	China	0.491	0.107	0.083
110	Cambodia	0.157	0.094	0.090
116	Philippines	0.849	0.090	0.036
127	Taiwan	0.488	0.076	0.062
144	Mongolia	0.331	0.054	0.047
191	Japan	0.028	0.014	0.014
209	Korea, South	0.003	0.003	0.003
221	Korea, North	0.000	0.000	0.000

Source: Desmet, Ortuño-Ortín, and Weber (2009).

Note: The number appearing in the first column is the order in which countries are ranked according to the *B* index, starting with the largest value of the index.

but the linguistic distance that separates them is small. While more disaggregated data are preferable, they should be matched with an appropriate functional form of the index.

The findings of the Soviet project have been extensively used by researchers working in various disciplines. We would like, however, to take the opportunity here to dispel a misconception that emerged in the burgeoning fractionalization literature. Most studies mistakenly view ELF as an index of ethnolinguistic fractionalization. ELF is not an index but rather an impressive data set. What the literature mistakenly refers to as the ELF index is in fact Greenberg's *A* index based on the ELF data set, which had already been calculated by Taylor and Hudson (1972). Likewise, the Muller and Rogers measures in Easterly and Levine (1997) are values of Greenberg's *A* index for the Muller and Rogers data sets, respectively, and have nothing to do with ELF. The same comment applies to recent studies of fractionalization that use the *A* index (or some other index) based on *Ethnologue*'s trees, *Britannica*, the *CIA World Fact Book*, or any other recently constructed data set. In short, calling an index ELF without relying on the Soviet 1964 data set prolongs confusion.

TABLE 6.2. (cont.) Indices for 218 countries (Europe)

Number	Country	A Index	B Index	PI Index
	Northern Europe			
30	Estonia	0.476	0.457	0.451
71	Greenland	0.242	0.242	0.242
99	Finland	0.140	0.121	0.120
118	Sweden	0.167	0.088	0.083
125	Latvia	0.595	0.077	0.065
156	Lithuania	0.339	0.044	0.042
187	Denmark	0.051	0.018	0.017
211	Iceland	0.019	0.001	0.001
	Central and Eastern Europe			
76	Slovakia	0.307	0.196	0.180
78	Russia	0.283	0.183	0.165
79	Bulgaria	0.224	0.178	0.172
84	Hungary	0.158	0.153	0.153
93	Romania	0.168	0.134	0.130
98	Moldova	0.589	0.122	0.091
101	Serbia and Montenegro	0.359	0.112	0.096
137	Ukraine	0.492	0.066	0.053
146	Bosnia and Herzegovina	0.416	0.053	0.044
166	Belarus	0.397	0.037	0.033
174	Albania	0.257	0.028	0.026
185	Slovenia	0.174	0.021	0.020
195	Croatia	0.087	0.010	0.010
199	Czech Republic	0.069	0.008	0.008
205	Poland	0.060	0.006	0.006
	Western Europe			
91	Netherlands	0.389	0.137	0.113
102	Belgium	0.734	0.110	0.065
106	France	0.272	0.097	0.087
121	Switzerland	0.547	0.079	0.067
132	Luxembourg	0.498	0.069	0.061
133	Germany	0.189	0.067	0.063
157	United Kingdom	0.139	0.044	0.042
159	Austria	0.540	0.042	0.033
173	Ireland	0.223	0.028	0.027
180	Andorra	0.574	0.024	0.020
184	Monaco	0.521	0.022	0.019
197	Liechtenstein	0.128	0.010	0.010

2. DISENFRANCHISEMENT INDICES

We now consider a multilingual society in which every member is characterized by her linguistic repertoire, represented by the languages she is proficient in. Assume that the society faces the problem of selecting

TABLE 6.2. (cont.) Indices for 218 countries (Europe)

Number	Country	A Index	B Index	PI Index
	Southern Europe			
20	Gibraltar	0.498	0.498	0.498
41	Cyprus	0.366	0.361	0.358
74	Macedonia	0.566	0.212	0.152
153	Spain	0.438	0.046	0.037
160	Greece	0.175	0.041	0.039
162	Italy	0.593	0.039	0.031
169	San Marino	0.494	0.032	0.032
189	Malta	0.016	0.016	0.016
192	Portugal	0.022	0.011	0.011
225	Vatican State	0.000	0.000	0.000

Source: Desmet, Ortuño-Ortín, and Weber (2009).

Note: The number appearing in the first column is the order in which countries are ranked according to the B index, starting with the largest value of the index.

a subset of languages to be used in official documents, for communication between institutions and citizens, for debates in official bodies, and the like. Call these languages *core* languages. Their choice may have a major negative impact on the well-being of some members by limiting their access to laws, rules and regulations, and debates in their parliament. In some cases, these limitations could even violate the basic principles of the society. To determine the optimal set(s) of core languages, one has to weigh the costs of linguistic disenfranchisement against the benefits of standardization, as suggested in chapter 2. Here we focus on the construction of disenfranchisement indices for various choices of core languages. Applications of disenfranchisement indices are presented in chapter 7, where we also examine the optimal choice of languages in the EU, for each given number of languages.

We calculate disenfranchisement by using two alternative approaches. Like Greenberg (1956), we distinguish between *dichotomous* and *distance-adjusted indices*. An individual is disenfranchised under the dichotomous approach (Ginsburgh and Weber 2005) if she speaks no core language; she is not disenfranchised if she speaks at least one core language. This assumption is quite restrictive. If the individual speaks no core language, some of these languages may nevertheless have common roots with her native tongue and could be considered to reduce the degree of her disenfranchisement. As an example, we can consider Ana, who speaks only Spanish, and compare her attitude toward two potential sets of core languages, each consisting of a single language, Italian or German. Even though Ana speaks none of these,

TABLE 6.2. (cont.) Indices for 218 countries
(islands, Indian and Pacific Oceans)

Number	Country	A Index	B Index	PI Index
Indian Ocean				
7	Mauritius	0.641	0.564	0.499
34	Mayotte	0.459	0.433	0.410
135	Seychelles	0.067	0.066	0.066
136	Reunion	0.066	0.066	0.065
183	Comoros	0.551	0.022	0.016
214	Maldives	0.010	0.001	0.001
219	British Indian Ocean Terr.	0.000	0.000	0.000
Pacific Ocean				
161	Australia	0.126	0.039	0.038
Melanesia				
4	Papua New Guinea	0.990	0.598	0.038
9	New Caledonia	0.834	0.542	0.462
10	East Timor	0.897	0.540	0.119
19	Fiji	0.607	0.503	0.493
58	Solomon Islands	0.965	0.295	0.033
72	Vanuatu	0.972	0.238	0.016
Micronesia				
29	Guam	0.640	0.458	0.317
46	Northern Mariana Islands	0.642	0.341	0.234
67	Nauru	0.596	0.254	0.172
97	Micronesia	0.792	0.124	0.049
175	Marshall Islands	0.027	0.027	0.027
188	Kiribati	0.033	0.017	0.017
200	Palau	0.077	0.007	0.007

the cultural and linguistic proximity of Spanish and Italian ensures she would be better off with the choice of Italian. This shows that it could be worthwhile to examine indices adjusted for linguistic proximity (Ginsburgh, Ortuño-Ortín, and Weber 2005).

A second distinction can be made between disenfranchisement indices based on native languages of an individual, say the native Portuguese of Maria, and all other languages she is proficient in. In terms of disenfranchisement, Maria may judge the set of core languages on the basis of only one criterion—whether Portuguese is included in the core set or not. In most cases the native language substantially improves the ability of an individual to read, write, and communicate with others. Even if Maria is perfectly fluent in one of the core languages, say, Spanish, the noninclusion of Portuguese in

TABLE 6.2. (cont.) Indices for 218 countries
(islands, Indian and Pacific Oceans)

Number	Country	A Index	B Index	PI Index
Polynesia				
38	French Polynesia	0.596	0.385	0.284
109	New Zealand	0.102	0.095	0.094
117	American Samoa	0.116	0.088	0.086
130	Niue	0.071	0.071	0.071
139	Cook Islands	0.379	0.064	0.052
145	Tokelau	0.054	0.054	0.054
182	Wallis and Futuna	0.407	0.022	0.017
204	Tuvalu	0.139	0.006	0.006
210	Samoa	0.002	0.002	0.002
215	Tonga	0.015	0.000	0.000
222	Norfolk Island	0.000	0.000	0.000
Other islands				
122	Saint Pierre and Miquelon	0.134	0.078	0.076
220	Falkland Islands	0.000	0.000	0.000
223	Pitcairn	0.000	0.000	0.000
224	Saint Helena	0.000	0.000	0.000

Source: Desmet, Ortuño-Ortín, and Weber (2009).

Note: The number appearing in the first column is the order in which countries are ranked according to the B index, starting with the largest value of the index.

the core set may adversely affect her sense of national pride. But she may also accept communicating in Spanish, without losing anything. We therefore examine both possibilities: (1) disenfranchisement is calculated on the basis of native languages only, and (2) the entire set of languages known by an individual is taken into account.

This leads us to consider the four indices represented in table 6.3: D^n, dichotomous, based on native languages; D^l, dichotomous, based on all spoken languages; C^n, continuous (distance-adjusted), based on native languages; and C^l, continuous (distance-adjusted), based on all languages spoken by individuals. The distinction between

TABLE 6.3. Types of disenfranchisement indices

	Native	All Languages
Dichotomous index	D^n	D^l
(Distance)-adjusted index	C^n	C^l

native and non-native languages has an important implication in our analysis. If we consider native languages only, it is sufficient to disaggregate the society into groups according to native languages. If there is a native language that is spoken by everybody, such as in France or Germany, data collection is easy, since the number of speakers (almost) coincides with the total population. However, if disenfranchisement is determined on the basis of the entire linguistic repertoire of individuals, the division according to native languages is too coarse. If Spanish is a core language but Portuguese is not, Maria can reduce her disenfranchisement by utilizing Spanish, whereas a monolingual Portuguese speaker would still be disenfranchised. Since the distribution of linguistic repertoires within each group is not uniform, we have to disaggregate into *clusters* of individuals with identical linguistic repertoires. For, example in a society with two spoken languages, e and f, there will be three clusters: monolingual speakers of e, monolingual speakers of f, and bilingual individuals who speak both languages.

To proceed with our derivations, we introduce some simple notation. There will be K linguistic groups, where a typical group whose native language is k has a population share s_k. Every linguistic group is partitioned into several clusters i of individuals with identical linguistic repertoires $L(i)$, which could be e, f, or ef. The share of each such cluster is denoted by s_i.

Now suppose that a set of the core languages T consists of the native languages of some but not all groups.[17] To illustrate the discussion, we consider the following example.

Example. Suppose that there are three linguistic groups with population sizes E, F, and G and native languages, e, f, and g. Since some individuals may speak one or two other languages, the distribution of linguistic repertoires within each group is not uniform. Thus, as indicated above, we disaggregate each group into four clusters of members with an identical repertoire.

Group e is partitioned into $\bar{e}$ (monolingual speakers), ef (speakers of e and f), eg (speakers of e and g), and efg (speakers of e, f, and g). Similar partitions can be made for groups f and g. This leads to twelve clusters.

Table 6.4 gives the detailed (hypothetical) data. We assume that the linguistic distances are 0.2 between e and f, 0.5 between e and g, and 0.3 between f and g.

[17]If the set T consists of all spoken languages, the society incurs no disenfranchisement, and the value of all four indices for this comprehensive set is equal to 0.

TABLE 6.4. An example of dichotomous disenfranchisement indices

	Total	Only e	Only f	Only g	Both e, f	Both e, g	Both f, g	All Three e, f, g
Group e	200	100	—	—	50	30	—	20
Group f	300	—	150	—	40	—	90	20
Group g	500	—	—	300	—	100	100	—

To compute disenfranchisement indices, and similar to what was done for fractionalization indices, we need the following:

1. the functional form of an index;

2. data on language proficiency (both native and acquired) of individuals in a given country or group of countries (the EU, for example), which are usually provided by survey or census data;

3. distances between languages, as discussed in chapter 3.

2.1. Dichotomous Indices

Native Languages Only

For every potential set of core languages T, index $D^n(T)$ is simply equal to the population share of those groups whose native language is not included in T. Thus, the functional form of $D^n(T)$ is

$$D^n(T) = \sum_k s_k,$$

where the sum $\sum_k$ is taken over all groups whose native language is not included in T.

All Spoken Languages

For every possible set of core languages T, index $D^l(T)$ evaluates the share of those who, in the total population, speak no language in T. Here we take into account cluster disaggregation, and the functional form of $D^l(T)$ is

$$D^l(T) = \sum_i s_i,$$

where we count only those clusters whose language repertoire $L(i)$ has no common languages with T. The dichotomous index D^l differs from D^n in that here we also account for individuals who know *any* language included in the core set T, even if it is not their native language.

If the core set contains only one language, D^l coincides with a linguistic index studied by Gunnemark (1991), who examines the number of individuals who do not speak the official or the most widely spoken language in the country. It is also related to Van Parijs's (2005) principle of *minimal exclusion*. In his search for maximal communication, Van Parijs looks for a language that guarantees that the number of individuals who do not speak the language is the smallest possible.

2.2. Continuous (Distance-Adjusted) Indices

Disenfranchisement is again calculated with respect to a given set of core languages T, and the calculation refers to individuals who speak no language in T. But here, instead of considering disenfranchisement to be dichotomous (an individual knows or does not know a certain language), we take into account distances between languages. If the individual knows another language, the distance is 0; if not, we mitigate her disenfranchisement rate by replacing the value of 1 by the distance from her (native or spoken) linguistic repertoire to the set of core languages.

Native Languages Only

Again, we utilize here a coarser group partition. Similar to the shift from Greenberg's A index to his B index, the functional form of C^n differs from D^n by introducing the continuous variable $d_k(T)$, which represents the distance between the native language k and the closest to it in T:

$$C^n(T) = \sum_k s_k d_k(T).$$

The summation is made over all groups whose native language is not included in T. Otherwise, the corresponding term $d_k(T)$ is equal to 0.

All Spoken Languages

The functional form of C^l differs from D^l, as now distances are introduced:

$$C^l(T) = \sum_i s_i d_i(T).$$

TABLE 6.5. Comparing society's disenfranchisement rates

Sets of Core Languages	D^n	D^l	C^n	C^l
e	0.80	0.64	0.31	0.22
f	0.70	0.53	0.19	0.14
g	0.50	0.34	0.19	0.10
$\{e, f\}$	0.50	0.30	0.15	0.09
$\{e, g\}$	0.30	0.15	0.06	0.03
$\{f, g\}$	0.20	0.10	0.04	0.02
$\{e, f, g\}$	0.00	0.00	0.00	0.00

The societal disenfranchisement rates for all four indices D^n, D^l, C^n, and C^l examined in this section are calculated in section 5, and summarized in table 6.5. They are based on the data in table 6.4.

In the table, notice first that all values of D^n are larger than the corresponding values of D^l for all sets of core languages (except, of course, for efg, where the value of all indices is 0). The reason is obvious. Under the D^l index, the ability to speak one of the core languages is a clear disenfranchisement-reducing device for multilingual individuals whose native language does not belong to the set of core languages, even if they prefer to speak their native tongue.

Similarly, disenfranchisement indices C^n are larger than the corresponding values C^l for all sets of core languages (with the exception of the set efg) since, in addition to their native language, multilingual individuals may use other languages they know.

Indices D^n and C^n differ only in that the distance-adjusted index C^n allows individuals who do not speak a core language to use other languages they know to reduce their disenfranchisement. Thus, all the positive values of C^n are smaller than the corresponding entries for D^n.

Finally, the distance-adjusted index C^l allows individuals who do not know a core language to use the languages they know to reduce their disenfranchisement as well. Thus, all positive values of C^l are smaller than the corresponding entries for D^l.

2.3. Identification of Groups and Data

Since here one is dealing with the language repertoire of each individual of a society, region, or country, one has to use census or survey data, as long as they include questions on the whole repertoire of each individual and not only on the native language or the language that is spoken at home. In addition to those basic questions, it is useful to have some idea on the proficiency of the languages, and this is rarely dealt with in censuses, more often in surveys.

When dealing with cross-country censuses or surveys, there is often a problem with the formulation of questions, which is hardly identical in all countries. This is not so with the regularly conducted surveys of the EU member states. They include questions on the repertoire and depth of knowledge, and are identical in all states. In all cases, however, one should note that the data are self-reported, and over- or underconfidence may be problematic.

Here are some details of such a survey that we exploit in section 2 of chapter 7. This survey (Special Eurobarometer 243, 2006) was carried out in November 2005 in all member countries of the EU, plus Bulgaria and Romania (which were not yet members in 2005) and two candidate countries, Croatia and Turkey. In most countries, 1,000 citizens were interviewed. The exceptions are Germany (1,500), the United Kingdom (1,300), Luxembourg (500), and Malta (500). The total number of usable interviews amounts to 28,694. Among the technical specifications, it is worth mentioning the following recommendations:

> [T]he survey covers the national population of citizens ... that are residents in those countries and have a sufficient command of one of the respective national language(s) to answer the questionnaire. The basic sample design applied in all states is a multi-stage, random (probability) one. In each country, a number of sampling points was drawn with probability proportional to population size (for a total coverage of the country) and to population density.

> In order to do so, the sampling points were drawn systematically from each of the "administrative regional units," after stratification by individual unit and type of area. They thus represent the whole territory of the countries surveyed according to the distribution of the resident population of the respective nationalities in terms of metropolitan, urban and rural areas. In each of the selected sampling points, a starting address was drawn, at random. Further addresses (every Nth address) were selected by standard "random route" procedures, from the initial address. In each household, the respondent was drawn, at random (following the "closest birthday rule"). All interviews were conducted face-to-face in people's homes and in the appropriate national language. As far as the data capture is concerned, CAPI (Computer Assisted Personal Interview) was used in those countries where this technique was available.

For each country a comparison between the sample and the universe was carried out. The universe description was derived from Eurostat population data or from national statistics offices. For all countries surveyed, a national weighting procedure, using marginal and intercellular weighting, was carried out based on this universe description. In all countries, gender, age, region and size of locality were introduced in the iteration procedure. For international weighting (i.e. EU averages), TNS Opinion & Social applies the official population figures as provided by EUROSTAT or national statistics offices.

The data that we used were taken from the answers to the following questions:

1. D48a. What is your mother tongue? (do not probe—do not read out—multiple answers possible).

   Follows a list of thirty-four languages that include the twenty-three member states' official languages, as well as Arabic, Catalan, Chinese, Croatian, Luxembourgish, Russian, Turkish, Basque, Galician, Other regional languages, Other.

2. D48b to D48d. Which languages do you speak well enough in order to be able to have a conversation, excluding your mother tongue? (do not probe—do not read out—multiple answers possible).

   Follows the same list of thirty-four languages. This question was asked for first, second, and third foreign languages.

3. D48f. Is your (language cited in 48b, 48c, and 48d) very good, good, basic? (show card with scale).

Table 6.6 provides an overview of the official languages spoken in the EU as of 2006. The lower part of the table lists some additional languages spoken in Europe, including those that have been proposed as contenders for official language status (Basque, Catalan, and Galician), those of the candidate countries (Croatian and Turkish), Russian, and those of the main immigration communities (Arabic, and languages of the Indian subcontinent).

The table is divided into several columns. Columns 1 and 2 display the number of those who are native speakers of each language or who report their linguistic skills as good or very good, both in the native country or countries (for instance, German in Austria and Germany, English in the United Kingdom and Ireland) and elsewhere in the EU,

TABLE 6.6. Linguistic groups in the European Union and worldwide (millions)

	EU		Worldwide	
	Home (1)	Abroad (2)	Native (3)	All (4)
Bulgarian	7.6	0.2	n.a.	9.0
Czech	10.2	1.8	n.a.	12.0
Danish	5.4	1.0	5.0	5.3
Dutch	23.3	0.7	20.0	n.a.
English	63.3	119.3	400.0	1,500.0
Estonian	1.2	0.1	1.0	n.a.
Finnish	5.2	0.5	4.7	6.0
French	67.8	29.4	72.0	122.0
German	89.6	32.1	n.a.	120.0
Greek	11.8	1.1	12.0	n.a.
Hungarian	10.1	2.9	12.0	14.5
Irish	0.6	0.3	0.03	n.a.
Italian	56.8	8.0	57.0	63.0
Latvian	2.1	0.1	1.5	n.a.
Lithuanian	3.4	0.2	4.0	n.a.
Luxembourgish	0.4	0.0	0.4	n.a.
Maltese	0.4	0.0	0.3	n.a.
Polish	37.6	3.3	n.a.	44.0
Portuguese	10.5	1.7	175.0	187.0
Romanian	21.3	0.9	20.0	26.0
Slovak	5.2	2.0	5.0	n.a.
Slovenian	2.0	0.8	2.2	n.a.
Spanish	42.2	11.9	270.0	350.0
Swedish	9.0	1.8	9.3	n.a.

denoted as "Abroad." Columns 3 and 4 give the worldwide numbers of speakers estimated by Crystal (1999).

Some general remarks are in order. First, the table clearly shows that cross-border mobility is limited in the EU: English, French, German, Italian, Polish, and Spanish are the only languages with more than three million native speakers outside their native countries. Hungarian has 2.9 million speakers abroad, but this includes large indigenous populations of ethnic Hungarians in Slovakia and Romania. Second, as expected, English, French, German, and Spanish are the most widespread languages. Russian, a nonofficial and indeed a non-EU language, is spoken well or very well by 22 million EU citizens. As such, it is the eighth largest language in the EU, after English (183 million), German (122 million), French (97 million), Italian (65 million), Spanish (54 million), Polish (41 million), Dutch (24 million), and Romanian (22

TABLE 6.6. (cont.) Linguistic groups in
the European Union and worldwide (millions)

	EU		Worldwide	
	Home (1)	Abroad (2)	Native (3)	All (4)
Basque	1.1	0.2	0.6	n.a.
Catalan	5.4	0.4	4.0	9.0
Galician	2.9	0.1	3.0	n.a.
Other regional		13.8		
Croatian		1.7	4.8	n.a.
Turkish		2.6	59.0	n.a.
Russian		22.4	170.0	290.0
Arabic		2.5	200.0	n.a.
Indian SC		2.6		
Other		6.3		

Source: Fidrmuc, Ginsburgh, and Weber (2007).
Note: Columns 1 and 2 report the number of people who are either native speakers or assess their linguistic skills as good or very good (those with basic skills and those unable to assess their skills are not included) in their native country (home) or abroad. Columns 3 and 4 show the worldwide numbers of speakers for each language according to Crystal (1999). Note that these are sometimes smaller than those given for more restricted areas in columns 1 and 2. The native countries for English are the United Kingdom and Ireland, German is attributed to Germany and Austria, France, Belgium, and Luxembourg are taken as the native countries for French, Dutch is native in the Netherlands and Belgium, Greek is native in Greece and Cyprus. We assume that Catalan, Basque, and Galician are native only to Spain, and Hungarian to Hungary (although sizable ethnic Hungarian minorities live in Slovakia and Romania). Indian SC includes the languages of the Indian subcontinent: Hindi, Urdu, Punjabi, Gujarati, and Bengali. Indian SC languages, Arabic, and Russian are assumed not to be native in any of the EU countries.

million). The accession of Turkey would add 73 million speakers of Turkish, propelling that language into fourth position. While six or seven languages dominate in the EU, English is clearly a step ahead of the others.

3. LINKS BETWEEN FRACTIONALIZATION, DISENFRANCHISEMENT, AND COMMUNICATION INDICES

The concept of disenfranchisement is based on the notion that individuals are adversely affected if the languages they speak, in particular the native one, do not receive full-fledged status and support from the center. One of the important reasons is that excluding a language from the set of core languages limits the channels of communication of its speakers with the center, where decisions are made and official documents are produced, edited, translated, and distributed. Communication with the center and the ability of the latter to represent the will of its members is one of the basic principles of democratic institutions.

It is therefore interesting to examine the link between disenfranchisement index D^n, Greenberg's (1956) communication index H, and its extension H_b by Lieberson (1964), described in section 2.1 of chapter 3. Consider a society that consists of two groups, S and C. Group S is formed by *citizens*, and group C (the center) by *bureaucrats*. Assume that all citizens in group S speak only their native language, whereas every bureaucrat speaks all the languages included in the set T of core languages. The communicative distance between S and C, represented by the Lieberson two-sided index H_b, is the probability that a randomly chosen individual in S can communicate with a randomly chosen bureaucrat in the center. In our setting, this amounts to the probability that the native language of a randomly chosen member of S is included in T. This is the dichotomous index D^n of group S, subtracted from 1.

The interpretation of index D^l is quite similar. The only difference with respect to D^n is a change in our assumption, since now we accept that individuals in S can communicate with the center in any language they speak. The communicative distance between S and C, represented by H_b, is determined by the probability that a randomly chosen pair of individuals, one from group S and another from group C, have at least one common language and can communicate with each other. It is the value of the dichotomous index D^l of group S, subtracted from 1.

The link between distance-adjusted indices C^n and C^l, examined in this chapter, and other communication and fractionalization indices is more subtle. Consider all linguistic groups in S identified by speakers of the same native language. The value of the disenfranchisement index C^n for S is determined by the average linguistic distance between the native languages of all members of S and the center C. This is the value of the peripheral index PI of Desmet, Ortuño-Ortín, and Weber (2005), which measures the average linguistic distance between all peripheral clusters and the center.

To embed the value of C^l into the communication distances framework, we need to modify the previous argument. If one wants to calculate the average linguistic distance between S and the center C while taking into account the entire linguistic repertoire of the society's members, a partition into linguistic groups determined by native languages does not suffice. Indeed, there could be individuals whose non-native languages would reduce the distance to the center. To overcome this difficulty, one needs to disaggregate S into groups of individuals with identical linguistic repertoires, the clusters considered in sections 2.1 and 2.2 of this chapter. Then the value of the peripheral index PI over clusters in S would represent the average communicative distance when all spoken languages of members of S are accounted for. The latter is precisely the value of the distance-adjusted disenfranchisement index C^l. Note that if a member of S speaks a language from T, she makes an identical contribution to the disenfranchisement values D^l and C^l. However, if she speaks no language from T, rather than assigning the value of 1, as is done under the dichotomous index D^l, under C^l we take the shortest linguistic distance between two languages, one in her repertoire and one in T.

4. SUMMARY

In this chapter we have discussed the measurement of diversity based on a set of societal attributes that allows identifying the number and size of various groups. We examined fractionalization, polarization, and disenfranchisement indices of two types. The first type of index takes into account only the number and size of groups, the second type also takes into account the linguistic distances between various groups. If one adopts the dichotomous approach, in which the distance between every pair of different groups is set to 1, size-based indices can be viewed as special cases of the second type.

While recognizing differences between the various types of indices, we think it is important to underline their common features. We therefore devoted the last section to a discussion of the links between fractionalization, disenfranchisement, and communication indices. We also described the nature of the data sets used to compute such indices.

5. Appendix: Numerical Calculation of the Various Disenfranchisement Indices

Native Languages Only

If the core set T consists of one language, then all individuals in the other two groups are disenfranchised. Thus, $D^n(e) = (F+G)/1,000 = 0.8$, $D^n(f) = (E+G)/1,000 = 0.7$, and $D^n(g) = (E+F)/1,000 = 0.5$.

If the core set T consists of two languages, then only individuals in the third group are disenfranchised. Thus, $D^n(ef) = G/1,000 = 0.5$, $D^n(eg) = F/1,000 = 0.3$, and $D^n(fg) = E/1,000 = 0.2$.

All Spoken Languages

If the core set contains only a single language, say e, then only those individuals in f and g who do not speak e will be disenfranchised. Thus, we have to count only clusters $\bar{f}$, fg, $\bar{g}$, and gf, which gives us $D^l(e) = (150 + 90 + 300 + 100)/1,000 = 0.64$. A similar count for the core set f yields $D^l(f) = (100 + 30 + 300 + 100)/1,000 = 0.53$, and for g it is $D^l(g) = (100 + 50 + 150 + 40)/1,000 = 0.34$.

If the core set contains two languages, say e, f, then only monolingual individuals in g will be disenfranchised, as they speak neither e nor f. Their share in the total population is $300/1,000$, and $D^l(ef) = 0.3$. Similarly, the shares of monolingual individuals in f and e give us the values $D^l(eg) = 150/1,000 = 0.15$, and $D^l(fg) = 100/1,000 = 0.1$, respectively.

Native Languages Only

As for index D^n, if the core set T contains one language only, only individuals in the other two groups are disenfranchised. However, the calculations for D^n have to be adjusted for distance.

Consider the set $T = e$. The distance $d_{fe} = 0.2$, and $d_{ge} = 0.5$. Thus, $C^n(e) = (300 \times 0.2 + 500 \times 0.5)/1,000 = 0.31$. Similarly, for $T = f$, $d_{ef} = 0.2$ and $d_{gf} = 0.3$. Then $C^n(f) = (200 \times 0.2 + 500 \times 0.3)/1,000 = 0.19$. Finally, for $T = g$, $d_{eg} = 0.5$ and $d_{fg} = 0.3$. Thus, $C^n(g) = (200 \times 0.5 + 300 \times 0.3)/1,000 = 0.19$.

If the core set T consists of two languages, then only the third group is disenfranchised. For the set $T = ef$ there are 500 members in g for whom of the two languages e and f, f is closer, so that $d_{gf} = 0.3$. Hence, $C^n(ef) = (500 \times 0.3)/1,000 = 0.15$. For $T = eg$, there are 300 members of f and $d_{fe} = 0.2$. Then $C^n(eg) = (300 \times 0.2)/1,000 =$

0.06. Finally, for $T = fg$, there are 200 members of f and $d_{fe} = 0.2$, yielding $C^n(fg) = (200 \times 0.2)/1{,}000 = 0.04$.

All Spoken Languages

As for the D^l index, if the core set T consists of one language, then only individuals in the other two groups are disenfranchised. However, the analysis here becomes a bit more delicate.

Consider the set $T = e$. Group e and clusters fe, feg, and ge (360 individuals in total), speak e and do not contribute to the disenfranchisement index. Clusters $\bar{f}$, fg, and gf (340 individuals in total) are at a distance 0.2 from e. The rest of the society, namely, 300 monolingual individuals in g, is at a linguistic distance of 0.5 from e. Thus, $C^l(e) = (340 \times 0.2 + 300 \times 0.5)/1{,}000 = 0.218$.

Similarly, for $T = f$, group f and clusters ef, efg, and gf (470 individuals in total) speak f. Clusters $\bar{e}$, eg, and ge (230 individuals in total) are at a distance 0.2 from e. Only 300 monolingual individuals in g are at a distance 0.3 from f. Thus, $C^l(f) = (230 \times 0.2 + 300 \times 0.3)/1{,}000 = 0.136$.

If $T = g$, group g and clusters eg, efg, fg, and feg (660 individuals in total) speak g. Clusters $\bar{f}$, fe, and ef (240 individuals in total) are at a distance 0.2 from g, while 100 monolingual individuals in e are at distance 0.5 from g. Thus, $C^l(g) = (240 \times 0.2 + 100 \times 0.5)/1{,}000 = 0.098$.

If the core set T consists of two languages, then only monolingual individuals in the third group are disenfranchised. For the set $T = ef$, there are 300 of those in cluster $\bar{g}$ with $d_{gf} = 0.3$, and $C^l(ef) = (300 \times 0.3)/1{,}000 = 0.09$.

For $T = eg$, 150 monolingual members of $\bar{f}$ are at a distance 0.2 from e, and $C^l(eg) = (150 \times 0.2)/1{,}000 = 0.03$.

In the case of $T = gf$, 100 monolingual members of cluster $\bar{e}$ are at a distance 0.2 from f, and $C^l(gf) = (100 \times 0.2)/1{,}000 = 0.02$.

Chapter 7

DIVERSITY AND DISENFRANCHISEMENT: APPLICATIONS

> Civilizations should be measured by the degree of
> diversity attained and by the degree of unity retained.
> —*W. H. Auden*

WHEN, SEVERAL YEARS AGO, *one of us visited the Higashi Honganji Temple in Kyoto, the ancient capital of Japan, he saw two sentences written on the wall: "Living together in diversity. Learning to accept our differences." Easier said than done. The political and economic success of societies and countries, not to mention civilizations, is in many ways determined by their degree of cohesiveness. To sustain the degree of unity of a diverse society as articulated by W. H. Auden, one of the most celebrated poets of the twentieth century, is a tough challenge. The way societies deal with diversity (or fail to do so) has crucial implications for their economic and political development. This is also so for languages: Linguistic policies may disenfranchise certain groups, and then the trouble is just around the corner. Or even closer.*

History is full of examples of societal failures to overcome internal division. The example of postcolonial Africa offers a succession of sad case studies. In chapter 2 we mentioned the challenges of linguistic policies and disenfranchisement in Ghana. The cocoa story offers another painful aspect of the country's linguistic and ethnic fractionalization. In the 1950s and early 1960s, Ghana was the world's largest cocoa producer. Production was concentrated in the region of the Ashanti group, whose dominance in pre-colonial times was resented by coastal Akan communities. When in 1954 the world price of cocoa trebled, Prime minister Kwame Nkrumah, himself from a coastal Akan group, Nzema, decided to divert this windfall profit to national development, rather than allowing the cocoa farmers of the Ashanti group area to reap the benefit. The Ashanti-based government, led by Kofi Busia, took power in 1969. One of its first acts was to raise the producer prices of cocoa. The ruling coalitions changed often and furiously until 1981, the beginning of the twenty-year reign of Jerry Rawlings, but for about thirty years, cocoa producers in the Ashanti area were the target of punitive taxation as the share of the world price of cocoa received by producers plunged from 89 percent in 1949 to only 6 percent in 1983. Production dropped accordingly from 450,000 tons per year to 159,000 tons in 1983–84.[1]

Not all development stories are that gruesome. There are societies consisting of a large number of diverse groups that give hope that cultural, linguistic, ethnic, and religious diversity could even enhance economic development. Sassen (1994) claims that the cultural diversity of residents of London, Paris, New York, and Tokyo was crucial in the development of finance and specialized services. Similarly, Bairoch (1998) argues that urban diversity is the engine of economic growth. Moreover, as numerous studies demonstrate (see section 1.3), fractionalized societies are not necessary more prone to civil conflicts than their more homogeneous counterparts.

In this chapter we discuss applications of fractionalization, polarization (section 1) and disenfranchisement (section 2) indices, introduced in chapter 6.

1. FRACTIONALIZATION AND POLARIZATION INDICES

Does diversity (linguistic and ethnic, in our case) have a positive or negative impact on the performance and progress of a society? A beautiful quote by Canadian painter and naturalist Robert Bateman (2002, 78–79) puts the dilemma in a very eloquent way:

> North America, like the rest of the world, is going through turbulent times. It is as if we are in a canoe that has hit rapids—and there's rough water ahead as far as the eye can see. We have the choice to steer or not to steer, but we do not have the option of getting out of the canoe. We might even paddle to one side and hold in an eddy while we look ahead and challenge many of the assumptions underlying our current philosophy, assumptions like bigger is better, you can't stop progress, no speed is too fast, globalization is good. We have to replace these notions with some different beliefs: small is beautiful, roots and traditions are worth preserving, variety is the spice of life, the only work worth doing is meaningful work, biodiversity is the necessary precondition for human survival.

[1] See Clark (1994) and Easterly and Levine (1997).

The answer to the question of whether diversity is a good thing or not is, like almost everything in economics, context dependent. We thus embark on a journey that will take us in three different directions: yes, no, and don't know. Before doing so, we would like to make another point that could be useful for sailing through this chapter. There are so many different policies and outcomes, including economic growth, degree of solidarity and redistribution, provision of public goods, level of decentralization, and intensity of civil conflicts, that could be influenced by diversity. The menu of various diversity indices does not make it obvious which index to apply to which question. We address this issue as well.

1.1. Size-Based Fractionalization Indices

Diversity Is Good

Florida (2002) and Florida and Gates (2001) show that metropolitan regions with a higher degree of diversity in terms of education, cultural background, sexual orientation, and country of origin have a higher level of economic development. Lian and O'Neal (1997) and Collier (2001) argue that more fractionalized societies could, under some conditions, perform in a better way than more homogeneous ones.

A more diversified environment attracts creative individuals, ventures, businesses, and capital. The success of Silicon Valley in the late 1990s is often attributed to the varied backgrounds of the scientists, engineers, and entrepreneurs who flocked to California from all corners of the world, including India, China, Taiwan, and Israel. In fact, Saxenian (1999) points out that more than 30 percent of businesses in Silicon Valley had an Asian-born co-founder. However, this diversity did not prevent and in fact even reinforced the commonality of workers' purpose and goals. Saxenian (1996) describes how workers in Silicon Valley enjoyed frequent and intensive exchanges of information through a variety of formal and informal contacts. These exchanges were facilitated by frequent moves of workers across firms (the average time spent by an individual in a firm was about two years) and a flexible industry structure. It is often claimed that in Silicon Valley, "a firm is simply a vehicle allowing an individual to work."

The innovative and creative aspect of diversity is also studied in theoretical papers by Lazear (1999a,b), who considers a "global team" one whose members come from different cultures or countries. Combining workers with different cultures, legal systems, and languages imposes costs on the firm that would not be present otherwise.

TABLE 7.1. Linguistic shares in selected metropolitan areas in 1990 (%)

	English	German	Italian	Spanish	Chinese	Other	A index
Atlanta	93.4	0.5	0.1	2.6	0.4	3.0	0.137
Chicago	80.4	0.9	0.8	9.4	0.6	7.9	0.355
Cincinnati	96.2	0.8	0.2	0.9	0.1	1.8	0.080
Dallas	85.0	0.4	0.1	11.2	0.5	2.9	0.265
El Paso	32.2	0.9	0.1	65.6	0.2	1.1	0.473
Indianapolis	96.3	0.5	0.1	1.4	0.1	1.6	0.070
Los Angeles	57.0	0.5	0.3	30.0	2.5	9.7	0.591
New York	64.5	0.7	2.8	17.7	3.2	11.1	0.550
Philadelphia	92.2	0.7	0.9	2.6	0.3	3.4	0.148
Pittsburgh	95.8	0.5	0.8	0.8	0.2	2.0	0.080
San Francisco	67.9	0.9	0.6	10.7	8.7	11.2	0.620
Washington, DC	85.7	0.7	0.3	5.3	0.0	7.1	0.278

Source: Ottaviano and Peri (2005, table 2).

However, the benefit of complementarity workers' skills offsets the costs of cross-cultural interaction.

Ottaviano and Peri (2005) turn their attention to U.S. cities and investigate whether and how linguistic diversity affects the wages of U.S.-born, forty- to fifty-year-old white men. Using census data from 1970, 1980, and 1990 in 160 cities, they find that richer diversity is systematically associated with higher hourly wages.

The twenty-year span between 1970 and 1990 substantially changed urban diversity, given the large influx of Hispanics and to some extent of Chinese. The share of Spanish and Chinese speakers went from 3.9 percent and 0.1 percent in 1970 to 13.2 percent and 1.5 percent in 1990. Since the share of English speakers remained constant (80 percent in 1970, 78.9 percent in 1990), the shares of all other linguistic groups (German, Italian, all other) decreased from 12.9 to 5.2 percent. The linguistic diversity across various important metropolitan areas in 1990 is illustrated in table 7.1.

The two largest metropolises, New York and Los Angeles, are also among the most linguistically diverse, though San Francisco is even more so, owing to three large groups of speakers of English, Spanish, and Chinese. Midwestern cities such as Cincinnati and Indianapolis exhibit a much smaller degree of diversity. Ottaviano and Peri (2006, 31) point out that San Francisco, which has a linguistic fractionalization index equal to 0.62, is at the level of Malawi, Pakistan, or Afghanistan. Cincinnati and Pittsburgh have a level of fractionalization equal to 0.08, identical to that of very homogeneous Sweden.

Ottaviano and Peri run regressions with 480 observations (160 cities times three years, 1970, 1980, and 1990) in which they explain the (logarithm) of average hourly wages of white men by linguistic diversity (measured by the A index) and a certain number of other variables: average schooling of the population, proportion of college-educated people, proportion of whites, unemployment, other forms of diversity (skills, state of birth, racial fractionalization) and city effects that capture other geographic characteristics. The effect of linguistic diversity turns out to be positive and quite large, since an increase of 0.20 in the index (for example, living in Chicago instead of Atlanta, or in Dallas instead of Cincinnati) increases the average hourly wage by 15 to 20 percent, all other things being equal. Thus, there is a definite positive effect of linguistic diversity on labor productivity.

But Not Always

Indeed, in some countries that consist of linguistically, ethnically, or economically fragmented groups, diversity can, as in the case of Ghana, impede economic development. Mauro (1995) argues that ethnic fragmentation, measured by the ELF-based A index, decreases institutional efficiency, political stability, and bureaucratic efficiency and increases corruption. All correlation coefficients are very significantly different from zero. The relationship between the quality of institutions and ethnolinguistic fractionalization is examined and confirmed in an extensive empirical study by La Porta et al. (1999), who, however, suggest that other variables, such as countries' legal origins, could be even more significant. Alesina et al. (2003) account for a larger number of group characteristics by constructing three A indices, based on ethnicity, language, and religion, for a sample of countries larger than that examined by the Soviet team in 1964, described in section 1.3 of chapter 6. Their results are, in general, consistent, with those of La Porta et al. (1999) in the sense that ethnic and linguistic fractionalization are negatively correlated with government quality.

Alesina, Baqir, and Easterly (1999) find that in the United States, ethnically fragmented communities run larger deficits and exhibit lower spending shares on basic public goods, including education, than their more homogeneous counterparts.[2] Kuijs (2005) indicates that similar results hold in other countries as well. Annett (2001) shows

---

[2]These findings are consistent with James (1993), who used Shannon's linguistic entropy index to study investment gaps in private and public secondary education.

that ethnic fractionalization leads to political instability and excessive government consumption, which in turn may have a negative impact on growth.

Easterly and Levine (1997) focus on growth, education, political stability, consensus on policy choices, and infrastructure in sub-Saharan Africa between 1960 and 1990. They show that all these measures are negatively correlated with ethnolinguistic fragmentation (using the A index based on ELF, but also on other data sets).[3] They forcefully illustrate the economic importance of ethnolinguistic diversity and its devastating impact on the "long-run growth tragedies" in Africa.[4] They make a very interesting and illuminating comparison of growth rates between African and East Asian countries, and try to understand how much of the difference is due to ethnolinguistic fractionalization. They estimate that on average, 1.4 percent of the 3.5 percent growth difference per year is due to fractionalization. They also try to estimate this number for two extremes of the ethnolinguistic index, Tanzania and Japan, and find that the index accounts for half of the growth difference. These conclusions have important consequences far beyond sub-Saharan Africa since many of the results are not specific to that region and apply to a broad cross-section of countries.

Though the correlation between ethnic fractionalization and growth seems to be negative, the strength of the link is mitigated by the benefits of production complementarity.[5] This observation is consistent with Collier's (2001), who combines an A index of ethnic diversity with an index of political rights and freedoms and shows that ethnic diversity has no adverse effects on growth and productivity in fully democratic societies, whereas it has a negative impact in less democratic societies, especially in dictatorships.[6] It is difficult to disentangle the effects of democracy, level of income, and productivity. Since most rich countries are (somewhat) democratic, the conclusions by Alesina and La Ferrara (2005) give support to Collier's assertion that ethnolinguistic fragmentation has a lesser impact in more democratic

---

[3] It is often claimed that the borders of African nations, imposed by European powers in the nineteenth century, did split ethnic communities between neighboring countries and, as Easterly and Levine (1997, 1213) put it, "exasperated preexisting high levels of ethnic and linguistic diversity." Englebert, Tarango, and Carter (2002) find that "boundaries do matter and that Africa paid a substantial price for the particularly arbitrary natures of the ones it inherited from colonialism."

[4] One of the few successful exceptions, Botswana, which adopted growth-enhancing public policies, only confirms the rule. In fact, Botswana is one of the most ethnically homogeneous countries in Africa.

[5] Lazear (1999 a,b), Berliant and Fujita (2008), Fujita and Weber (2009).

[6] See also a comprehensive empirical study by Lian and O'Neal (1997).

countries.[7] Interestingly, Campos, Saleh, and Kuzeyev (2007) indicate that the effect of ethnic fractionalization on economic growth is also weak in the context of twenty-six transitional, formerly centrally planned economies of Eastern and Central Europe, Central Asia, and Mongolia, that exhibit various degrees of democratization. However, if the dynamic aspects of fractionalization are taken into account—and indeed, some of those countries have undergone tremendous ethnic shifts over the past twenty years—and diversity, represented by the A index, is treated as an endogenous variable, Campos, Saleh, and Kuzeyev (2007) find a robust negative link between fractionalization and economic growth.

And Sometimes the Outcome Is Not Clear-Cut

Fractionalization indices may also fail to provide clear-cut answers. While ethnic fractionalization seems to be an impediment to economic growth, Fearon and Laitin (2003), as well as Collier and Hoeffler (2004), show that it does not explain civil wars and conflicts. Annett (2001) argues that there is no obvious link between fractionalization and the likelihood of civil conflicts.

In describing applications of the A index in various disciplines, we must mention that the first extensive wave of such studies goes back to the 1950s. Bachi (1956) uses this index to study the linguistic heterogeneity of Jewish populations in Palestine and Israel. Rustow (1967), who made the Soviet ELF database known in Western countries, used the A index in his research on political modernization. Lieberson (1969) uses a form of the A index to examine linguistic diversity in three main Canadian cities (Montreal, Toronto, and Vancouver). In his later 1981 paper, he looks at the dynamic aspects of linguistic diversity in a sample of thirty-five countries. Bell's (1954) index of isolation, another variant of the A index, played an important role in the development of research on segregation. Earlier applications of A-type indices in economics and sociology, dealing in particular with issues of urbanization and industrial diversification, include, among others, Mueller and Shuessler (1961), Gibbs and Martin (1964), Amemiya (1963), Labovitz and Gibbs (1966), and Gibbs and Browning (1966).

[7] See also Easterly (2001).

1.2. Distance-Based Fractionalization Indices

The incorporation of linguistic distances into empirical research is relatively recent. This explains the relatively small number of papers on that topic, which remains the subject of active ongoing research.

Laitin (2000) uses Greenberg's B index to study the patterns of linguistic diversity in six former Soviet republics: Estonia, Latvia, Kazakhstan, Ukraine, Bashkortostan, and Tatarstan.[8] In doing so, he relies on a very interesting data set collected by Jerry Hough and himself, as well as the LANGFAM linguistic distances described in chapter 3. Laitin argues that the conclusions generated by his B index calculations lead to more intuitive and better results than those generated by the A index.

Desmet, Ortuño-Ortín, and Weber (2009) study the effect of ethnolinguistic fractionalization on income redistribution in 160 countries. They use both A indices and distance-adjusted indices B and PI, defined in section 1 of chapter 6. They find that distance-adjusted indices perform much better and lead to statistically significant results, while A indices do not. This effect is found to be highly robust and quantitatively important. Compared to an average level of redistribution of 9.5 percent of GDP, the model predicts that an increase in diversity by one standard deviation lowers redistribution as a share of GDP by about one percentage point. Comparing this with the existing literature, we note that incorporating distances into the measurement of diversity has important consequences, which is consistent with the findings of Alesina et al. (2003).

There is a small but growing literature that utilizes genetic distances[9] to measure societal diversity. Spolaore and Wacziarg (2009) explore the relation between diversity and bilateral income differences. They use a B index with genetic distances, since they analyze the way in which genes capture the divergence in characteristics that are, in the long run, transmitted across generations. These differences act as barriers to the diffusion of development from the world technological frontier. Ashraf and Galor (2008) study the precolonial time relationship between genetic diversity within a society and its economic development, measured by population density. They find that the relation is non-monotonic: higher population density is associated with intermediate levels of genetic diversity. Desmet et al. (2009) introduce a structural model in which agents vote on the optimal level of public spending. Larger nations benefit from increasing returns in

[8]At the time, the last two countries had no full-fledged Union Republic status.
[9]Genetic distances are introduced in chapter 3.

the provision of public goods but bear the costs of greater cultural diversity, represented by genetic distances between groups. They assume that there exists a "home bias" or strong identification (in the sense of Esteban and Ray's polarization) whereby individuals prefer consuming public goods within a community of similar individuals. They calibrate the model to Europe and show that it can account for the breakup of Yugoslavia and the dynamics of its disintegration. They also predict some "weak links" in the European map, including the Basque Country, Scotland, and Sardinia.

In other disciplines, the B index has been introduced by Nei and Li (1979) as the nucleotide genetic diversity index, or the NL coefficient. It is now routinely used to measure genetic similarity between various DNA sequences. The B index, also known as "quadratic entropy," was introduced by Rao (1982) in studies of biodiversity. A more general form of the index is suggested by Ricotta and Szeidl (2006). It subsumes both the Rao index and Shannon's entropy index. Obviously, the A index, or, as it is called in biodiversity studies, the Sampson index, is included in this class as well.

1.3. Polarization Indices

Polarization is an area of growing interest in various disciplines. Again, as in the case of fractionalization indices, the size-based index RQ, defined in section 1.3 of chapter 6, has a simpler functional structure than the ER index, which takes into account linguistic distances. RQ proves to be an easier tool for empirical research. Montalvo and Reynal-Querol (2005) argue that RQ explains in a significant way the incidence of civil wars,[10] whereas the A index fails to do so. They also find that a higher level of ethnic polarization has an indirect negative effect on growth through the increased likelihood of civil conflict, which usually reduces investment. Montalvo and Reynal-Querol (2002) also argue that more polarized societies (with larger RQ indices) endure longer wars and civil conflicts.

Desmet, Ortuño-Ortín, and Wacziarg (2009) examine various political economy outcomes, including civil conflict and redistribution. They construct extensive linguistic trees describing the genealogical relationship between all world languages, and use the A fractionalization index and the RQ polarization index at different levels of linguistic aggregation. They find that deep cleavages, created thousands of years ago, are more accurate predictors of civil conflict and

[10]Esteban and Ray (1999) provide theoretical support for this claim.

patterns of redistribution (or lack thereof) than differences generated by recent breakups and divisions. Recent cleavages, however, and finer distinctions between languages do better in explaining the impact of linguistic diversity on growth.

Desmet, Ortuño-Ortín, and Weber (2009) consider five indices—two fractionalization indices, A and B, the peripheral index PI, and two polarization indices, ER and RQ—and examine their link with the degree of solidarity or redistribution in 218 countries.

Although the functional form of all these indices is different, in practice, some of them may yield similar conclusions. In fact, the correlation between all these indices is relatively high, and the only factor that is important in empirical analysis is whether one uses size-based (A or RQ) or distance-based (B, PR, or ER) indices. The distinction within each group does not seem to be empirically relevant, but distance-based indices do a better job. Again, as Fearon (2003) argues in the case of fractionalization measures, linguistic or genetic distances matter.

2. DISENFRANCHISEMENT INDICES: THE EXAMPLE OF THE EU

"Broken English spoken perfectly."
Sign in a shop on the island of Cozumel, Coast of Mexico
—*Charlie Croker, Lost in Translation*

It is unavoidable that a multilingual society, such as the current EU, will have to consider a certain degree of linguistic standardization, and the disenfranchisement that it generates. The analysis that follows is based on the comprehensive survey data set on languages and their use, the Special Eurobarometer 243 survey (2006), which is briefly described in section 2.3 of chapter 6.[11] We focus on the extent of linguistic disenfranchisement of EU citizens that would result if the set of languages were limited to a particular single core language or a combination of such languages. We formulate a procedure for selecting subsets among all eligible twenty-three official languages in order to minimize the EU-wide disenfranchisement rate.

The assumption is that members of the EU Council would, implicitly or explicitly, take such information into account when casting their vote for or against a specific standardization proposal. This procedure

---

[11]This and the following sections are largely based on Fidrmuc, Ginsburgh, and Weber (2007).

is implemented for different subsets consisting of one, two, three, …
languages, focusing on the obvious subset consisting of the following
six languages: English, French, German, Italian, Spanish, and Polish.

2.1. Who Does Not Speak English?

The choice of core languages should take into account the number
of EU citizens who speak each language, including those who do not
live in the country where this language is native. As emphasized in
chapter 6, the concept of linguistic disenfranchisement quantifies the
number of citizens in every country (and in the EU as a whole) who
would find themselves unable to communicate if their native language
(or any other language they know) did not belong to the group of core
languages (consisting of one, two, three, … languages).

Table 7.2 exhibits, for each EU member country, the rates for the
seven most widespread languages. The concept of disenfranchisement
rate that we use is relatively strict: it comprises not only those who do
not speak the language in question but also those who say they have
only a basic knowledge of it. The results lead to several observations.
First, even though English is the most widely known language, it would
nevertheless disenfranchise 62.6 percent of EU citizens if it were the
only core language. Moreover, there are only seven countries where
less than 50 percent of the population would be disenfranchised. But
the EU-wide disenfranchisement rate rises to 75.1 and 80.1 percent
if English were replaced by German or French, respectively, and it
would be even worse if Italian or Spanish were chosen (86.7 and
88.9 percent). Second, with the exception of English, German, French,
Italian (and Russian), no language is spoken by more than 5 percent
of the population in more than two European countries. Finally, even
though Russian is not an EU-official language, it disenfranchises fewer
people in the EU than many official languages, such as Bulgarian,
Czech, Danish, Estonian, Finnish, Greek, Hungarian, Irish, Latvian,
Lithuanian, Maltese, Portuguese, Slovak, Slovenian, and Swedish.

Young people often speak foreign languages more readily. We therefore report also EU-wide disenfranchisement rates for four age groups
(fifteen to twenty-nine, thirty to forty-four, forty-five to fifty-nine, and
sixty or older). The data in Table 7.3 show that English is the only
language for which disenfranchisement rates are significantly lower
among younger generations.

This is so in all twenty-seven countries. Details for English are
given in table 7.4. Overall, if English were the only EU language,
disenfranchisement would drop from 62.6 percent to 44.6 percent

TABLE 7.2. Disenfranchisement in European languages, all respondents (%)

	English	German	French	Italian	Spanish	Polish	Dutch
Austria	55	1	94	95	98	100	100
Belgium	59	87	29	97	97	99	32
Bulgaria	84	94	96	99	99	100	100
Cyprus	49	98	95	99	99	100	100
Czech Republic	84	81	98	100	100	98	100
Denmark	34	73	97	99	98	100	100
Estonia	75	92	100	100	100	100	100
Finland	69	95	99	100	100	100	100
France	80	95	1	95	93	100	100
Germany	62	1	92	99	98	98	100
Greece	68	94	95	98	100	100	100
Hungary	92	91	100	99	100	100	100
Ireland	1	98	91	100	99	99	100
Italy	75	96	90	3	97	100	100
Latvia	85	97	100	100	100	99	100
Lithuania	86	96	99	100	100	87	100
Luxembourg	61	12	11	95	99	100	99
Malta	32	99	95	65	99	100	100
Netherlands	23	43	81	100	97	100	1
Poland	82	90	99	99	100	2	100
Portugal	85	98	91	99	96	100	100
Romania	86	97	90	98	99	100	100
Slovak Republic	83	82	99	100	100	98	100
Slovenia	59	79	98	91	99	100	100
Spain	84	98	94	99	2	100	100
Sweden	33	88	97	99	99	100	100
United Kingdom	1	98	91	99	98	100	100
EU	62.6	75.1	80.1	86.7	88.9	91.6	95.1

Source: Fidrmuc, Ginsburgh, and Weber (2007).

TABLE 7.3. Disenfranchisement rates for main languages,
all respondents and age groups, EU (%)

		Age Groups (yr)			
	All	15–29	30–44	45–59	⩾60
English	62.6	43	57	67	74
German	75.1	73	74	74	74
French	80.1	78	80	80	81
Italian	86.7	86	86	86	86
Spanish	88.9	86	88	89	89
Polish	91.6	91	91	91	91
Dutch	95.1	95	95	95	95

Source: Fidrmuc, Ginsburgh, and Weber (2007).

in the EU if the whole population were as knowledgeable in English as is the youngest fifteen- to twenty-nine-year-old cohort. Therefore, one could expect that some thirty to forty years from now, English would be known by more than half the EU population, as well as in sixteen individual countries. Bulgaria, the Czech Republic, France, Hungary, Italy, Latvia, Poland, Portugal, Romania, the Slovak Republic, and Spain would still suffer from disenfranchisement rates larger than 50 percent. The knowledge of English is bound to increase, given that more and more students take foreign language courses, as is shown in the last column of table 7.4, which contains the shares of students in upper secondary education who study at least one foreign language, mainly English, but to some extent also French and German.[12]

A similar calculation for German or French would lead to global disenfranchisement rates of 73 and 77 percent, and only three countries would enjoy rates below 50 percent. These would be Austria, Germany, and Luxembourg for German and Belgium, France, and Luxembourg for French, which clearly shows that neither German nor French is gaining speakers among today's youngest generation. Italian, Spanish, and Dutch would even do worse.

2.2. English Only Would Not Work

It should appear obvious that no single language, even English, could bring disenfranchisement to a reasonable level. We now address the question of whether a subset of official languages could do better. Calculating disenfranchisement for every couple, triple, of the twenty-three languages would be a cumbersome task, and nobody could read the millions of tables that would be the outcome of such a computation. Therefore, we chose a procedure that yields the subsets of languages that minimize disenfranchisement in the EU as a whole, for every given number of languages. Let m take the values 1, 2, 3, ..., 23. Then, for every m, we search for the subset of twenty-three languages that minimizes the disenfranchisement rate over all sets with m languages.

Though this calculation is conceptually simple, it would, in practice, still require a very large number of computations if the number of languages among which the core languages are chosen is large.[13] However, since European languages differ considerably in the numbers of people who speak them, the scope of the analysis can be

---

[12] See *Eurostat Newsrelease* 137/2009, September 24, 2009.

[13] For example, if $m = 6$, the number of arrangements of six languages among the twenty-three is equal to $18 \times 19 \times 20 \times 21 \times 22 \times 23$, which is of the order of 72.6 million.

TABLE 7.4. Disenfranchisement rates for English,
all respondents and age groups (%)

| | All | Age Groups (yr) | | | | Learning Other Languages in High School |
		15–29	30–44	45–59	≥60	
Austria	55	41	45	58	78	98
Belgium	59	39	49	61	80	99
Bulgaria	84	57	83	94	99	99
Cyprus	49	18	33	61	72	n.a.
Czech Republic	84	64	81	90	97	100
Denmark	34	9	19	36	57	100
Estonia	75	33	67	87	94	99
Finland	69	29	55	76	92	100
France	80	67	74	84	90	100
Germany	62	38	53	67	78	n.a.
Greece	68	40	56	80	93	99
Hungary	92	76	89	96	98	99
Ireland	1	2	1	1	0	81
Italy	75	54	77	84	93	98
Latvia	85	55	91	97	99	98
Lithuania	86	49	89	95	99	99
Luxembourg	61	50	53	58	80	100
Malta	32	10	18	39	46	97
Netherlands	23	11	12	20	40	100
Poland	82	57	85	93	96	99
Portugal	85	62	74	87	99	n.a.
Romania	86	69	82	96	99	100
Slovak Republic	83	57	85	90	96	100
Slovenia	59	22	52	78	94	99
Spain	84	65	85	93	96	96
Sweden	33	5	17	37	61	100
United Kingdom	1	2	2	1	1	48
EU	62.6	43.2	57.3	66.6	74.3	n.a.

Source: Fidrmuc, Ginsburgh, and Weber (2007). Last column from *Eurostat Newsrelease* 137/2009, 24 September 2009.

narrowed substantially. For instance, it is clear that English should be introduced first, followed by French or German, then the other large languages (Italian, Spanish, and Polish), and so on. In this way, identifying the most suitable combination is often easy and, at any stage in the analysis, the number of possibilities to be considered is relatively small.

It could nevertheless happen that a language enters into the optimal set and then moves out when one or two more languages are added. Assume, for instance, that the optimal set with three languages contains English, German, and French. Assume further that moving to the set with four languages produces an optimal set containing English, German, Italian, and Spanish. That is, Italian and Spanish replace French, which belongs to the same group of Romance languages. Fortunately, this does not happen in our case. Once a language is in the optimal set containing three languages, it would stay there, whatever the number of additional languages in optimal sets containing more languages.

The results of these computations are reproduced in tables 7.5 and 7.6, respectively, for all respondents and respondents who are less than thirty years old.[14] Each column indicates which language should be added to the subset formed by the languages reported in the preceding columns so as to minimize EU's disenfranchisement. Consider first the results when all respondents are taken into account. The optimal set of one language contains English. For two languages, the optimal set contains English and German, and so on.[15]

The marginal contribution of each additional language to reducing disenfranchisement falls to less than 1 percent of the EU population once the number of languages exceeds thirteen, and the differences between marginal contributions attributable to further candidate languages are often minute. To save space, we report on only the first eleven languages.

English is clearly the first language in any sequence, as it is spoken well or very well by more than one-third of the EU population. German and French are in a close race for the second position: German, with a 49.3 percent disenfranchisement rate, fares a little better than French at 50.6 percent. The bundle of three languages leads to a disenfranchisement rate of 37.8 percent. Italian, Spanish, or Polish would each make almost the same contribution to reducing disenfranchisement further, with Italian slightly ahead of the other two languages. Spanish in turn performs only marginally better than Polish. With the six largest languages included, 16 percent of the EU population would still remain disenfranchised. Adding Romanian brings the residual disenfranchisement rate down further, to 13 percent. Of course, important differences across countries can be noticed. Several (Bulgaria, Czech Republic, Estonia, Finland, Greece, Hungary,

[14] For further details on the calculation and additional results, see Fidrmuc, Ginsburgh, and Weber (2007).

[15] Note that there are instances where two languages result in approximately the same reduction in disenfranchisement at a particular step in the sequence. For example, the tenth language could be Czech or Greek. If Czech is taken as the tenth language, Greek then appears again as the eleventh language.

TABLE 7.5. Disenfranchisement in the sequence of
optimal language sets, all respondents (%)

Number of Languages	1 EN	2 GE	3 FR	4 IT	5 SP	6 PL	7 RO	8 HU	9 PT	10a CZ	10b GR	11 CZ&GR
Austria	55	0	0	0	0	0	0	0	0	0	0	0
Belgium	59	56	18	18	18	18	18	18	18	18	18	18
Bulgaria	84	81	79	79	78	78	78	78	78	77	77	77
Cyprus	49	49	49	48	48	48	48	48	48	48	0	0
Czech Republic	84	69	69	69	69	67	67	66	66	0	66	0
Denmark	34	31	31	31	31	30	30	30	30	30	30	30
Estonia	75	70	70	70	70	69	69	69	69	69	69	69
Finland	69	67	67	67	67	67	67	67	67	67	67	67
France	80	77	1	0	0	0	0	0	0	0	0	0
Germany	62	1	1	1	1	1	1	1	1	1	1	1
Greece	68	64	63	63	63	63	63	63	63	63	0	0
Hungary	92	85	85	85	85	85	84	0	0	0	0	0
Ireland	1	1	1	1	1	1	1	1	1	1	1	1
Italy	75	74	69	1	1	1	1	1	1	1	1	1
Latvia	85	83	83	83	83	82	82	82	82	82	82	82
Lithuania	86	82	82	82	82	71	71	71	71	71	71	71
Luxembourg	61	8	1	1	1	1	1	1	1	1	1	1
Malta	32	31	31	31	31	31	31	31	31	31	31	31
Netherlands	23	18	18	18	18	18	18	18	18	18	18	18
Poland	82	77	76	76	76	1	1	1	1	1	1	1
Portugal	85	84	81	81	79	79	79	79	0	0	0	0
Romania	86	85	81	80	79	79	1	1	1	1	1	1
Slovak Republic	83	72	72	72	72	70	70	57	57	44	57	44
Slovenia	59	50	50	45	45	45	45	45	45	45	45	45
Spain	84	84	81	80	1	1	1	1	1	1	1	1
Sweden	33	33	33	33	33	33	33	33	33	33	33	33
United Kingdom	1	1	1	1	1	1	1	1	1	1	1	1
EU	62.6	49.3	37.8	29.5	22.4	16.4	12.9	10.9	9.2	7.7	7.7	6.2

Source: Fidrmuc, Ginsburgh, and Weber (2007).
Note: One language is added to the previous ones in each column. In columns 10a,
and 10b, two languages result in the same percentage reduction in disenfranchisement. In column 11, they are both added to the set. Languages are abbreviated
as follows: Czech (CZ), English (EN), French (FR), German (GE), Greek (GR),
Hungarian (HU), Italian (IT), Spanish (SP), Polish (PL), Portuguese (PT), Romanian
(RO).

Latvia, Lithuania, Portugal, and Slovakia) face disenfranchisement
rates greater than 50 percent. The most dramatic case is Hungary,
where only 16 percent of the population can speak one of the first seven
languages. Not surprisingly, Hungarian becomes the eighth language
in the sequence. This also has a positive impact on Slovakia, where
the disenfranchisement rate declines from 70 percent to 57 percent.
Portuguese is the ninth language, followed by Czech and Greek tied in
the tenth position.

The disenfranchisement rates in table 7.5 give a snapshot of the situation at the time of the survey (end of 2005). However, language proficiency changes over time. In particular, the pattern of learning foreign languages may change both with respect to the languages that are popular and the frequency with which people learn other languages. Indeed, table 7.4 shows that younger generations are more likely to speak foreign languages, especially English. Therefore, we calculated a sequence of optimal sets based on the disenfranchisement rate of the youngest generation (fifteen to twenty-nine years old) only. This sequence is presented in table 7.6.

The first difference is that German, which was second to enter the sequence in table 7.5 (whole population), is replaced by French. This is because 60 percent of the German and Austrian youngest generation know English, so that German becomes less useful to reduce EU-wide disenfranchisement. Beyond the first two languages, the sequence is essentially the same as before, and includes English, French, German, Italian, Spanish, Polish, Romanian, Hungarian, Portuguese, Czech, Greek and Bulgarian, Dutch, and Finnish, Slovak, Lithuanian, and Latvian (the last four languages, along with Russian, are all in a tie for the fourteenth position). The criterion used before (a language's contribution to reducing disenfranchisement should be at least 1 percent) now results in ten languages. The disenfranchisement rate that would prevail among the youngest generation with ten official languages is 3.9 percent. This rate is likely to decrease even further as more and more children in upper secondary education study languages (essentially English, but also French and German).

Table 7.7 reports the results of an identical exercise that takes into consideration Dyen, Kruskal, and Black's (1992) linguistic distances between languages. In constructing the sequence, individual disenfranchisement at each stage is adjusted proportionately to the distance between the language of an individual and the closest language that is already included in the sequence. In the single-language (English-only) scenario, accounting for linguistic proximity reduces the EU-wide disenfranchisement rate considerably, from 62.6 percent to 43.1 percent. Adding French reduces disenfranchisement also in all Romance language countries, bringing the EU-wide rate to 24 percent. A deviation from the two sequences reported above is that Polish is now in third place, just ahead of German. Italian is the fifth language, followed by Hungarian and Spanish. Greek ties with Romanian for eighth place. The requirement of at least 1 percent contribution to reducing disenfranchisement cuts off the sequence at nine languages, with the resulting disenfranchisement rate of 2.9 percent. Adding

TABLE 7.6. Disenfranchisement in the sequence of optimal language sets, young respondents (%)

Number of Languages	1 EN	2 FR	3 GE	4 IT	5 SP	6 PL	7 RO	8 HU	9 PT	10 CZ	11a GR	11b BG	12 GR&BG
Austria	40	40	1	1	1	1	1	1	1	1	1	1	1
Belgium	39	8	8	8	8	8	8	8	8	8	8	8	8
Bulgaria	56	56	53	53	53	53	52	52	52	52	51	3	3
Cyprus	18	18	18	18	18	18	17	17	17	17	1	17	1
Czech Republic	64	64	52	52	52	50	50	50	50	0	0	0	0
Denmark	9	8	6	6	6	5	5	5	5	5	5	5	5
Estonia	33	33	29	29	29	29	29	29	29	29	29	29	29
Finland	29	29	29	29	29	29	29	29	29	29	29	29	29
France	67	0	0	0	0	0	0	0	0	0	0	0	0
Germany	38	38	0	0	0	0	0	0	0	0	0	0	0
Greece	40	40	36	36	36	36	36	36	36	36	0	36	0
Hungary	76	76	64	64	64	64	63	0	0	0	0	0	0
Ireland	2	2	2	2	2	2	2	2	2	1	1	1	1
Italy	54	51	49	1	1	1	1	1	1	1	1	1	1
Latvia	55	55	54	54	54	53	53	53	53	53	53	53	53
Lithuania	49	49	45	45	45	36	36	36	36	36	36	36	36
Luxembourg	50	2	1	1	1	1	1	1	0	0	0	0	0
Malta	10	10	10	10	10	10	10	10	10	10	10	10	10
Netherlands	11	11	10	10	10	10	10	10	10	10	10	10	10
Poland	57	56	50	49	49	1	0	0	0	0	0	0	0
Portugal	62	60	60	60	59	59	59	59	0	0	0	0	0
Romania	68	62	62	61	59	59	2	0	0	0	0	0	0
Slovak Republic	57	57	39	39	39	38	38	31	31	23	23	23	23
Slovenia	22	22	17	15	15	15	15	15	15	15	15	15	15
Spain	65	63	63	62	1	1	1	1	1	1	1	1	1
Sweden	5	5	5	5	5	5	5	5	5	5	5	5	5
United Kingdom	2	2	2	2	2	1	1	1	1	1	1	1	1
EU	44.6	34.5	25.8	19.9	14.4	10.4	7.8	6.3	5.1	3.9	3.1	3.1	2.3

Source: Fidrmuc, Ginsburgh, and Weber (2007).

Note: One language is added to the previous ones in each column. In columns 11a, and 11b, two languages result in the same percentage reduction in disenfranchisement. In column 12, they are both added to the set. Languages are abbreviated as follows: Bulgarian (BG), Czech (CZ), English (EN), French (FR), German (GE), Greek (GR), Hungarian (HU), Italian (IT), Spanish (SP), Polish (PL), Portuguese (PT), Romanian (RO).

more languages (Czech, Finnish, Bulgarian, Swedish, and Portuguese) brings the residual disenfranchisement rate to 0.9 percent. The gains from adding the remaining languages (Danish, Dutch, Estonian, Irish, Latvian, Lithuanian, Maltese, Slovak, and Slovene) are negligible.

These three sequences of sets that minimize EU's global rate of disenfranchisement are used in our analysis of the political feasibility of linguistic reforms in chapter 8.

TABLE 7.7. Distance-adjusted disenfranchisement in the
sequence of optimal language sets, all respondents (%)

Number of Languages	1 EN	2 FR	3 PL	4 GE	5 IT	6 HU	7 SP	8a GR	8b RO	9 GR&RO	10a CZ	10b FI	10c BG
Austria	23	23	23	0	0	0	0	0	0	0	0	0	0
Belgium	33	8	8	3	3	3	3	3	3	3	3	3	3
Bulgaria	64	62	29	28	28	28	28	28	28	28	20	33	2
Cyprus	41	40	40	39	39	39	39	0	39	0	0	0	0
Czech Republic	59	58	19	16	16	15	15	15	15	15	0	14	14
Denmark	14	14	13	9	9	9	9	9	9	9	9	9	9
Estonia	60	60	35	34	34	28	28	28	28	28	15	11	15
Finland	65	65	65	64	64	45	45	45	45	45	45	0	45
France	60	0	0	0	0	0	0	0	0	0	0	0	0
Germany	26	26	24	0	0	0	0	0	0	0	0	0	0
Greece	55	54	53	50	50	50	50	0	50	0	0	0	0
Hungary	88	87	86	84	84	0	0	0	0	0	0	0	0
Ireland	1	1	1	1	1	1	1	1	1	1	1	1	1
Italy	57	15	15	14	1	1	1	1	1	1	1	1	1
Latvia	65	64	27	27	27	27	27	27	27	27	8	8	8
Lithuania	64	64	27	26	26	26	26	26	26	26	13	13	13
Luxembourg	28	3	3	0	0	0	0	0	0	0	0	0	0
Malta	31	31	31	31	30	30	30	30	30	30	30	30	30
Netherlands	9	9	9	3	3	3	3	3	3	3	3	3	3
Poland	61	60	1	1	1	1	1	1	0	0	0	0	0
Portugal	64	24	24	24	18	18	10	10	10	10	10	10	10
Romania	66	35	35	34	28	26	25	25	1	1	1	1	1
Slovak Republic	59	59	19	17	17	13	13	13	13	13	3	10	10
Slovenia	41	39	20	17	16	16	16	16	16	16	15	16	16
Spain	64	22	22	22	18	18	1	1	1	1	1	1	1
Sweden	14	14	14	10	10	10	10	10	10	10	10	10	10
United Kingdom	1	1	1	1	1	1	1	1	1	1	1	1	1
EU	43.1	24.0	16.6	11.4	9.0	6.9	5.2	4.0	4.1	2.9	2.1	2.1	2.1

Source: Fidrmuc, Ginsburgh, and Weber (2007).
Note: One language is added to the previous ones in each column. In columns 8a, and 8b, two languages result in the same percentage reduction in disenfranchisement. In column 9, they are both added to the set. In columns 10a, 10b and 10c, three languages compete for the 10th place. Languages are abbreviated as follows: Bulgarian (BG), Czech (CZ), English (EN), French (FR), German (GE), Greek (GR), Finnish (FI), Hungarian (HU), Italian (IT), Spanish (SP), Polish(PL), Romanian (RO).

3. SUMMARY

Fractionalization and polarization indices are used in more and more econometric studies to check how diversity affects economic outcomes. A rather large number of studies show that diversity exerts negative effects, though this also depends on whether countries are more or less democratic. Negative effects are more likely in dictatorial regimes. Recent papers point to the fact that distance-based indices often have more explanatory power than size-based indices.

Disenfranchisement indices are used to examine outcomes of linguistic standardization. In this chapter they were applied to examine the consequences of restricting the number of languages in some uses in the EU. Whether these restrictions can be implemented is the topic of chapter 8.

Chapter 8

MULTILINGUALISM IN THE EUROPEAN UNION: A CASE STUDY IN LINGUISTIC POLICY

THE FIRST SECTION OF THIS CHAPTER deals with the difficulties faced by European society, including European institutions themselves, which can hardly cope with the burden of so many languages. Section 2 suggests some simple solutions that do not contradict the generous European cultural idea that all languages are official.

1. TWENTY-THREE LANGUAGES, AND MORE TO COME

> —I don't speak English. Kurdish I speak, and Turkish, and gypsy language. But I don't speak barbarian languages.
> —Barbarian languages?
> —English! German! Ya! French! All the barbarian.
> *Yasar Kemal*[1]

BABYLON IN BRUSSELS. *And the whole of Europe was of several speeches. And it came to pass, as they journeyed from the West and the East, that they found a place in the land of Belgium; and they dwelt there. And they said one to another, Go to, let us make brick, and burn them thoroughly. And they had brick for stone, and slime had they for mortar, and asbestos to protect them against the fire of the Lord. And they said, Go to, let us build several towers, one for the Commission, one for the Parliament, and many others, whose tops may reach unto heaven; and let us make us a name, lest we be scattered abroad upon the face of the whole continent. And the Lord came down to see the city and the towers, which the children had built. And the Lord said, Behold, the people are several, and they have many languages. Go to, let us go*

---

[1] Kemal is a Turkish writer whose words are quoted by Paul Theroux in *The Great Railway Bazaar.*

down, and there give them one language, that they may understand one another's speech. But the children turned the Lord down. He returned to his own land, thinking of what he had done wrong some 5,700 years ago. And so they are now, living in Babylon in Brussels. (Genesis 11:1–9, King James Version (Adapted))

In this section we describe the linguistic rules set by the EU and its institutions (section 1.1). We then look at whether the rules are really implemented (section 1.2), how the EU itself as well as the European Court "changed" some of them (section 1.3), and what European citizens and bureaucrats think (sections 1.4 and 1.5).

1.1. Linguistic Rules of the European Union

In 1958, the Treaty of Rome and Regulation 1/1958 recognized Dutch, French, German, and Italian as official languages. Danish, English, Finnish, Greek, Portuguese, Spanish, and Swedish were added at later stages. The 2004 enlargement resulted in adding Czech, Estonian, Hungarian, Latvian, Lithuanian, Maltese, Polish, Slovak, and Slovene. Irish was given the same status in 2005, but it was agreed that the decision would be implemented only as of January 2007. Bulgarian and Romanian became official languages as of that date as well, in the wake of those countries' accession to the EU. All these languages enjoy the same privileges as the original four. Without a reform, the list of official EU languages is likely to grow even longer as more countries enter the EU: at present, Croatia and Turkey are the only candidates for membership, but in the future they may be joined by other Balkan countries. Turkish may become an official language even without Turkey's accession as a member state as a result of the possible reunification of Cyprus. Furthermore, as has happened with Irish, languages that currently enjoy national or regional official status in their own countries without being used at the EU level can eventually become official EU languages. Luxembourgish, Catalan, Basque, Welsh, or Russian may therefore follow suit.

Allowing multiple official languages is costly. The EU with fifteen member states (EU15) was spending some 686 million euros annually on translation and interpretation.[2] In the wake of further enlargements, this cost has risen to 1,045 million euros.[3] The latest figure

[2]Unofficial estimates are even larger. *Le Monde*, November 30, 1999, put the cost at 1.8 billion euros.

[3]Of which 806 million went for translation of official documents and 238 million for interpreting oral statements. See European Commission (2005a,b).

available puts the cost at 1,123 million in 2005. This pays for 2,500 staff, or a tenth of the commission's workforce.[4] At the outset of the European integration process, meetings involving six countries with four languages were relatively simple and manageable. With each enlargement of the EU, the combinations of languages requiring translations grew. At present, with EU membership having grown to twenty-seven and the number of languages to twenty-three, providing translation and interpretation services is not an easy task. In practice, costs have been kept in check by scaling down the scope of services provided. The new Directorate-General for Translation carefully identifies the documents that need translation into all languages and those that do not.[5] Its director, Juhani Lönnroth, also mentions that the average length of a commission communication has decreased from thirty-seven pages to fifteen pages during his time as head of the department.[6] EU bodies increasingly use relay translations (that is, translating a text or speech first into one of the core languages, and then translating the same text again into the target language) or two-way translations (into and out of a principal language). Relay and two-way translations may result in misunderstanding, misrepresentation, or outright errors, so revisions by a native speaker of the target language are often necessary (Lönnroth 2006).[7] The issue of the validity of legal documents is also important. National delegations may agree on a text prepared in a single language, such as English. The text that is eventually incorporated into national law and becomes legally binding, however, is the translated text.

In principle, each country can freely decide what happens on its own turf. But even this limited aspect of multilingualism could be problematic. Indeed, the French regulation that insurance contracts must be written in French was found to be in violation of EU law. A compromise was finally reached so that, unless subscribers want to use another language, contracts are written in French, a decision that could not have been reached without the commission's consent.[8]

---

[4] Europa Languages Portal, Frequently asked questions, http://europa.eu/languages/en/document/59 (last accessed on June 11, 2009).

[5] "The highest priority is given to legal acts and similar documents which have major legal or financial implications. ... [There is a distinction] between core documents, which should in principle be translated in-house, and non-core documents which can be outsourced. ... [There are] strict guidelines on the maximum length of different types of documents. ... Finally ... two thirds of the documents are written in English ... [and] authors now work in a language which is not their own" (Lönnroth 2006).

[6] See http://euobserver.com/9/25712.

[7] See also De Swaan (2008) on the problems generated by relay translations.

[8] Truchot (2003, 107).

Multilingualism may also have other important drawbacks. For example, in May 2004, the implementation of new directives on financial regulation and transparency of securities information had to be delayed because they were not translated in time.[9] As the EU had in the meantime expanded, the directives had to be translated into nine additional languages, necessitating a delay of six months.

Another compelling case, in terms of both cost and speed, concerns patent applications filed with the European Patent Office (EPO).[10] By filling out an application in English, French, or German, it is possible to obtain protection in all thirty-one EPO member countries. However, once the patent is granted by the EPO, it must be validated, translated into each language of the country where the firm wants to be protected, put into force, and renewed in each national system. Translation costs alone for the thirteen frequently cited countries[11] are estimated at 13,600 euros, while the total filing for twenty years costs 129,000 euros (the same filing costs 16,500 euros in the United States and 17,300 euros in Japan). But as Van Pottelsberghe and François (2006) point out, the total cost is not the only issue. They show that both the incoming workload of examiners and their output are three to four times larger in the United States than at the EPO. The procedure takes twenty-seven months in the United States, and forty-nine months in Europe. As a consequence, the number of claims (a patent application is composed of an average of seven claims in Japan, eighteen in Europe, and twenty-three in the United States) amounts to 1 million in Europe, 3 million in Japan and 8 million in the United States, though the European market consisting of the thirteen countries is the largest.

Here are the linguistic provisions for the most important institutions of the EU.[12]

European Parliament: In accordance with the multilingualism principle, all documents discussed must be drawn in all languages; all members of the European Parliament (MEPs) can address the Parliament in one of the official languages; simultaneous interpretation is provided in public deliberations. However, there is some flexibility for committee and delegation meetings as long as attending members agree.

[9] See "A Welcome Break," *Wall Street Journal Europe*, May 17, 2004, A8.

[10] The reader is referred to Van Pottelsberghe and François (2006) for more detailed information.

[11] Austria, Belgium, Denmark, Finland, France, Germany, Ireland, Italy, Netherlands, Spain, Sweden, Switzerland, and the United Kingdom.

[12] See Athanassiou (2006), who includes a discussion of linguistic regimes adopted by other institutions. See also Phillipson (2003, chap. 4) and Pujadas (2006).

Council of the European Union: This is the institution where legislation is adopted (more and more frequently in collaboration with the European Parliament), and documents are made available in all official languages.

European Commission: Full translation and interpretation are available on formal occasions, full multilingualism should prevail in external communications, and legislative initiatives are drafted in all official languages, but otherwise there is no provision for a language regime except for a few, relatively vague references to official, working, and authentic languages.[13] In practice, the main languages are English and French; German is used much less frequently.[14] English, French, and German are the so-called procedural languages, used for day-to-day communication within the EU bureaucracy and for the preparation of drafts of official documents. The vast majority of EU documents are prepared in English (62 percent in 2004), French (26 percent), and German (3 percent), with the remaining languages accounting for some 9 percent of all inputs. According to the director-general of the commission's translation department,[15] the share of English jumped to 72 percent in 2008.

European Court: Each case examined by the Court is usually conducted in the language decided by the applicant of the case; "judges and advocates general are entitled to use any language and to require translation of any document into the language of their choice, [but] internally the [Court] deliberates in French,"[16] which is also the language of its administration.[17]

Ministerial meetings: Meetings on topical issues and diplomatic meetings are simultaneously translated into the three procedural languages only. Of the approximately 4,000 meetings held every year (before the two last enlargements), 75 percent did not require simultaneous translation.[18]

Communication of European institutions with citizens of the EU: Every citizen can communicate in his or her own language.

Other international organizations tend to be more restrictive and clearer than the EU with respect to the endorsed languages. While the

[13] Athanassiou (2006, 20).
[14] See also Krämer (2010).
[15] http://euobserver.com/9/25712.
[16] Athanassiou (2006, 22).
[17] For an extensive discussion, see Gaudissart (2010).
[18] Truchot (2003, 102).

official languages at the UN since 1973 have been Chinese, English, French, Russian, Spanish, and Arabic, its bureaucracy uses mainly English and French.[19] Speeches given in one of the official languages are translated simultaneously into the remaining official languages only. Delegates who wish to address the UN Assembly in any other language can do so as long as they arrange translation into one of the official languages. English is the language used by the OECD, NATO, the IMF, the World Bank, and other international organizations. But these examples are not necessarily relevant for the EU, since none of these organizations has the ambition of achieving political integration.

1.2. Linguistic Reality

Most institutions of the EU have found compromises on the number of languages effectively used when full multilingualism is either difficult or impossible to achieve, or when so-called rules of procedure limit the number of languages. The basic distinction that has to be drawn can be summarized as follows: (1) multilingualism (that is, twenty-three languages) is the rule for communications between an EU institution and EU citizens, (2) certain restrictions are accepted for administrative procedures of the various institutions, and (3) the choice of language(s) to be used internally is determined by the institution itself and is driven by its internal functioning and objectives. In short, selected languages (essentially English, French, and to a lesser extent German) are used internally by the administration, and though there is no need for interpretation in many high-level meetings, the doctrine is that all twenty-three languages are on the same level.

Unfortunately, the European Parliament, which should certainly be the multilingual institution per excellence, has also made some compromises,[20] as pointed out by Wright (2007, 2009) in two very interesting papers. After spending several months in 2006 with MEPs, in Strasbourg, Brussels, and in the corridors of the commission, Wright (2009) finds that

> there is a considerable mismatch between policy and practices in linguis-
> tic matters. … Only a restricted number of languages are regularly used
> as working languages [English, French, and, to a much lesser degree,

[19] In 2001, official representatives were asked in which language (English, French, or Spanish) they wanted to receive their emails; 185 members replied; 126 chose English (including 14 from French-speaking countries), 39 chose French, and 20 chose Spanish (Calvet 2002, 154).

[20] This is also true of the communication of institutions with European citizens.

German] and among these English is coming to dominate. In consequence, political actors without knowledge of the working languages,
particularly English, find it increasingly difficult to do their job. Interestingly, monolingual native English speakers do not tend to perform
well in the multilingual setting of the Parliament ... either they may be
ineffectual in large meetings and fail to fulfill their goals in interaction
... The multilingual principle has been undermined in another very
important area. The undertaking that citizens can communicate with the
institutions in their own language cannot be guaranteed in all settings.
... These are just some instances drawn from the abundant evidence
that the policy to promote multilingualism has not succeeded.

In her 2007 paper, Wright gives some details on the behavior of
several groups of MEPs. She distinguishes among (1) native English
speakers, (2) native French speakers, (3) MEPs from the Central European countries, (4) Mediterranean and Southern European MEPs, and
(5) MEPs from the Nordic-, Dutch- and German-speaking countries.
It is worth quoting her at some length. A summary would not do full
justice to her account.

1. Native English speakers

The Irish and UK MEPs split into two clear camps. In one group, some
respondents were very aware of the need to respond very carefully and
tactfully to the tendency within the Parliament for increased use of
English as the language of the political process. ... They felt that their
contribution should be to confine (themselves) to a standard format
in order to be understood, to boil down their style, to observe the
parliamentary rule of KISS (keep it short and sweet). They saw no
place for rhetorical flourishes and extravagant style since this could
hamper comprehension in a multilingual setting. In the plenary sessions,
parliamentary procedure discourages this practice anyway, as speakers
are allocated a precise and short time to make their point and are cut off
if they run over their allotted slot.

Another group of English native speakers was much less linguistically
aware. From observation of their performance in the parliament and in
other public forums, it was clear that they were not making a conscious
effort to meet the linguistic needs of those using English as a second language. Their oral performance suffered from one or more of the following
problems: too many metaphors, archaic idiom, colloquialisms, rambling
syntactic structures, a failure to articulate clearly and a tendency to
speak very fast. ... Some members of this group that could be termed

less linguistically aware were judged as arrogant by those native English speakers who do take pains to facilitate communication.

Analysed more closely it seems clear that in the parliament not all English mother tongue speakers are at an advantage. Those who rely entirely on English and believe that there is no need for them to make an effort to learn the communication rules of Brussels may well be marginalised and out of the loop of much of the trans-national information flows.

2. Native French speakers

The French native speaker group bore some resemblance to the English native speaker community, in that its members also divide clearly into two sets, one militantly monolingual and the other pragmatic and ready to do what is necessary to further its political projects.

3. MEPs from Central Europe

The language repertoires among this group are very diverse with three main profiles discernible. [Some are competent in Western languages, in particular the Hungarians, but] they are critical of any translation or interpretation offered in Hungarian which is not first class. Sometimes the translation is quite unspeakable! [Among the Baltic-Slavic group, there are those] who are only able to read European documents confidently and comfortably once they have been translated into their national language. [They] are often disadvantaged because the translation of essential documents and amendments may take longer to appear in the small languages than in the big, and may sometimes arrive too late to be studied properly before the meeting. Those who can read other languages but only draft in their first language are also handicapped and must rely on assistants with linguistic skills.

Outsiders to this group reported the difficulties in interacting with some of its members. A Hungarian reporting on working with a Lithuanian in a committee said, "I go away from all our meetings thinking she hasn't understood." A Dutch respondent said, "The Poles I work with are on the outside of the group. We often do not know what they want or think."

4. Mediterranean and Southern MEPs

Portuguese is one of the languages that is interpreted into the majority of languages through the relay system, i.e. it is rendered first into English or French and then into Estonian, Czech etc. The Portuguese respondents were extremely critical of the relay system which they felt generated inaccuracies and lost information. Because of this, some reported that they often give their speeches in English or French, reasoning that at least the message was their message at the point of interpretation into the majority of languages. Those who do not do this, asked colleagues to check the accuracy of the French and English interpretations or gave interpreters summaries of their speech beforehand.

The high number of Brazilian interpreters was an issue for the Portuguese. Respondents stated that they were irritated by interpretation into a language that they saw as allied to their own, but not their own.

5. MEPs from the Nordic-, Dutch-, and German-speaking countries

Respondents from these language groups proved to be among the least interested in my research project. One very frank German interviewee told me that my work was probably counter productive in that it drew attention to a problem which is in the process of resolving itself.

6. And to top things off

Many informants have been quite clear that, in their opinion, some MEPs are excluded from certain aspects of the process of the parliament and are disadvantaged by present language practices. Some MEPs are marginalised in their committees. Some MEPs are disadvantaged as they wait for documents to be translated into their language. Where they cannot read the early versions in English and French, they have less time to formulate responses. Some MEPs are never contacted informally by those outside their language group because there is no easy way to do this. This prohibits all quiet negotiation and deal making. Bringing people on side is done in public and through interpretation, and committee rapporteurs report that this is difficult and makes compromise less likely.

1.3. Challenges to the Rules by EU Institutions

The Treaty of Rome established the principle of "equal authenticity" of treaties and legal documents adopted by the EU, whereby each translated version is considered correct and legally binding (Athanassiou 2006). But translating official documents into several languages leads to delicate interpretation problems.

A decision that weakens the rule that legal documents have to be translated into all languages was made by the EU Council. The rule can be broken if this is "decided unanimously by the Council on grounds of urgency."[21] Additional steps taken by the EU Council before the 2004 enlargement allow voluntary restrictions by countries. A system of interpretation on request has recently been implemented for preparatory meetings of the council.

That standardization is also legally possible is the topic of a judgment of the European Court of Justice in *Kik v. Office for Harmonization in the Internal Market (Trade Marks and Design) OHIM*,[22] which held that Article 314 of the treaty (on multilingualism and official languages) does not enshrine an absolute community law principle of the "equality of all languages":[23]

Paragraph 85. Regulation No. 1 [on official and working languages], in particular Article 4, requires that regulations and other documents of general application be drafted in the eleven [now twenty-three] official languages of the Union. It follows from that provision, and from Article 191 of the EC Treaty (now Article 254 EC) requiring publication in the *Official Journal of the European Union* of regulations, directives, and decisions adopted in accordance with the procedure referred to in Article 189b of the EC Treaty (now, after amendment, Article 251 EC), read in conjunction with Article 5 of Regulation No. 1, which provides for the publication of the *Official Journal* in the official languages, that an individual decision need not necessarily be drawn up in all the official languages, even though it may affect the rights of a citizen of the Union other than the person to whom it was addressed, for example a competing operator.

Paragraph 87. Nor can the second paragraph of Article 248 of the Treaty, as amended by the Treaty of Amsterdam, or the Court's case-law on the interpretation of Community law be relied on in support of a possible principle of equality of languages. Although equal account must be taken of all the authentic versions of a text when interpreting that text, that holds good only in so far as such versions exist and are authentic. Consequently, even if an individual decision is published in the *Official Journal of the European Union* and is therefore translated into all the languages for the information of citizens, only the language used in the relevant procedure will be authentic and will be used to interpret that decision.

[21] Council of the European Union, Council's Rules of Procedure and Rules for the Organization of the Proceedings of the European Council, Brussels: European Communities, 2007, Article 14.

[22] Case C-361/01 P, September 9, 2003.

[23] Athanassiou (2006, 11).

This is also the clear message of an interesting case[24] that went to the European Court and had to be examined first on the basis of its wording, since the various versions could lead to different outcomes. We are not particularly interested in the case itself but in the linguistic issues that were raised concerning Article 23 of the "Partnership and Cooperation Agreement between the European Communities and the Russian Federation—Freedom of movement of workers—Limit on the number of players from countries outside the EEA—Football." It is worth quoting in full that part of the opinion of Advocate General Stix-Hackl concerned with the interpretation of the article:

14. The starting point for assessing Article 23 of the Agreement in isolation must be its wording. In so doing, it must be borne in mind that Community legislation is drafted in various languages and that the different language versions are all equally authentic. An interpretation of a provision of Community law thus involves a comparison of the different language versions.

15. Such a comparison of the various versions of Article 23(1) shows that its wording and meaning do not correspond in all of them. The ten language versions that were authentic at the time of signature give the following picture: while seven (Danish, German, English, French, Italian, Portuguese and Russian) indicate an obligation, in the general sense of "ensure", three-language versions (Greek, Spanish and Dutch) point to an obligation to use endeavours. According to the Greek version, "the Community and its Member States shall use every endeavour", according to the Spanish version "they shall watch that..." and according to the Dutch version "they shall take care that...."

16. In order to determine the meaning of Article 23, one might take the common minimum of all the language versions as the starting point and accept that there is merely an obligation to use endeavours. However, such a method is supported neither by convincing arguments nor by the practice found in the Court's case-law.

17. Another solution would be to determine the clearest text, hence to eliminate texts that are not typical [three cases cited] or versions which contain a translation error [one case cited]. It is true that such an approach is in principle possible and is also found in the Court's case-law, but in the circumstances of the present case, in which it is not just

[24]Case C-265/03, *Igor Simutenkov v. Ministerio de Educación y Cultura and Real Federacíon Española de Fútbol,* opinion of Advocate General Stix-Hackl, delivered on January 11, 2005, in German.

one text that diverges from all the others, the approach does not permit a convincing solution.

18. A method of interpretation referred to by the Commission, namely that the language versions forming the majority prevail, would support the view that preference is to be given to the language versions laying down an obligation. This method also finds expression in the Court's case-law [two cases cited]. That may, however, be countered by the Court's line of argument under which, in certain circumstances, a single language version is to be favoured over the majority [five cases cited].

19. This indicates that recourse should be had to a quite different method, namely the method under which one proceeds on the basis of the original text, hence the version of the Agreement which served as the source text for the translation into the other languages, English. This text ("shall ensure") clearly imposes an obligation.

20. In view of the linguistic divergences it appears, however, to be necessary to consider the intention of the parties and the object of the provision to be interpreted [seven cases cited].

21. It is to be noted that this step in the examination is not always distinguished from the second step [three cases cited], namely taking into account of the object, purpose, essence or the like of the agreement.

22. The intention of the parties is of decisive importance for the interpretation of Article 23(1). The documents which have been submitted by the Commission that were used in preparing for the negotiations on the Agreement support the view that the parties wanted to lay down a clear obligation going beyond an obligation merely to use endeavours.

23. A comparison with similar agreements also supports the view that Article 23(1) is in the nature of an obligation. A comparison with Article 24(1) of the agreement with Ukraine and Article 23(1) of the agreement with Moldova reveals that these parallel provisions expressly contain the words "shall endeavour to ensure."

24. Further support for the view that Article 23(1) lays down an obligation going beyond an obligation merely to use endeavours is provided by the circumstance, revealed by the documents for negotiating the Agreement, that Russia expressed a wish to that effect.

25. The restriction at the beginning of Article 23(1) ("Subject to the laws, conditions and procedures applicable in each Member State…") might indicate that Article 23 is not in the nature of an obligation and therefore does not have direct effect.

26. However, under the case-law of the Court of Justice on a similar provision in the Europe agreements, the words "subject to the conditions and modalities applicable in each Member State" cannot be interpreted in such a way as to allow Member States to make the application of the principle of non-discrimination set out in that provision subject to conditions of discretionary limitations inasmuch as such an interpretation would render the provision meaningless and deprive it of any practical effect [two cases cited].

27. The outcome of the analysis of Article 23(1) in isolation is, therefore, that the—English—original text and the majority of the language versions as well as the intention of the negotiating parties indicate that a clear obligation is imposed on the Community and the Member States and thus that the provision has a direct effect.

The translation and interpretation system, the largest in the world, suffers from a certain number of sometimes unavoidable shortcomings. The opinion of Advocate General Stix-Hackl just discussed clearly shows that this was not the first case encountered with translation "errors," since it cites other cases that have been resolved in different ways: the Court does not have a clear policy to resolve such cases. Though the number of such cases that go to court is relatively small, it does not mean that the number of translation "errors" is small. They may simply go unnoticed as long as they do not generate too much trouble. Nevertheless, the opinion also shows that the original text may be considered the one that matters (though here other arguments reinforced the opinion). If this is so, then "a citizen whose only language of command is say, Slovak, can not rely on the Slovak version of Community law published in the *Official Journal* without comparing it with other language versions ... [but this] comparison may not guarantee that the actual meaning and purpose of the law will be revealed to him/her."[25] If so, why should the EU bother about the translation of legal documents into all official languages?

1.4. What Do EU Citizens Think?

As discussed earlier, standardization usually breeds disenfranchisement, and it is important to gauge the support for linguistic disenfranchisement among citizens of the EU. The short analysis that follows is based on the answers to some specific questions in the Special Eurobarometer 255 (2006) survey. They are summarized in table 8.1.

[25] See Glézl (n.d.).

TABLE 8.1. Attitudes on linguistic policies and usefulness of languages (%)

	Single EU Lang. (1)	Common Lang. (2)	One Add. Lang. (3)	Two Add. Lang. (4)	Treat All Equally (5)	EN (6)	GE (7)	FR (8)	SP (9)
Austria	48	60	75	44	76	19	73	2	15
Belgium	59	75	92	60	72	68	83	9	54
Bulgaria	34	43	70	27	70	28	65	34	11
Cyprus	59	69	96	70	91	79	93	17	34
Czech Republic	53	72	88	45	89	18	68	56	5
Denmark	44	54	91	48	74	93	92	56	7
Estonia	51	53	91	63	88	60	71	14	2
Finland	36	45	77	41	78	92	86	18	8
France	51	76	86	32	62	31	81	19	2
Germany	62	78	86	36	62	20	81	5	27
Greece	58	65	92	74	90	68	74	30	21
Hungary	65	66	83	68	67	13	57	52	3
Ireland	44	65	75	34	74	43	4	37	58
Italy	55	62	84	67	74	28	82	15	25
Latvia	58	63	92	65	69	39	70	17	3
Lithuania	56	71	89	69	86	24	85	27	4
Luxembourg	48	71	89	52	71	41	37	60	82
Malta	50	76	85	55	94	40	88	5	12
Netherlands	48	75	90	35	61	89	93	48	19
Poland	69	74	89	75	90	27	70	45	5
Portugal	50	66	73	52	83	63	51	5	31
Romania	46	56	70	37	69	61	63	18	33
Slovak Republic	44	61	84	31	78	22	70	60	4
Slovenia	54	50	80	47	87	77	79	61	4
Spain	56	71	79	63	69	26	72	11	32
Sweden	41	60	90	27	71	94	96	39	12
United Kingdom	48	69	79	49	80	47	4	29	63
EU	54.3	69.4	83.4	49.4	72.3	37.5	67.3	22.3	25.0

Source: Fidrmuc, Ginsburgh, and Weber (2007).

Note: Columns 1 through 5 report percentages that tend to agree with the following statements: "The European institutions should adopt one single language to communicate with European citizens," "Everyone in the European Union should be able to speak a common language," "Everyone in the European Union should be able to speak one language in addition to their mother tongue," "Everyone in the European Union should be able to speak two languages in addition to their mother tongue," and "All languages spoken within the European Union should be treated equally." Columns 6 to 9 report the percentages that mentioned each language in response to the question "Which two languages, apart from your mother tongue do you think are the most useful to know for your personal development and career?" Only languages that were mentioned by at least 15 percent of the EU population are included.

They show that a majority of EU citizens support some degree of linguistic standardization. Fifty-four percent of the population "tend to agree" that European institutions should adopt one single language to communicate with European citizens and 69 percent "tend to agree" that everyone in the EU should be able to speak a common language; 83 and 49 percent believe that everyone should be able to speak one or two languages in addition to his or her mother tongue. On the other hand, and in contradiction to what precedes, 72 percent think that all languages should be treated equally. Hence, and though attitudes vary, sometimes substantially, across countries, a clear majority of Europeans hold a generally pragmatic attitude toward linguistic policies, recognizing that ensuring effective communication may require that the EU should use a single language or that EU citizens should learn and use foreign languages. While a majority also support equal treatment of all languages, this does not necessarily contradict the aforementioned pragmatic stance. On the contrary, taken together with the prevailing support for using a single language, this attitude seems to suggest that Europeans would prefer a regime based on a single official language rather than on a larger set of privileged core languages. It is interesting to note that Europeans also display a great deal of agreement on which languages are important. The language that most Europeans consider useful is English, cited by 67 percent of EU citizens (not counting native speakers). French (25 percent), German (22 percent), and Spanish (15 percent) follow, with a substantial gap. Russian (3.4 percent, cited almost exclusively in postcommunist countries), Italian (3.2 percent), and Chinese (1.5 percent) receive even less support. No other language is seen as useful by more than 1 percent of the EU population.[26]

1.5. Who Is Afraid of Standardization?

The Lisbon Treaty (in particular Article 342 TFUE), which became effective on December 1, 2009, suggests a "simplified" mechanism to replace many of the remaining unanimity requirements by the lighter qualified majority mode. Such shifts would, however, need to be approved unanimously by all member states (Article 48.7 TEU).

Changes in the linguistic regime of the EU are, however, still subject to a unanimous vote cast by the European Council (Article 290 EC).

---

[26]The following languages were mentioned by more than 0.5 percent but less than 1 percent: Arabic (0.7 percent), Dutch (0.7 percent), Portuguese (0.5 percent), and Swedish (0.5 percent).

The mere principle of accepting a discussion of standardization would probably require unanimous agreement. Therefore, even the Lisbon Treaty may not make a change in linguistic regime easier.

The negative reactions that the authors of this book often received from EU civil servants, as well as from some distinguished European linguists, when they tried to discuss standardization bear some clarification. The standardization scenarios that are suggested do not oppose the principle that each member state is "represented" by its official language and that all official languages should be used in the European Parliament and in contacts between EU institutions and citizens. But they open up the possibility of translating regulations and legal documents into a restricted number of languages (central or core languages), with translation into other languages decentralized to individual countries, which conceivably could be compensated for doing this work. This was suggested by Fidrmuc and Ginsburgh (2007) and is further developed in section 2. It would allow member states either to implement their own preferred translation and interpretation regimes (possibly on a different scale than the current EU regime) or to forgo linguistic services altogether and instead divert the compensatory transfers to alternative uses.

2. Possible Solutions

> I speak Spanish to God, Italian to women,
> French to men, and German to my dog.
> —*Emperor Charles V*

REMODELING BABYLON. *And then, the Lord read chapter 8:1–5. And changed his mind. Genesis, Apocryphal Writings.*

Section 2.1 of this chapter examines the issue of how to determine the set of core languages. Section 2.2 uses the provisions of the Lisbon Treaty and Penrose's Law to simulate the type of linguistic reform that could pass qualified majority voting (once the issue of linguistic regime is no longer ruled by unanimity). Section 2.3 presents an alternative to reducing costs. It explores ways of sharing between countries the total cost of translation and interpretation. Clearly, the results of sections 2.1 to 2.3 can be combined, and countries whose languages are not chosen as core languages can be compensated using a variant of the method used in section 2.3.

2.1. How Many Languages Does the EU Need?

A functional multilingual society requires willingness on behalf of the participating linguistic groups to make compromises and to accept some sort of linguistic standardization. As Queen Beatrix of the Netherlands stated in an opening speech to the European Parliament, "I am addressing you today in Dutch. At the same time, I am convinced that cooperation in Europe will increasingly demand concessions of us in this field."[27] To be more specific about its linguistic challenges, note that the EU consists of twenty-seven countries. Germany and Austria share a common language, German; Greece and the Greek part of Cyprus share a common language, Greek; three countries, France, the Netherlands, and Belgium, share two languages, French and Dutch. Since Luxembourg did not insist on the recognition of Luxembourgish as an official language, there are "only" twenty-three languages forming the set of EU official languages.

A decision on which languages to use at the EU level can have wide-ranging implications. It could affect the legitimacy of decision making and may induce citizens who do not speak or understand those languages to refuse participation in the political process. The EU proudly asserts that its "policy of official multilingualism as a deliberate tool of government is unique in the world. The EU sees the use of its citizens' languages as one of the factors which make it more transparent, more legitimate and more efficient."[28]

Determining the set of core languages for a multilingual society confronts the trade-off between costs (limited communication) and benefits (improved communication and administrative efficiency, among others). The analysis must weigh the benefits of multilingualism against its costs, which can be quite substantial. Even before the 2004 enlargement the institutions of the EU were the largest recruiter of interpreters and translators in the world.[29] In 1999 the total translation and interpretation costs for the commission alone amounted to 30 percent of its internal budget.[30] The basic principles of political accountability and equality among citizens require that all, or at least a substantial part of the full-fledged translation services, will have to be maintained in some of the EU institutions (Council of the European Union, European Council, European Parliament).[31]

[27] Address by the queen to the European Parliament in Strasbourg, October 26, 2004.
[28] See the EU Web portal "Languages and Europe," http://europa.eu.int/languages/en/home.
[29] Cole and Cole (1997, 59).
[30] De Swaan (1993, 2001, 172).
[31] Mamadouh (1995, 55–56), and Council of the European Union (2002).

Moreover, a failure to provide translation services by the EU may simply shift the provision of the service to individual countries, leading to duplications that could raise the total cost of services,[32] as well as to divergent translations and interpretations. The burden of maintaining official languages is not limited to the direct costs of translation and interpretation. Communication[33] constitutes an even more serious challenge in societies with a large number of languages. Translation and interpretation errors, as well as delays necessitated by translation, may end up paralyzing multilateral discussions and negotiations.[34]

If costs depended only on the number of core languages, the search for an optimal linguistic regime would, as shown in section 2 of chapter 7, boil down to achieving the lowest possible EU disenfranchisement for a given number of languages.

Ginsburgh, Ortuño-Ortín, and Weber (2005) take the examination of this issue a step farther. They look at optimal sets of official languages, which are determined by two parameters. One is the society's sensitivity toward language disenfranchisement of its members. The other is the degree of comprehensiveness of its *language regime*, which can take any intermediate form between two polar cases: under *full interpretation*, at one extreme, all documents and discussions in meetings are translated into all languages, whereas under *minimal interpretation*, at the other extreme, all documents are translated into one core language. In practice, the language regime is chosen somewhere between these two extremes. The society's objective is to find a set of languages that minimizes the weighted sum of total EU disenfranchisement and costs. (In fact, the weight assigned to costs can be set to 1.) The weight attached to total disenfranchisement represents society's "sensitivity" toward linguistic concerns of its citizens. If the sensitivity parameter is high, then society cares about the disenfranchisement of its citizens and will implement a large number of core languages; in the extreme case, all languages spoken in the society would belong to the set of core languages. If the sensitivity parameter is low and cost considerations become more important, the society would shrink the set of core languages, and in the extreme case would select one language only.

The derivation of the cost function in Ginsburgh, Ortuño-Ortín, and Weber (2005) is based on the following idea. There are cases in which the proper functioning of institutions becomes impractical if too

---

[32] Mamadouh and Hofman (2001).
[33] De Swaan (2001, 173).
[34] Mamadouh (1998, 8).

many languages are used. Imagine a meeting where every participant speaks her own language without being understood by the majority of other participants. This generates a cost function whose values are prohibitively high if the number of official languages exceeds a certain threshold. But even if this is not the case, the total cost of sustaining several languages depends on the nature of the language regime imposed by the society. Assume that there is a fixed cost c generated by translation, interpretation, and communication between any two official languages, and that there is a uniform stream of demands from all languages. Under a full interpreting regime, which requires every important document to exist in all official languages, the total cost of sustaining k languages is given by ck^2, which also includes the cost of printing all the documents.[35] If the society adopts a minimal standard interpreting regime, which requires translating into one core language, the total cost of sustaining k languages is approximately ck—actually it is $c(k - 1)$ because the documents in all languages except the core one should be translated. The society can also adopt an intermediate standard interpreting regime, in which case the cost would take values ck^β, where $1 < \beta < 2$. To accommodate various language regimes, it is assumed that $C = ck^\beta$, where k stands for the number of core languages and the parameter β ($1 \leqslant \beta \leqslant 2$) represents the degree of comprehensiveness of the language regime, including the two polar cases $\beta = 1$ and $\beta = 2$ described above.

Since one does not know what the weight "sensitivity to disenfranchisement," as well as β, "the degree of comprehensiveness of the language regime," should be, one can run simulations with different values of these weights.[36] The simulations show that it could be unwise to select English as unique working language not only because it is not always optimal, but also because it is optimal only for very small values of the weight that represents sensitivity to disenfranchisement. The best choice of three languages is English, French, and German, though Italian could be a very reasonable substitute for French. This is so for the EU before and after the 2004 enlargement. Spanish is obviously not a good choice within the EU if no account is taken of Mexico and Latin America and the growing importance of Spanish in the South and West of the United States. One can argue that it might

---

[35]This is an approximation, since with k languages, only $k(k - 1)$ translations are necessary, not k^2.

[36]See also Grin (2003), who argues that there must be an optimum, since "it is reasonable to assume that the benefits of diversity increase at a decreasing rate, while its costs increase at an increasing rate."

be reasonable for the EU to adopt four working languages, three—English, French, and German—for general use, with Spanish added because of its importance in the rest of the world.[37]

2.2. EU Politicians and Linguistic Reforms

The decision on the set of core languages is inevitably a political one and boils down to deciding what extent of disenfranchisement is tolerable.

Traditionally, most EU decisions were made by unanimous agreement of the European Council. However, as the EU continued to expand, unanimous agreement became increasingly difficult,[38] and therefore the EU has been gradually moving toward greater application of qualified majority voting (QMV), in particular with the adoption of the Single European Act in 1986. The Nice Treaty and the Lisbon Treaty subsequently confirmed this trend. While this extended the range of issues for which QMV is used, the EU language regime remains subject to the unanimity rule. This is, however, inherently undemocratic. In the context of linguistic policies, it implies that a Maltese or an Estonian citizen has more weight than a Pole or an Italian. Thus, to avoid the EU becoming overwhelmed by dozens of languages, and to enhance the democratic legitimacy of EU policies, the EU will have to shift its emphasis from national concerns to those of individual citizens.

Therefore, we now examine under which conditions a linguistic reform could pass under the QMV rules stipulated by the (outdated) Nice Treaty, the Lisbon Treaty, or under Penrose's law.[39] The question can be formulated as follows: What would be the minimal number of official languages required under alternative voting rules, given a uniform (but sensitivity-adjusted) disenfranchisement rate that all countries would find acceptable?

The differences between the two treaties are interesting to analyze. Under the Nice Treaty, each member state has a fixed number of votes (see column 2 of table 8.2, with an EU-wide total of 345. Populations, listed in column 3 of table 8.2, and the number of countries are also taken into account. For a decision to pass, the following three requirements apply: (1) the proposal must backed by a majority of states (fourteen of twenty-seven), (2) it must be supported by 255 of the

[37] See also Pool (1996) for a different approach to the problem.
[38] See, for example, Baldwin et al. (2000, 2001) and Baldwin and Widgrén (2004).
[39] See also Fidrmuc, Ginsburgh, and Weber (2009).

345 votes, and (3) the states backing the votes must represent at least 62 percent of the EU population (or 303 million). Under the Lisbon Treaty, for a decision to pass, it must be supported by 55 percent of the countries (fifteen out of twenty-seven) and by 65 percent of the EU population (318 million). It is worth pointing out that the voting rules under the Lisbon Treaty are exactly the same as under the previous draft of the European Constitution, which was rejected.

To discuss the possible variants of QMV, we consider a setup with all twenty-seven member countries of the EU. Suppose that the EU adopts a specific variant of QMV (Nice, Lisbon, any other) that imposes restrictions on the number and configuration of the countries required to support a decision.

Suppose that each country of the EU chooses a maximum acceptable disenfranchisement rate that serves as a threshold determining whether it would support a specific subset of core languages. It is then straightforward to compute the set of countries that would vote in favor of a reform stipulating, say, five languages. Assume that each country whose disenfranchisement rate was smaller than the threshold of, say, 50 percent would vote for a reform. Consider now the disenfranchisement rates obtained in table 7.5, with English, German, French, Italian, and Spanish as core languages. Then the following countries would vote for the reform: Austria, Belgium, Cyprus, Denmark, France, Germany, Ireland, Italy, Luxembourg, Malta, Netherlands, Slovenia, Spain, Sweden, and the United Kingdom. These fifteen countries, representing 362 million citizens (that is, 74 percent of EU's population), would vote for the proposition, which would pass the requirements of, for example, the Lisbon Treaty. Under the Nice Treaty, this proposal would need seven languages to pass.

However, not all countries have the same *sensitivity* to language issues. Therefore, instead of assuming that the acceptable disenfranchisement rate is uniform over all countries, it is computed as follows. We start with an acceptable *average* disenfranchisement rate r (r takes the following values: 0.10, 0.20, 0.30, 0.40, and 0.50) and modify it according to the sensitivity of each country. To estimate sensitivity, we use the percentage of citizens in each country who tend to agree with the following statement (one of the questions in the Special Eurobarometer 243 [2006] survey): "The European institutions should adopt one single language to communicate with European citizens," reported in column 4 of table 8.2. These percentages ρ_k are then normalized by the EU-wide weighted response to that question, denoted by ρ and the countries' rates r_k are computed as

$$r_k = r\rho_k/\rho, \quad r = 0.10,\ldots,0.50.$$

TABLE 8.2. Number of votes, population, and
sensitivity of citizens to language issues

Country (1)	No. of Votes (units) (2)	Population (million) (3)	Sensitivity Answers (%) (4)	Index (5)
Austria	10	8.2	48	0.87
Belgium	12	10.4	59	1.09
Bulgaria	10	7.4	34	0.63
Cyprus	4	0.7	59	1.09
Czech Republic	12	10.2	53	0.98
Denmark	7	5.4	44	0.81
Estonia	4	1.3	51	0.94
Finland	7	5.2	36	0.66
France	29	60.6	51	0.94
Germany	29	82.5	62	1.14
Greece	12	11.1	58	1.07
Hungary	12	10.1	65	1.20
Ireland	7	4.1	44	0.81
Italy	29	58.5	55	1.01
Latvia	4	2.3	48	1.07
Lithuania	7	3.4	56	1.03
Luxembourg	4	0.5	48	0.88
Malta	3	0.4	50	0.92
Netherlands	13	16.3	48	0.88
Poland	27	38.2	69	1.27
Portugal	12	10.5	50	0.92
Romania	14	22.3	46	0.85
Slovak Republic	7	5.4	44	0.81
Slovenia	4	2.0	54	0.99
Spain	27	43.0	56	1.03
Sweden	10	9.0	41	0.76
United Kingdom	29	60.0	48	0.88
Total	345	489.2	54.3	1.00

Source: Fidrmuc, Ginsburgh, and Weber (2009).
Note: Column 4 reports percentages of citizens who that "tend to agree" with the following statement: "The European institutions should adopt one single language to communicate with European citizens." Column 5 is obtained by dividing these percentages by the EU weighted average (54.3 percent).

The values of ρ_k / ρ are reproduced in column 5 of table 8.2. The smaller the index, the more sensitive is the country, and the less easily it will accept disenfranchisement.

Table 8.3 presents the results of our calculations for the optimal sets based on all respondents, as well as on the young generation aged 15–

TABLE 8.3. Voting scenarios: minimal number of
languages satisfying qualified majority voting

Acceptable Average Disenfranchisement Rate (%)	Minimal Number of Languages		
	Nice Treaty	Lisbon Treaty	Penrose's Law
All respondents			
10	11	11	9
20	10	10	8
30	9	10	7
40	9	8	7
50	7	5	6
Young respondents ($\leqslant 29$ years)			
10	9	9	7
20	7	5	6
30	7	5	6
40	5	3	4
50	4	2	3
With distances—all respondents			
10	10	10	8
20	5	5	5
30	3	3	3
40	3	2	2
50	3	2	2

Source: Fidrmuc, Ginsburgh, and Weber (2009).

Note: Nice: approved if 255 votes and fourteen countries, representing 62 percent of the population (303 million), vote for the reform; Lisbon: approved if fifteen countries, representing 65 percent of the population (318 million), vote for the reform; Penrose: approved if 65 percent of the sum of the square roots of individual countries' populations vote for the reform.

29 only and on distance-adjusted disenfranchisement rates (tables 7.5, 7.6, and 7.7).

Consider, for instance, the case in which all respondents are taken into account. Assume that the representatives of countries for which the chosen set of languages results in an acceptable disenfranchisement rate that is on average smaller than or equal to 10 percent would vote for the proposal. Then, under the application of the Nice or Lisbon QMV rules, all eleven languages listed in table 7.5 would be required for the reform to pass.

The number of languages needed to pass a vote decreases as the acceptable average disenfranchisement rate increases, and it decreases faster under the Lisbon rules. The provision that is constraining in the case of the Nice Treaty is the fixed number of votes allocated to each country. This criterion is abandoned in the Lisbon Treaty, while the two remaining criteria are made somewhat stricter than those of the Nice Treaty (fifteen countries instead of fourteen and 65 percent of the EU population instead of 62 percent). The combined effect leads nevertheless to a reduction in the number of core languages. Overall, the results show the following (under the Lisbon Treaty QMV rules):

1. *All respondents.* A linguistic reform would be possible if it maintains between five (English, German, French, Italian, Spanish) and eleven (those five plus Polish, Romanian, Hungarian, Portuguese, Czech, and Greek) core languages as the acceptable average disenfranchisement rate goes from 50 to 10 percent.

2. *Young generation aged 15–29 years.* Between two (English, French) and nine (English, French, German, Italian, Spanish, Polish, Romanian, Hungarian, and Portuguese) core languages would be required to make the reform politically feasible (again depending on the acceptable rate of disenfranchisement).

3. *All respondents, adjusted for linguistic distances.* The numbers of languages needed to satisfy the Nice Treaty or the Lisbon Treaty are similar to those generated for young respondents only.

The provisions of both the Nice Treaty and the Lisbon Treaty assign unequal voting power to countries of different size. The important principle advocated by Penrose (1946, 56) in his seminal contribution is that every voter should have equal power in what he called "a world assembly":

This situation, however, can only arise in an assembly of nations of equal sizes, each enfranchized to the same degree. To award nations voting powers proportional to their populations would give the spokesmen for larger nations too much power in relation to the number of their sponsors. On the other hand, if, as at present arranged [in the United Nations], large and small nations have equal voting powers, the spokesmen for small nations are felt to be too significant, and artificial rules about the meanings of votes and vetoes should be constructed to redress the balance.

Indeed, an average citizen in a large country is less powerful than her counterpart in a smaller country, and Penrose shows that the voting power of a single citizen in a world assembly is proportional to the inverse of the square root of her country's population. Thus, to guarantee equal distribution of voting power in the two-tier voting system, each country should be assigned a voting weight proportional to the square root of its population. In the context of the EU, the Penrose weight allocation ensures an equal influence of every EU citizen on decisions of the European Council.[40]

In the last column of table 8.3 we use Penrose weights and assume that a proposal supported by 65 percent of the square root of EU's total population would pass.[41] As can be seen, the Penrose method would make it possible to restrict the number of core languages quite substantially. A regime with six core languages (English, French, German, Italian, Spanish, and Polish) is likely to be accepted at a reasonably low 20 to 30 percent acceptable average disenfranchisement rate. Using distances between languages allows reaching the threshold of five languages with an acceptable disenfranchisement rate as low as 20 percent.

Note that in this group of languages (English, French, German, Italian, Spanish, and Polish), there is at least one language belonging to each of the main families of Indo-European languages (Romance, Germanic, and Slavic). The group includes English (which is at some distance from other Germanic languages, as figure 4.1A shows) but excludes the small group of two Baltic languages (Latvian and Lithuanian), Greek, and the three non–Indo-European languages (Finnish, Hungarian, and Maltese). The fact that all large language families are represented implies that translations to other languages belonging to the same family would be made somewhat easier. The oddity is the overrepresentation of Romance languages (French, Italian, and Spanish), which results from two factors. First, the number of speakers of each of these languages in the EU is rather large. Second, the countries in which these three languages are native tend to ignore most other European languages (see table 7.2). One may argue that Spanish is also important in the rest of the world, with 300 million speakers outside Spain, and is worth keeping in the group. This is, however, not the case with Italian, which is spoken almost exclusively in Italy.

[40]Laurelle and Widgrén (1998).

[41]We select the same threshold as that stipulated by the Lisbon Treaty. Alternatively, one can use a 62 percent threshold, as suggested by Slomczynski, Zastawniak, and Zyczkowski (2006) in their so-called Jagiellonian compromise.

If implemented, the six-language scenario would result in a relatively modest overall disenfranchisement of 16 percent. Adding more languages would lower the disenfranchisement rate further, but the gains attributable to each additional language would be small and limited to the native country of that language. An important feature is that the six-language scenario could be seen as broadly consistent with Europeans' preference for linguistic pragmatism as well as with the equal treatment of languages described in table 8.1: the languages included are all spoken in large EU member countries with a population of approximately 40 million or more. If more languages were to be included, the next two should optimally be Romanian and Hungarian. That, however, would be difficult to justify. Introducing Romanian would indeed add a fourth Romance language and one spoken by only 21 million people; Hungarian is spoken by 12 million people (in Hungary and to some extent in Slovakia, Romania, Serbia, and Austria), while other languages spoken by similar numbers of people (most notably Dutch, spoken by 22 million citizens) would be left out.

Finally, the results in table 7.2 show that most European citizens speak the official language of the country in which they were born and in which they live. Therefore, an appropriate disenfranchisement rate to incorporate national pride considerations could be based entirely on the number of native speakers of each language. A sequence constructed on this notion would obviously lead to the same optimal set, since the six languages belong to the most populated countries (and include German-speaking Austria and the 40 percent of Belgians whose native language is French). These countries account for 75.7 percent of the EU population.

2.3. Sharing Costs or Compensating Losers?

Dutch appears in no case among the first eleven languages in the sequence of optimal sets of tables 7.5, 7.6, or 7.7. Actually, it would enter the sets as number 13 only. It is spoken by over 22 million citizens (of whom 16 million live in the Netherlands and 6 million in Belgium), that is, equal to or more than the numbers who speak some languages in the optimal set introduced before Dutch: Romanian (with 22.3 million speakers), Greek (11.1 million), Portuguese (10.5 million), Czech (10.2 million), Hungarian (10.1 million), and Bulgarian (7.4 million). This is due to the fact that both the Dutch and the Flemings speak English, German, or French, and their rate of disenfranchisement is at 18 percent as long as these three languages are introduced in the optimal set. If their language is not part of the set of core languages, it is because they are fluent in other important languages. Though Denmark, Malta, and Sweden have fewer inhabitants than the Netherlands, they are also proficient in English, and the likelihood of their languages belonging to a core set is even more remote. In some sense, these countries may feel punished because their citizens made the effort to learn foreign languages.

Conversely, as can be seen from the numbers in table 7.2, Italian, Spanish, and Polish inhabitants hardly speak any foreign language, and their languages are little used elsewhere in Europe. They enter the optimal set at a very early stage (numbers 4, 5, and 6) merely because Italy, Spain, and Poland have large populations (58.5, 43.0, and 38.2 million, respectively). So they seem to be favored.

The United Kingdom has 60 million inhabitants, but English is spoken by almost 120 million citizens in other European countries. English thus benefits from efforts made by many European citizens to learn the language, which in turn induces United Kingdom's inhabitants to refrain from learning any other language. The last column of table 7.4 shows that only some 48 percent of UK high school students learn another language, while this percentage is over 90 percent in most other countries. From the next to last line in table 7.2 (United Kingdom), one can check that some 9 percent of Britons know French, but this figure decreases to 2 percent for German and Spanish, 1 percent for Italian, and zero for Polish or Dutch. By being a large enough country and having their language known by many foreigners, Britons can communicate with many people. They therefore have little need to learn other languages, and know that their language will be learned by foreigners. The reason for this was set out chapter 5. The United Kingdom, and English, free-ride on other nations and languages.

There is thus a feeling of inequity. Some countries or languages are "lucky," while others are less so. The injustice results from the fact that this luck or misfortune is often a consequence of past events. Large populations are favored. History also played a role. Estonians, Finns, Hungarians, and Maltese do not speak Indo-European languages, and though Greek belongs to the Indo-European family, it is far from the other languages of the group. More recent events in which today's citizens have no responsibility have also taken their toll. The former countries of the communist bloc were isolated for a long time, and so were Spain until Franco's death and Portugal until the 1974 Carnation Revolution. On the other hand, the United Kingdom, a somewhat reluctant member of the EU, can communicate with a quarter of the world, since more than 1.5 billion people have a good knowledge of English, which is also the leading language in the EU.

A second reason for this variance across countries and languages is the unequal cost per citizen for translation and interpretation services. Assuming that the total cost is 1,123 million euros, as claimed by the European Commission, that all languages are treated equally (that is, each document or oral statement is translated into all languages), and that all twenty-three languages are equally costly to translate into and from, the average cost per language per year is roughly 50 million euros.[42] It is often argued by the commission and some of its commissioners that this amounts to a mere 2.30 euros per citizen, "the price of a cup of coffee."[43] As suggested by Fidrmuc and Ginsburgh (2007), a much better indicator is the cost per person who would be disenfranchised had EU documents not been provided in his or her native language. Such calculation reveals considerable differences across languages. Table 8.4 reports the average costs per language. Column 3 lists the population speaking each language appearing in column 1, taking account of the fact that some languages are spoken in more than one country (column 2). In columns 4 and 5, we show the disenfranchisement rates and the number of citizens who would be disenfranchised if only English, German, French, Italian, Spanish, and Polish were considered core languages. The average costs per disenfranchised head are reported in column 6. These are computed per language rather than per country, by dividing the average cost per language (50 million) by the disenfranchised population.

We assume here that no citizens are disenfranchised in any of the countries where one or several of the core languages are official. As can be seen, there are huge differences across the remaining countries. The cost of providing translations of a language reflects the combined effect of the number of people who speak the language and the number

---

[42]This is the total cost, divided by twenty-two, as we assume that a document prepared in any of the twenty-three official languages has to be translated into the remaining twenty-two languages.

[43]These words are attributed to Lord Neil Kinnock, who at the time was the vice president of the European Commission. They have since become buzzwords each time the cost of translation in the EU is invoked, as in the official document written by the European Commission, Directorate-General for the Press and Communication, "Many tongues, one family: Languages in the European Union" (July 2004). Lord Kinnock, in his new capacity as the chair of the British Council, the United Kingdom's international organization for cultural relations and educational opportunities, wrote in the introduction to Graddol's (2006) report: "the English language teaching sector directly earns £1.3 billions [at the time of writing this, the British pound was worth 1.3 euros] for the UK as invisible exports and our education related exports earn up to £10 billion a year more." Grin (2005) estimates the sum at some 17 to 18 billion euros, roughly the same amount as Kinnock. This is, Lord Kinnock, more than a cup of coffee per UK inhabitant, isn't it?

TABLE 8.4. Cost per disenfranchised citizen, assuming that core languages are English, German, French, Italian, Spanish, and Polish

Languages	Countries	Population (million)	Disenfr. Rate (%)	Population Disenfr. (million)	Cost Per Disenfr. Head (euros)
Bulgarian	Bulgaria	7.4	78	5.8	8.6
Czech	Czech Republic	10.2	67	6.8	7.4
Danish	Denmark	5.4	30	1.6	31.3
Dutch	Netherlands and Belgium (60%)	22.6	21	4.8	10.4
English	UK and Ireland	64.1	0	0.0	0.0
Estonian	Estonia	1.3	69	0.9	55.6
Finnish	Finland	5.2	67	3.5	14.3
French	France and Belgium (40%)	64.7	0	0.0	0.0
German	Germany and Austria	90.7	0	0.0	0.0
Greek	Greece and Cyprus	11.8	62	7.3	6.8
Hungarian	Hungary	10.1	85	8.6	5.8
Irish	Ireland	4.1	0	0.0	0.0
Italian	Italy	58.5	0	0.0	0.0
Latvian	Latvia	2.3	82	1.9	26.3
Lithuanian	Lithuania	3.4	71	2.4	20.8
Maltese	Malta	0.4	31	0.1	500.0
Polish	Poland	38.2	0	0.0	0.0
Portuguese	Portugal	10.5	79	8.3	6.0
Romanian	Romania	22.3	79	17.6	2.8
Slovak	Slovak Republic	5.4	70	3.8	13.2
Slovene	Slovenia	2.0	45	0.9	55.6
Spanish	Spain	43.0	0	0.0	0.0
Swedish	Sweden	9.0	33	3.0	16.7

of speakers of that language who are proficient in foreign languages. Hence, the more people speak a language, ceteris paribus, the lower the cost, but the more speakers of that language who speak one of the six core languages, the lower the need to provide translations and, correspondingly, the higher the cost per disenfranchised person. Because of these two effects, languages spoken by large populations are relatively inexpensive. Romanian, for example, costs little more per citizen than the average EU cost of 2.30 euros. The second tier is formed by linguistic groups that are medium-sized (Bulgarian, Czech, Greek, Hungarian, Portuguese) or relatively large but highly proficient in other languages (Dutch). These are in the range of approximately 5 to 10 euros per person. In contrast, languages spoken by relatively few people come out as expensive, especially if those people tend to be proficient also in other languages: Danish (31 euros), Estonian (54 euros), Finnish (14 euros), Latvian (26 euros) Lithuanian (21 euros), Slovak (13 euros), Slovene (56 euros), Swedish (17 euros). The highest cost is incurred by Maltese (500 euros).

While these costs are by no means excessive, they are all much higher than the cost of a mere "cup of coffee," and one might want to consider the trade-offs entailed in spending 30 to 100 euros per person per year on translating and interpreting instead of devoting this amount to other worthy causes. These costs would be even more substantial if one considered the younger group as representing the future, since their disenfranchisement rates are much lower.

The figures discussed above are back-of-the-envelope calculations. However, they give a good indication of the order of magnitude of the per-person costs of eliminating disenfranchisement with respect to the various European languages. A limitation of that analysis is that it ignores linguistic distances. Translation may be easier (and cheaper) if it involves two closely related languages. Translating a document from Spanish to Portuguese, from Swedish to Danish, or from Czech to Slovak costs less than translating the same document from English or French.

The question boils down to, who should be paying the costs of translation? Should countries whose languages are spoken by foreigners compensate them, since they bore the cost of learning the language? Should countries whose citizens do not know foreign languages and did not have to bear the cost of learning another language pay a contribution to other countries? Should countries whose languages are chosen as core languages compensate others?

Sharing Costs

In this section, we assume that all languages have identical rights and are all part of the set of core languages, that is, we consider the current situation with translation and interpretation being made from each to all other twenty-two languages. We simulate a situation in which the costs of translation and interpretation are borne by those who do not speak foreign languages.

We start with an example. Let us assume that we have four countries, Austria (A), France (F), Germany (G), and the UK (E), and three languages English (e), German (g), and French (f). Define the number of *nonspeakers* of a language in a country by the pair Xz, where X is the country and z the language. For example, Fg is the number of nonspeakers of German in France, while Gf is the number of nonspeakers of French in Germany. Let c_z be the cost of implementing language z. Finally, let E, G, and F represent the total number of speakers of English, German, and French. The data are presented in table 8.5, using the numbers of nonspeakers that can be extracted from table 7.2, columns 1 to 4, for each country and the countries' populations. The formula used to compute the share of the total cost to be borne by Austria is

$$t_A = \frac{Ae}{E}c_e + \frac{Ag}{G}c_g + \frac{Af}{F}c_f.$$

The first term $Ae \times c_e/E$ shares c_e, the total cost of maintaining English, according to the share of Austrians who do not speak English with respect to E, the total number of Europeans who do not speak it. The other two terms can be interpreted in the same way, to maintain German and French. Summing the three terms gives the contribution that Austria would have to pay to maintain all three languages. The reader can construct the formulas for the three other countries. The formulas can easily be extended to any number of languages and countries. Each equation would contain more terms (as many as there are languages), and there would be one such equation for each country.

Using the numbers from table 8.5, and assuming that the costs are all equal to c, one gets $t_A = 0.10c$, $t_F = 0.96c$, $t_G = 1.04c$, and $t_E = 0.90c$. It is easy to see that the total cost adds to $3c$ and is shared by the four countries according to the following percentages: 3.3, 31.9, 34.7, 30.0.

Germany will pay the largest share, just because it is the largest country, though disenfranchisement rates for the two other languages are roughly the same in Austria and Germany.

This is exactly what the inverse square root law of Penrose introduced in section 2.2 tries to correct, by taking the square roots of the populations instead of the absolute numbers. This would lead to the same calculation by taking the square roots of the number of nonspeakers in each country, and take as last row ("Total nonspeakers"), the sum column by column of the square roots. Redoing a

TABLE 8.5. Data for the computation of cost sharing

	English	German	French
Austria	$Ae = 4.5$	$Ag = 0.1$	$Af = 7.7$
France	$Fe = 48.5$	$Fg = 57.6$	$Ff = 0.6$
Germany	$Ge = 51.5$	$Gg = 0.8$	$Gf = 75.9$
United Kingdom	$Ee = 0.6$	$Eg = 58.8$	$Ef = 54.6$
Total nonspeakers	$E = 104.7$	$G = 117.3$	$F = 138.8$

Note: Ae is the number of nonspeakers of English living in Austria, for example. These figures provide the basis for determining the costs of translation and interpretation borne by countries in which some citizens do not speak foreign languages.

comparable calculation with these new numbers leads to the following percentages: 9.4, 30.3, 30.6, 29.6. The three large countries will now pay less, while the payment made by Austria becomes larger. This is also more reasonable, since, as was mentioned, disenfranchisement rates are roughly equal, and the square roots of the populations of nonspeakers make them closer to each other.

There is also the possibility of considering weighted costs, based for example on the proportions of the various languages used to draft original documents. According to the last statistics, English is used in 72 percent of the cases, French in some 25 percent, and the remaining 3 percent goes to German.[44] Then the only change needed is to set $c_e = 0.72, c_f = 0.25$, and $c_g = 0.03$.

The calculations for the EU are given in table 8.6 for four different cases: number of citizens, square root (Penrose's law) of that number, crossed with equal costs and weighted costs. As can be checked, the use of square roots decreases the shares of larger countries and slightly increases those of smaller countries. Still, the largest burden falls on large countries: France, Germany, Italy, Poland, Spain, and the United Kingdom. If costs are weighted costs, the United Kingdom (and Ireland) have less to support, since English is the language used most often in drafting documents, and little has to be translated into English.

[44] In 2004, English accounted for 62 percent, French for 26 percent, and German for 3 percent, with the remaining languages accounting for some 9 percent of all inputs. We assume that in 2008, English took away the share of all other languages. This assumption is easy to change, but it will have little impact on the final calculation.

TABLE 8.6. Sharing the costs of multilingualism (%)

	Populations		"Penrose" populations	
	Equal Costs	Weighted Costs	Equal Costs	Weighted Costs
Austria	1.6	1.5	3.0	2.9
Belgium	2.1	1.7	3.4	3.1
Bulgaria	1.5	2.0	2.9	3.4
Cyprus	0.1	0.1	0.9	0.9
Czech Republic	2.1	2.7	3.3	4.0
Denmark	1.1	0.8	2.4	2.1
Estonia	0.3	0.3	1.2	1.4
Finland	1.1	1.2	2.4	2.6
France	12.4	11.8	8.2	7.4
Germany	16.7	16.8	9.5	9.7
Greece	2.3	2.5	3.5	3.8
Hungary	2.1	2.9	3.4	4.1
Ireland	0.8	0.3	2.0	0.9
Italy	12.0	14.2	8.1	9.1
Latvia	0.5	0.6	1.6	1.9
Lithuania	0.7	0.9	1.9	2.3
Luxembourg	0.1	0.1	0.7	0.6
Malta	0.1	0.1	0.6	0.6
Netherlands	3.1	1.8	4.1	3.1
Poland	7.9	10.1	6.5	7.6
Portugal	2.2	2.8	3.4	4.0
Romania	4.6	6.0	5.0	5.9
Slovak Republic	1.1	1.4	2.4	2.9
Slovenia	0.4	0.4	1.5	1.5
Spain	8.9	11.4	6.9	8.1
Sweden	1.8	1.3	3.1	2.7
United Kingdom	12.3	4.2	8.1	3.4
Total	100.0	100.0	100.0	100.0

Compensating Losing Countries

Instead of charging countries whose disenfranchised citizens need translation and interpretation, one can think of compensating countries whose languages are not part of the set of core languages, using the savings the EU would be able to make if only say, the six languages discussed in section 2.2 were translated. Fidrmuc and Ginsburgh (2007) suggested giving each such country the same amount, obtained by dividing the remainder of the 1,123 million, after subtracting the costs of translating and interpreting the six core languages.

Here the compensation scheme that we suggest is based on the number of people in each country who ignore all six core languages.[45]

The formula used to compute, say, s_B the share of the total cost to be borne by Belgium is

$$s_B = \frac{B\,noCORE}{noCORE},$$

where $B\,noCORE$ and $noCORE$ represent the number of Belgians and the number of EU citizens who speak none of the six core languages. Table 8.7 gives an overview of these shares in two cases: populations and square roots of populations (taking again into account Penrose's law). The countries that would benefit from the largest compensations are the former members of the Soviet bloc, Greece, and Portugal.

The above formula is derived from a simple rule of thumb. One can also use sharing rules endowed with a certain number of desirable properties. Ginsburgh and Zang (2001, 2003) provide such a rule they call the museum pass sharing, which is itself related to the Shapley value (Shapley 1953).[46]

It is convenient to describe the museum pass sharing here, since it is very intuitive and based on a concrete situation. Assume that several competing museums offer a joint entry pass that gives visitors (tourists or residents) unlimited access to the participating museums during a limited period of one to several days (perhaps a whole year for residents). Since this scheme involves more than one museum, the issue of how to share the joint income from the pass program has to be addressed. Such passes have become very common in many cities and even countries. Some passes are even international.[47]

To make our point, we assume that each pass allows a single visitor free unlimited entry into all the museums that participate in the program, and that the full income of the joint pass program has to be shared among those museums. Such a system involves several steps. First there is the membership issue, which defines which museums are included or excluded. Once the group of participants is formed, a price (cost to the visitor) has to be set for the pass. Finally, a rule should be devised to share among museums the net income from the sale of passes. Here we abstract from the first two steps, concentrate only on income allocation, and recommend a rule based on game theory.

[45]To simplify, we assume that countries whose official languages are among the core languages are not allowed to any compensation, even if there are citizens who do not understand the official language of the country. See notes to table 8.7.

[46]See also Wang (2008).

[47]A Google search on "museum pass" led to over 39 million hits in January 2010, compared to 4,000 in 2004.

TABLE 8.7. Compensating countries whose languages
do not belong to the set of core languages (%)

	Populations	"Penrose" Populations
Austria	0.0	0.0
Belgium	2.4	4.0
Bulgaria	7.4	7.0
Cyprus	0.5	1.8
Czech Republic	8.8	7.7
Denmark	2.1	3.7
Estonia	1.2	2.8
Finland	4.5	5.5
France	0.0	0.0
Germany	0.0	0.0
Greece	9.0	7.7
Hungary	11.0	8.6
Ireland	0.1	0.6
Italy	0.0	0.0
Latvia	2.4	4.0
Lithuania	3.1	4.6
Luxembourg	0.0	0.0
Malta	0.2	1.0
Netherlands	3.8	5.0
Poland	0.5	1.8
Portugal	10.7	8.4
Romania	22.6	12.3
Slovak Republic	4.8	5.7
Slovenia	1.2	2.8
Spain	0.0	0.0
Sweden	3.8	5.0
United Kingdom	0.0	0.0
Total	100.0	100.0

Note: In the calculations, we assume that countries whose official languages are among the core languages are not allowed to any compensation, even if there are citizens who do not understand the official language (for example, Turks in Germany or Afghanis in England). This is the case for Austria, France, Germany, Italy, Luxembourg, Spain, and the United Kingdom. It is not so for Poland, since that country has Romanian and Hungarian minorities.

Every pass is likely to be used by a visitor to visit several museums (or the same museum several times), some of which are more in demand than others. Therefore, museums should be rewarded according to their relative contributions to overall income, or alternatively, according to their attractiveness or importance. Game-theoretic concepts are used to evaluate the contribution of a museum to the program by assessing the income that can be attributed to that particular museum. This yields the measure of its contribution. The process draws its theoretical foundations from the concept of allocation fairness, which follows a set of natural and desirable properties that have to be satisfied by an acceptable allocation rule. Here is a list of these properties:

1. *Full distribution*: The total income is fully allocated among the participating museums.

2. *Symmetry*: If a museum contributes the same additional income to each subgroup of museums,[48] then this will be the income allocated to this museum.

3. *Anonymity*: The income allocated to the various museums does not change if the order in which the museums are processed changes.

4. *Additivity*: If pass buyers are split into two classes, say tourists and residents, and the income allocation of each museum within each class of buyers (tourists and residents) is computed, then the sum of those two income allocations should be equal to the income allocation obtained by applying the formula to the unsplit population of buyers.

Applying these properties as requirements leads to a *unique, fair* allocation known as the Shapley value. It can be shown that, in the museum context, this gives the following very simple and intuitive rule:

> *The proceeds from each pass should be equally distributed among the museums actually visited by the pass holder.*

Sharing the costs of translating and interpreting languages can be put into the same format. Each language can be assimilated to a museum, and each European citizen in each member country to

---

[48]Consider, for example, a particular museum, say A, and consider the income obtained from the sales of passes that were used to visit only museums in a certain group, say $W = (B, C, D)$. Suppose that this income is 1,000. Consider now the income from the sales of passes that were used to visit only museums in the expanded group (A, B, C, D) (that is, group W plus A). Suppose that this sales figure is 1,150. The difference between the two is 150. We then say that museum A contributes an additional income of 150 to the subgroup $W = (B, C, D)$. If 150 is the contribution of museum A to each subgroup of museums (that excludes A), then the symmetry property says that its overall income share has to be 150.

TABLE 8.8. Data on language nonproficiency in country A

Number of Citizens Who Do Not Know	English	German	French
English only	18		
German only		1	
French only			22
English and German	1	1	
English and French	56		56
German and French		1	1
None of the three	1	1	1

the holder of a museum pass who will contribute a fixed amount to maintain the languages that he *does not* know. If we assume that each member country pays the contribution of its citizens, the calculation that follows has to be done for each country:

The contribution from each citizen in a given country should be equally distributed among the languages that this citizen does not know.

We now illustrate the calculations necessary to implement the allocation, assuming an almost imaginary country with 100 inhabitants. The basic data showing the number of citizens who *do not* speak English, German, or French is illustrated in table 8.8.

According to the rule, English will be attributed to the following number of citizens: the eighteen whose only unknown language is English, plus one-half of the unique citizen who knows neither English nor German, plus one-half of the fifty-six who know neither English nor French, plus one-third of the one citizen who knows none of the three languages, that is

$$18 + 1/2 + 56/2 + 1/3 = 46.83$$

out of 100, or 46.83 percent. Similarly, German will receive

$$1 + 1/2 + 1/2 + 1/3 = 2.34,$$

and French will be allocated:

$$22 + 56/2 + 1/2 + 1/3 = 50.83.$$

Note that these three numbers add up to 100, the total number of citizens. Similar calculations have to be made for each country, and one has to make the political decision about how much each citizen or each country has to contribute. This step corresponds to setting the price of the museum pass. One possibility is to impose on each citizen equally (for example, 2.30 euros, the price of Neil Kinnock's cup of coffee). Another is to make each country pay the same amount. This is a calculation that is tedious but feasible using the detailed results of Special Eurobarometer 243 (2006) survey.

Adding the contributions of all countries, calculated as above, gives the amount each language would have to pay. If two or more countries share the same language (Germany and Austria, for example), they must find a way to share the joint cost and revenue.

3. Summary

The policy of official multilingualism is one of the most fundamental principles of the EU and is guaranteed by its treaties, but is the subject of exceptions and shortcomings, as illustrated by Wright (2007, 2009), by the decisions of the European Court, and by the European institutions themselves. Extensive multilingualism at a time when the EU is expanding its membership nevertheless translates into rapidly rising costs of translation and interpretation, which may have important human, legal, and economic implications. Multilingualism is also associated with nonmonetary costs, such as delays in implementing new laws and regulations, erroneous or confusing translations, and potential conflicts arising from the fact that all translated versions of international treaties are considered legally binding even if they may occasionally lend themselves to different legal interpretations.

In this chapter, we have analyzed the effects of linguistic policies and of a variety of potential linguistic reforms in the EU. Our analysis offers a formal framework for addressing the merits and costs of extensive multilingualism. In chapter 7 we determined, for any given number of languages, the set of languages that minimizes linguistic disenfranchisement across the EU. This allowed us to construct a nested sequence of core languages, in fact, a menu of possible choices for policymaking. In this chapter we proceeded by discussing the political economy framework and various voting rules that support a sustainable number of official languages. It turns out that if the choice of core languages could be decided by using the currently valid QMV rules, a six-language scenario may turn out to be politically feasible. The core languages would then be English, French, German, Italian, Spanish, and Polish.

The standardization scenarios that we suggest do not question the principle that all official languages would be used in the European Parliament and in contacts between EU institutions and citizens. There is much less reason to continue this rule in other bodies (where it is anyway not used in practice) or for translations of documents. Individual countries should have the opportunity to do this if they feel the need. This raises two questions: (1) Where should the translations into official languages be done, and who should pay for this? and (2) Which version of a document should be binding? It is reasonable to assume that the translations into the restricted set of core languages should be centralized at the level of the European Commission, and that these, or the original draft only, as suggested in the opinion of Advocate General Stix-Hackl discussed in section 1.3, would be the binding version in case of divergent legal interpretations.

The amounts saved by the European Commission, given that there would be less to translate, could be transferred to those countries whose languages are not core languages. Fidrmuc and Ginsburgh (2007) suggest transferring the full cost (that is, roughly the total translation cost per language borne today by the EU) to each country. But other ways of calculating transfers are also envisaged. Each country would then have the choice of using the transfer at its own discretion. The commission would end up not saving on the cost of interpretation and translation, but countries would be given the right incentives and could possibly be held responsible for their own shortcomings.

Any of the linguistic reforms suggested in this chapter will change the incentives for acquiring skills in non-native languages. This in turn will modify the dynamics of learning foreign languages, and further changes to the set of core languages should be envisaged at some later time.

CONCLUSIONS

> If you talk to a man in a language
> he understands, that goes to his head.
> If you talk to him in his language,
> that goes to his heart.
> —*Nelson Mandela*

We have always taken for granted what is shown here: languages, and more generally ethnolinguistic divides, do matter since they are, in many cases, at the root of life or death. They help to explain underdevelopment, brutal changes of power, poor administration, corruption, and slacking growth. They impose frictions on trades between countries in which different languages are spoken. They influence migratory flows, and also the more mundane issues of literary translations or votes cast to elect winners in various contests.

The tour of linguistic diversity, which started with the Tower of Babel and its like in other mythologies, then moved on to the Rosetta stone and the banishment of Thomas Mowbray by Richard II, brought us to the bloody conflict in Sri Lanka and other problems faced today by multilingual societies. There are still serious linguistic challenges facing countries in Europe, Asia, Africa, and America, both North and South, and regional unions are already dealing or will have to deal with linguistic policies that may have an impact on their cohesiveness and progress. Regional approaches differ. While the European Union adopts and defends multilingualism, the Association of the South East Asian Nations (ASEAN) uses English as the only official language. The formation of a monetary union and a political federation of East African countries (Kenya, Uganda, Tanzania, Rwanda, and Burundi) is in a preliminary stage and will probably face formidable linguistic issues in the future.

Mankind probably started to speak systematically some 50,000 or 100,000 years ago, a time when there existed a unique language. Some disagree, but in any case the number of languages was probably small. This number grew with humans (*Homo sapiens*) migrating out of Africa, probably their very first home. Today we are all the descendants of these early humans, but became so *wise* that we dared adding a second *sapiens*. And languages changed, together with cultural traits and genes. We now live in a world that is facing globalization but in some sense has become even more diverse. As we gingerly look at the world's linguistic future, a trendy but nevertheless important question comes to mind: How will China affect the rest of the world? We briefly discussed several aspects of linguistic policies of another Asian giant, India, but the linguistic future of China (both externally and internally—after all, not everybody in China speaks Mandarin) opens up an important avenue for future research on optimal and effective linguistic policies. Will China adopt English as a lingua franca, or will the rest of the world learn Mandarin? Which languages will be learned in the coming years in Brazil, Russia, India, and elsewhere in the world?[49] What will happen to Spanish in the United States, which has no official language provision in its constitution?

As we have emphasized throughout the book, the development of optimal and sensible linguistic policies has to balance the will of the people and their attachment to traditions, history, and culture, with equity and efficiency considerations. It is a delicate balance. Are we ready to trade our languages in order to increase by a few percentage points our rate of economic growth?

One example to achieve this balance is suggested by the Lisbon Treaty, recently adopted by all twenty-seven member countries of the EU. The treaty breaks with the notion of equal veto power granted to every EU member and allows some sort of majority voting on issues such as asylum, border controls, fighting climate change, and energy security. The EU, however, retained the veto power of single members on important and sensitive issues such as foreign policy, defense, social security, and, yes, linguistic policies, implicitly indicating that culture may matter as much as, or even more than, efficiency. One reason to consider carefully the EU situation is that its linguistic policies offer an ongoing laboratory study whose findings can be useful to test linguistic policies. With its regulations, the EU cannot arbitrarily decide to stop translating certain languages. Some steps in this direction may be feasible, but they must be carefully negotiated, and compensating transfers may be needed, as suggested in chapter 8. If it comes to that, the way compensations are calculated will give us an estimation of the worth of single languages and their value to those who speak them. The methodology can then be used in other multilingual societies.

---

[49] Such as in Indonesia, where "in some families, the grandchildren cannot speak with the grandmother because they don't speak Bahasa Indonesia [but English only]. That's sad." "As English spreads, Indonesians fear for their language" (The *New York Times*, July 25, 2010).

Taking into account efficiency is unavoidable. As we repeated many times, diversity cannot be obtained or sustained for free. Excessive fragmentation and fractionalization weakens institutions, slows the path to their improvement, and causes political instability. The "African tragedy" seems to support policies that limit the number of languages used to conduct official business.

Standardization policies should, however, recognize the importance of the diversity of existing cultures and languages. Linguistic disenfranchisement, which limits the ability and opportunity of individuals and groups to fully use their native languages in communal, political, legal, business, and other spheres of life, may rock the foundations that lead to free cultural existence and to progress. The examples we introduced underscore how painful and devastating the limitation of full-fledged access to one's native language can be. Protecting our cultural and linguistic identity and diversity is especially important in an increasingly globalized environment. While the march of globalization is mostly conducted in English, the ascendance of English inevitably generates feelings of inferiority and discomfort, expressed by Dorfman (2002, 92): "Do you come from a place that is poor? ... Do you inhabit a language that does not have armies behind it, and smart bombs and modems and cell phones?"

But globalization also comes with migratory movements. Immigration from African and Asian countries to Europe is changing the cultural picture. Arabic is spoken by more and more people who immigrated recently, but also by their children, who became European citizens. The same is true for Hispanic immigrants to the United States. And while economic and political globalization is on the march, social globalization has unfortunately stagnated since 2001, and even declined in 2007, the last year for which the index is available.[50]

People speak different languages. More often than not, they care about their languages and cultural traits, and want their children to know and respect them. As Amartya Sen (1999, 32) writes:

> [I]n the freedom-oriented perspective the liberty of all to participate in deciding what traditions to observe cannot be ruled out by the national or local "guardians"—neither by the ayatollahs (or other religious authorities), nor by political rulers (or governmental dictators), nor by cultural "experts" (domestic or foreign).

The aim of linguistic policies is to take into account rigorous economic, linguistic, and sociological considerations while recognizing

[50] See KOF Index of Globalization 2010, press release, January 22, 2010, KOF Swiss Economic Institute, Eidgenössische Technische Hochschule Zürich.

differences and sensitives of all people, and to allow them to hope and achieve together. The success or failure of such policies will be judged according to W. H. Auden's yardstick, which we feel important enough to serve as the last sentence of this book:

> Civilizations should be measured by the degree of diversity attained and by the degree of unity retained.

BIBLIOGRAPHY

Abbott, Michael, and Charles Beach (1992). Immigrant earnings differentials in Canada: A more general specification of age and experience effects, *Empirical Economics* 17, 221–38.

Abrams, Daniel, and Steven Strogatz (2003). Modelling the dynamics of language death, *Nature* 424, 900.

Alesina, Alberto, Reza Baqir, and William Easterly (1999). Public goods and ethnic divisions, *Quarterly Journal of Economics* 114, 1243–84.

Alesina, Alberto, Reza Baqir, and Carole Hoxby (2004). Political jurisdictions in heterogeneous communities, *Journal of Political Economy* 112, 349–96.

Alesina, Alberto, Arvind Devleeschouwer, William Easterly, Sergio Kurlat, and Romain Wacziarg (2003). Fractionalization, *Journal of Economic Growth* 8, 155–94.

Alesina, Alberto, and Eliana La Ferrara (2005). Ethnic diversity and economic performance, *Journal of Economic Literature* 43, 762–800.

Alesina, Alberto, and Enrico Spolaore (2004). *The Size of Nations*, Cambridge, MA: MIT Press.

Alesina, Alberto, Enrico Spolaore, and Romain Wacziarg (2000). Economic integration and political disintegration, *American Economic Review* 90, 1276–96.

Alesina, Alberto, and Ekaterina Zhuravskaya (2008). Segregation and the quality of government in a cross-section of countries, NBER Working Paper 14316, National Bureau of Economic Research, Cambridge, MA.

Amemiya, Eiji (1963). Measurement of economic differentiation, *Journal of Regional Science* Summer, 85–87.

Anderson, James (1979). A theoretical foundation for the gravity equation, *American Economic Review* 69, 106–16.

Anderson, James, and Eric van Wincoop (2004). Trade costs, *Journal of Economic Literature* 42, 691–751.

Anderson, Simon, and Stephen Coate (2005). Market provision of broadcasting: A welfare analysis, *Review of Economic Studies* 72, 947–72.

Anderson, Simon, and Jean Gabszewicz (2006). The media and advertising: A tale of two-sided markets, in Victor Ginsburgh and David Throsby, eds., *Handbook of the Economics of Art and Culture*, Amsterdam: Elsevier.

Angrist, Joshua, and Alan Krueger (2001). Instrumental variables and the search for identification: From supply and demand to natural experiments, *Journal of Economic Perspectives* 15 (4), 69–85.

Annett, Anthony (2001). Social fractionalization, political instability, and the size of the government, *IMF Staff Papers* 46 (3), 561–92.

Ashraf, Quamrul, and Oded Galor (2008). Human genetic diversity and comparative economic development, CEPR Discussion Paper 6824, Centre for Economic Policy Research, London.

Athanasiou, Efthymios, Santanu Dey, and Giacomo Valetta (2007). On sharing benefits of communication, manuscript, CORE Université Catholique de Louvain.

Athanassiou, Phoebus (2006). The application of multilingualism in the European context, ECB Legal Working Paper 2, European Central Bank, Frankfurt.

Atlas Narodov Mira (1964). Miklucho-Maklai Ethnological Institute at the Department of Geodesy and Cartography of the State Geological Committee of the Soviet Union.

Aydemir, Abdurrahman, and Mikal Skuterud (2005). Explaining the deterioration entry earnings of Canada's immigrant cohorts, 1996–2000, *Canadian Journal of Economics* 38, 641–72.

Bachi, Roberto (1956). A statistical analysis of the revival of Hebrew in Israel, in Roberto Bachi, ed., *Scripta Hierosollymitana*, vol. 3, 179–247, Jerusalem: Magnus Press.

Bairoch, Paul (1998). Une nouvelle distribution des populations: Villes et campagnes, in Jean-Pierre Bardet and Jaques Dupaquer, eds., *Histoire des populations de l'Europe: La révolution démographique*, Paris: Arthème Fayard.

Baker, Mark (2001). *The Atoms of Language*, Oshkosh, WI: Basic Books.

Baldwin, Richard, Erik Berglöf, Franceso Giavazzi, and Mika Widgrén (2000). EU reforms for tomorrow's Europe, CEPR Discussion Paper 2623, Centre for Economic Policy Research, London.

—— (2001). Eastern enlargement and ECB reforms, *Swedish Economic Policy Review* 8, 15–50.

Baldwin, Richard, and Mika Widgrén (2004). Winners and losers under various dual majority rules for the EU Council of Ministers, CEPR Discussion Paper 4450, Centre for Economic Policy Research, London.

Bateman, Robert, with Rick Archbold (2002). *Thinking Like a Mountain*, Toronto: Penguin Canada.

Beine, Michel, Frédéric Docquier, and Çaglar Özden (2009). Diasporas, manuscript, Department of Economics, Université Catholique de Louvain.

Bell, Wendell (1954). A probability model for the measurement of ecological segregation, *Social Forces* 32, 357–64.

Belleflamme, Paul, and Jacques Thisse (2003). Sprechen Sie français? Yes I do: The economics of plurilingualism in the European Union, manuscript, CORE, Université Catholique de Louvain.

Berliant, Marcus, and Masahisa Fujita (2008). Knowledge creation as a square dance on the Hilbert cube, *International Economic Review* 49, 1251–95.

Berman, Eli, Kevin Lang, and Erez Siniver (2003). Language skill complementarity: Returns to immigrant language acquisition, *Labour Economics* 10, 265–90.

Biltereyst, Daniel (1991). Resisting American hegemony: A comparative analysis of the reception of domestic and US fiction, *European Journal of Communication* 6, 469–97.

Bisin, Alberto, and Thierry Verdier (2000). Beyond the melting pot: Cultural transmission, marriage and the evolution of ethnic and religious traits, *Quarterly Journal of Economics* 115, 955–88.

Bleakey, Hoyt, and Aimee Chin (2004). Language skills and earnings: Evidence from childhood immigrants, *Review of Economics and Statistics* 86, 481–96.

Bond, Karen (2001). French as a minority language in bilingual Canada, http://www3.telus.net/linguisticsissues/french.html (last accessed June 23, 2009).

Bossert, Walter, Conchita D'Ambrosio, and Eliana La Ferrara (2006). A generalized index of ethno-linguistic fractionalization, IGIER Working Paper 313, Università Bocconi, Milan.

Bossert, Walter, Prasanta K. Pattanaik, and Yongsheng Xu (2003). Similarity of options and the measurement of diversity, *Journal of Theoretical Politics* 15, 405–21.

Botta-Dukát, Zoltán (2005). Rao's quadratic entropy as a measure of functional diversity based on multiple traits, *Journal of Vegetation Science* 16, 533–40.

Bratsberg, Bernt, James Ragan, and Zafir Nasir (2002). The effect of naturalization on wage growth: A panel study of young male immigrants, *Journal of Labor Economics* 20, 568–97.

Breton, Albert (1978). *Bilingualism: An Economic Approach*, Montreal: C. D. Howe Institute.

Bretton, Henry (1976). Political science, language, and politics, in Jean O'Barr and William O'Barr, eds., *Language and Politics*, The Hague: Mouton.

Brown, Michael, and Sumit Ganguly (2003). *Fighting Words: Language Policy and Ethic Relations in Asia*, Cambridge, MA: MIT Press.

Bruine de Bruin, Wändi (2005). Save the last dance for me: Unwanted serial position effects in jury evaluations, *Acta Psychologica* 118, 245–60.

Burgess, Anthony (1984). Is translation possible? *Translation: The Journal of Literary Translation* 12, 3–7.

Calvet, Jean-Louis (2002). *Le marché aux langues*, Paris: Plon.

Campos, Nauro, Ahmad Saleh, and Vitaliy Kuzeyev (2007). Dynamic ethnic fractionalization and economic growth in the transition economies from 1989 to 2007, CEPR Discussion Paper 7586, Centre for Economic Policy Research, London.

Candolle, Alphonse de (1873). *Histoire des sciences et des savants depuis deux siècles*, Paris: Librarie Arthème Fayard.

Canning, David, and Marianne Fay (1993). Growth and infrastructure, discussion paper, Columbia University.

Canoy, Marcel, Rick van der Ploeg, and Jan van Ours (2006). The economics of books, in Victor Ginsburgh and David Throsby, eds., *Handbook of the Economics of Arts and Culture*, Amsterdam: Elsevier.

Carrington, William, Enrica Detragiache, and Tara Vishwanath (1996). Migration with endogenous moving costs, *American Economic Review* 86, 909–30.

Castelló, Xavier, Víctor Eguíluz, and Maxi San Miguel (2006), Dynamics of language competition: Bilingual and social structure effects, manuscript, Mediterranean Institute for Advanced Studies.

Catford, J. C. (1967). *A Linguistic Theory of Translation*, Oxford: Oxford University Press.

Cattaneo, Alejandra, and Rainer Winkelmann (2005). Earning differentials between German and French speakers in Switzerland, *Swiss Journal of Economics and Statistics* 143, 133–52.

Cavalli-Sforza, Luigi Luca (1997). Genes, peoples and languages, *Proceedings of the National Academy of Sciences of the USA* 94, 7719–24.

—— (2000). *Genes, Peoples, and Languages*, Berkeley and Los Angeles: University of California Press.

Cavalli-Sforza, Luigi Luca, and Francesco Cavalli-Sforza (1995). *The Great Human Diasporas. The History of Diversity and Evolution*, Cambridge, MA: Perseus Books.

Cavalli-Sforza, Luigi Luca, Paolo Menozzi, and Alberto Piazza (1994). *The History and Geography of Human Genes*, abridged ed., Princeton, NJ: Princeton University Press.

Caves, Richard (2000). *Creative Industries, Contracts between Art and Commerce*, Cambridge, MA: Harvard University Press.

Chiswick, Barry, and Paul Miller (2007). *The Economics of Language: International Analyses*, London: Routledge.

Church, Jeffrey, and Ian King (1993). Bilingualism and network externalities, *Canadian Journal of Economics* 26, 337–45.

CIA World Fact Book (2009). https://www.cia.gov/library/publications/the-world-factbook/index.html.

Clark, Nancy (1994). The economy, in La Verle Berry, ed., *Ghana: A Case Study*, Washington, DC: Library of Congress.

Cole, John, and Francis Cole (1997). *A Geography of the European Union*, 2nd ed., London: Routledge.

Collier, Paul (2001). Implications of ethnic diversity, *Economic Policy* 16 (32), 129–55.

Collier, Paul, and Anke Hoeffler (2004). Greed and grievance in civil war, *Oxford Economic Papers* 56, 563–95.

Constant, Amelie, Martin Kahanec, and Klaus Zimmermann (2006). The Russian-Ukraine earnings divide, CEPR Discussion Paper 5904, Centre for Economic Policy Research, London.

Corgan, Michael (2004). Icelandic confronts globalization, paper presented at the Center for Small States Studies Conference, Reykjavik, September 16–18, 2004.

Coser, Lewis, Charles Kadushin, and Walter Powell (1982). *Books: The Culture and Commerce of Publishing*, Chicago: University of Chicago Press.

Council of the European Union (2002). Use of languages in the Council in the context of an enlarged Union, Report of the Presidency, document 15334/1/02, December 6, 2002.

Crystal, David (1999). *A Dictionary of Language*, Chicago: University of Chicago Press.

—— (2003). *English as a Global Language*, Cambridge: Cambridge University Press.

Dalby, Andrew (2002). *Language in Danger: How Language Loss Threatens Our Future*, London: Allen Lane.

De Swaan, Abram (1993). The evolving European language system: A theory of communication potential and language competition, *International Political Science Review* 14 (3), 241–55.

—— (2001). *Words of the World*, Cambridge: Polity Press.

—— (2008). The language predicament of the EU since the enlargements, paper presented at the AILA Symposium 2008, Multilingualism in EU Institutions, Duisburg-Essen, August 28.

Desmet, Klaus, Ignacio Ortuño-Ortín, and Romain Wacziarg (2009). The political economy of ethnolinguistic cleavages, NBER Working Paper 15360, National Bureau for Economic Research, Cambridge, MA.

Desmet, Klaus, Michel Le Breton, Ignacio Ortuño-Ortín, and Shlomo Weber (2009). Stability of nations and genetic diversity, VIVES Discussion Paper 10, Catholic University of Leuven.

Desmet, Klaus, Ignacio Ortuño-Ortín, and Shlomo Weber (2005). Peripheral diversity and redistribution, CEPR Discussion Paper 5112, Centre for Economic Policy Research, London.

—— (2009). Linguistic diversity and redistribution, *Journal of the European Economic Association* 7, 1291–318.

deVotta, Neil (2003). Ethnolinguistic nationalism and ethnic conflict in Sri-Lanka, in Michael Brown and Sumit Ganguly, eds., *Fighting Words: Language Policy and Ethnic Relations in Asia*, Cambridge, MA: MIT Press.

—— (2004). *Blowback: Ethnolinguistic Nationalism, Institutional Decay, and Ethnic Conflict in Sri-Lanka*, Stanford, CA: Stanford University Press.

Docquier, Frédéric, Olivier Lohest, and Abdeslam Marfouk (2007). Brain drain in developing countries, *World Bank Economic Review* 21, 193–218.

Dorfman, Ariel (2002). The nomads of language, *American Scholar* 71, 89–94.

Duclos, Jean-Yves, Joan Esteban, and Debraj Ray (2004). Polarization: Concepts, measurement, estimation, *Econometrica* 72, 1737–72.

Dustmann, Christian (1994). Speaking fluency, writing fluency and earnings of migrants, *Journal of Population Economics* 7, 133–56.

Dustmann, Christian, and Arthur Van Soest (2001). Language fluency and earnings: Estimators with misclassified language indicators, *Review of Economics and Statistics* 83, 663–74.

—— (2002). Language and the earnings of immigrants, *Industrial and Labor Relations Review* 55, 473–92.

Dyen, Isidore (1965). A lexicostatistical classification of the Austronesian languages, *International Journal of American Linguistics*, Memoir 19.

Dyen, Isidore, Joseph B. Kruskal, and Paul Black (1992). An Indo-European classification: A lexicostatistical experiment, *Transactions of the American Philosophical Society* 82 (5).

Easterly, William (2001). *The Elusive Quest for Growth*, Cambridge, MA: MIT Press.

Easterly, William, and Ross Levine (1997), Africa's growth tragedy: Policies and ethnic divisions, *Quarterly Journal of Economics* 112, 1203–50.

Englebert, Pierre, Stacy Tarango, and Matthew Carter (2002). Dismemberment and suffocation: A contribution to the debate on African boundaries, *Comparative Political Studies* 35, 1093–118.

Esteban, Joan, and Debraj Ray (1994). On the measurement of polarization, *Econometrica* 62, 819–51.

—— (1999). Conflict and distribution, *Journal of Economic Theory* 87, 379–415.

Ethnologue (2009). *Languages of the World*, M. Paul Lewis, ed., Dallas, TX: SIL International.

European Commission (2005a). Interpretation: Where do we stand eight months after the enlargement?, press release, MEMO/05/9, January 13, 2005, http://europa.eu.int/rapid/pressReleasesAction.do?reference=MEMO/05/9&format=HTML&aged=0&language=EN&guiLanguage=en.

—— (2005b). Translation in the Commission: Where do we stand eight months after the enlargement?, press release, MEMO/05/10, January 13, 2005, http://europa.eu.int/rapid/pressReleasesAction.do?reference=MEMO/05/10&type=HTML&aged=0&language=EN&guiLanguage=en.

Falck, Oliver, Stephan Heblich, Alfred Lameli, and Jens Südekum (2010). Dialects, cultural identity, and economic exchange, IZA Working Paper 4743.

Fearon, James (2003). Ethnic and cultural diversity by country, *Journal of Economic Growth* 8, 195–222.

Fearon, James, and David Laitin (1999). Weak states, rough terrain, and large-scale ethnic violence since 1945, paper presented at the annual meeting of the American Political Science Association, Atlanta, GA.

—— (2003). Ethnicity, insurgency and civil war, *American Political Science Review* 97, 75–90.

Felbermayr, Gabriel, and Farid Toubal (2007). Cultural proximity and trade, manuscript, Paris School of Economics.

Fenn, Daniel, Omer Suleiman, Janet Efsathiou, and Neil Johnson (2005). How does Europe make its mind up? Connections, cliques, and compatibility between countries in the Eurovision Song Contest, arXiv:physics/0505071 v1, May 10.

Fidrmuc, Jan, and Victor Ginsburgh (2007). Languages in the European Union: The quest for equality and its cost, *European Economic Review* 51, 1351–69.

Fidrmuc, Jan, Victor Ginsburgh, and Shlomo Weber (2007). Ever closer union or Babylonian discord? The official-language problem in the European Union, CEPR Discussion Paper 6367, Centre for Economic Policy Research, London.

—— (2009). Voting on the choice of core languages in the European Union, *European Journal of Political Economy* 25, 56–62.

Flôres, Renato, Jr., and Victor Ginsburgh (1996). The Queen Elizabeth musical competition: How fair is the final ranking? *Journal of the Royal Statistical Society, Series D, The Statistician* 45, 97–104.

Florida, Richard (2002). *The Rise of the Creative Class, and How It's Transforming Work, Leisure, Community and Everyday Life*, New York, NY: Perseus.

Florida, Richard, and Gary Gates (2001). Technology and tolerance: The importance of diversity to high-tech growth, Brookings Institute Discussion Paper, Washington, DC.

Frith, Simon (1996). Does music cross boundaries?, in Annemoon van Hemel, Hans Mommaas, and Cas Smithuijsen, eds., *Trading Culture*, Amsterdam: Boekman Foundation.

Fry, Richard, and B. Lindsay Lowell (2003). The value of bilingualism in the U.S. labor market, *Industrial and Labor Relations Review* 57, 128–40.

Fujita, Masahisa, and Shlomo Weber (2009). Immigration quotas in the globalized economy, *Journal of the New Economic Association*, forthcoming.

Gabszewicz, Jean, Victor Ginsburgh, Didier Laussel, and Shlomo Weber (2009). Acquiring foreign languages: A two-sided market approach, manuscript, CORE, Université Catholique de Louvain.

Gabszewicz, Jean, Victor Ginsburgh, and Shlomo Weber (2011). Bilingualism and communicative benefits, *Annales d'Economie et de Statistique*, forthcoming.

Gabszewicz, Jean, Didier Laussel, and Nathalie Sonnac (2004). Programming and advertising competition in the broadcasting industry, *Journal of Economics and Management Strategy* 13, 657–69.

Galasi, Peter (2003). Estimating wage equations for Hungarian higher education graduates, manuscript, Budapest Working Paper 2003/4.

Gamkrelidze, Thomas, and Vjacheslav Ivanov (1990). The early history of Indo-European languages, *Scientific American* March, 82–89.

Ganne, Valérie, and Marc Minon (1992). Géographies de la traduction, in Françoise Barret-Ducrocq, ed., *Traduire l'Europe*, Paris: Payot.

Gatherer, Derek (2004). Birth of a meme: The origin and evolution of collusive voting patterns in the Eurovision Song Contest, *Journal of Memetics: Evolutionary Models of Information Transmission* 8, http://jom-emit.cfpm.org/2004/vol8/gatherer_d_letter.html.

—— (2006). Comparison of Eurovision Song Contest simulation with actual results reveals shifting patterns of collusive voting alliances, *Journal of Artificial Societies and Social Simulation* 9.

Gaudissart, Marc-André (2010). Le régime et la pratique linguistique de la Cour de Justice des Communautés Européennes, in Dominik Hanf, Klaus Malacek, and Elise Muir, eds., *Langues et construction européenne*, Bruxelles: PIE/Lang.

Geng, Difei (2009). Identifying the unique polarization index: A mean-preserving axiomatic approach, discussion paper, Southern Methodist University.

Gibbs, Jack, and Harley Browning (1966). Urbanization, technology and the organization of production in twelve countries, *American Sociological Review* 31, 81–92.

Gibbs, Jack, and Walter Martin (1964). Urbanization, technology and division of labor: International patterns, *American Sociological Review* 27, 667–77.

Gini, Corrado (1912). Variabilità e mutabilità, in *Studi Economico-Giuridici della R. Universitadi Cagliari* 3, 3–159, reprinted in Enrico Pizetti and Tomasso Salvemini, eds., *Memorie di metodologica statistica*, Roma: Libraria Eredi Virilio Vechi, 1955.

Ginsburgh, Victor (2003). Awards, success and aesthetic quality in the arts, *Journal of Economic Perspectives* 17, 99–111.

Ginsburgh, Victor, and Abdul Noury (2008). The Eurovision Song Contest: Is voting political or cultural?, *European Journal of Political Economy* 24, 41–52.

Ginsburgh, Victor, Ignacio Ortuño-Ortín, and Shlomo Weber (2005). Disenfranchisement in linguistically diverse societies. The case of the European Union, *Journal of the European Economic Association* 3, 946–64.

—— (2007). Learning foreign languages: Theoretical and empirical implications of the Selten and Pool model, *Journal of Economic Behavior and Organization* 64, 337–47.

Ginsburgh, Victor, and Juan Prieto (2010). Returns to foreign languages of native workers in the EU, *Industrial and Labor Relations Review*, forthcoming.

Ginsburgh, Victor, and Jan van Ours (2003). Expert opinion and compensation, *American Economic Review*, 93, 289–98.

Ginsburgh, Victor, and Shlomo Weber (2005). Language disenfranchisement in the European Union, *Journal of Common Market Studies* 43, 273–86.

Ginsburgh, Victor, Shlomo Weber, and Sheila Weyers (2007). The economics of literary translation: A simple theory and evidence, CEPR Discussion Paper 6432, Centre for Economic Policy Research, London.

Ginsburgh, Victor, and Israel Zang (2001). Allocating the subscription income of museum passes, *Journal of Museum Management and Curatorship* 19, 371–83.

—— (2003). The museum pass game and its value, *Games and Economic Behavior* 43, 322–25.

Giuliano, Paola, Antonio Spilimbergo, and Giovanni Tonon (2006). Genetic, cultural and geographical distances, CEPR Discussion Paper 5807, Centre for Economic Policy Research, London.

Glejser, Herbert, and Bruno Heyndels (2001). The ranking of finalists in the Queen Elisabeth International music competition, *Journal of Cultural Economics* 25, 109–29.

Glézl, Andrej (n.d.). Lost in translation: EU law and the official languages, manuscript, Faculty of Law, Comenius University, Bratislava.

Goldberger, Arthur S. (1964). *Econometric Theory*, New York: John Wiley & Sons.

Graddol, David (2006). *English Next: Why Global English May Mean the End of English as a Foreign Language*, London: British Council.

Gray, Russel, and Quentin Atkinson (2003). Language-tree divergence times support the Anatolian theory of Indo-European origin, *Nature* 426, 435–39.

Greenberg, Joseph (1956). The measurement of linguistic diversity, *Language* 32, 109–15.

Greenberg, Joseph (1987). *Language in the Americas*, Stanford, CA: Stanford University Press.

—— (2000). *Indo-European and Its Closest Relatives*, Stanford, CA: Stanford University Press.

Grenier, Gilles (1985). Bilinguisme, transferts linguistiques et revenus du travail au Québec: quelques éléments d'interaction, in F. Vaillancourt, ed., *Economie et langue*, Québec: Editeur officiel.

Grin, François (1996). Economic approaches to language and language planning: An introduction, *International Journal of the Sociology of Languages*, 121, 1–16.

—— (2003). On the costs of cultural diversity, in Philippe van Parijs, ed., *Cultural Diversity versus Economic Solidarity*, Bruxelles: de Boeck Université.

—— (2005). L'enseignement des langues étrangères comme politique publique, Paris: Haut Conseil de l'Evaluation de l'Ecole.

Grin, François, and François Vaillancourt (1997). The economics of multilingualism: Overview of the literature and analytical framework, in W. Grabe, ed., *Multilingualism and Multilingual Communities*, Cambridge: Cambridge University Press.

Grinblatt, Mark, and Matti Keloharju (2001). How distance, language, and culture influence stockholdings and trades, *Journal of Finance* 56, 1053–73.

Grogger, Jeffrey, and Gordon Hanson (2007). Income maximization and the sorting of emigrants across destinations, manuscript, University of California, San Diego.

Giuliano, Paola, Antonio Spilimbergo, and Giovanni Tonon (2006). Genetic, cultural and geographical distances, CEPR Discussion Paper 5807, Centre for Economic Policy Research, London.

Guilmoto, Christophe, and Frederic Sandron (2001). The international dynamics of migrations networks in developing countries, *Population: An English Selection* 13, 135–64.

Guiso, Luigi, Paolo Sapienza, and Luigi Zingales (2006). Does culture effect economic outcomes?, *Journal of Economic Perspectives* 20, 2–48.

Guiso, Luigi, Paola Sapienza, and Luigi Zingales (2009). Cultural biases in economic exchange, *Quarterly Journal of Economics* 124, 1095–1131.

Gunnemark, Eric (1991). *Countries, Peoples, and Their Languages: The Linguistic Handbook*, Gothenburg, Sweden: Lanstryckeriet.

Haan, Marco, Gerhard Dijkstra, and Peter Dijkstra (2005). Expert judgment versus public opinion. Evidence from the Eurovision Song Contest, *Journal of Cultural Economics* 29, 59–78.

Hagège, Claude (2000). *Le souffle de la langue*, Paris: Odile Jacob.

—— (2005). *Combat pour le français*, Paris: Odile Jacob.

—— (2009). *Dictionnaire amoureux des langues*, Paris: Plon and Odile Jacob.

Hägerstrand, Torsten, D. Hannerberg, and B. Odeving (1957). *Migration in Sweden*, Lund, Sweden: Lund Studies in Geography, Series B, 13.

Hall, Alastair R., and Fernanda P. M. Peixe (2003). A consistent method for the selection of relevant instruments, *Econometric Reviews* 22, 269–87.

Harris, Randy Allen (1993). *The Linguistic Wars*, Oxford: Oxford University Press.

Hart-Gonzalez, Lucinda, and Stephanie Lindemann (1993). Expected achievement in speaking proficiency, School of Language Studies, Foreign Service Institute, Department of State, Washington, DC.

Heilbron, Johan (1999). Towards a sociology of translation: Book translations as a cultural world system, *European Journal of Social Theory* 2, 429–44.

Hellerstein, Judith, and David Neumark (2003). Ethnicity, language, and workplace segregation: Evidence from a new matched employer-employee data set, *Annales d'Economie et de Statistique* 71/72, 19–78.

Hix, Simon, Abdul Noury, and Gérard Roland (2007). *Democratic Politics in the European Parliament*, Cambridge: Cambridge University Press.

Hjorth-Andersen, Christian (2001). A model of translations, *Journal of Cultural Economics* 25, 203–17.

Hofstede, Geert (1980). *Culture's Consequences*, Beverly Hills, CA: Sage.

—— (1991). *Culture and Organizations*, London: McGraw-Hill.

—— (2001). *Culture's Consequences: Comparing Values, Behaviors, Institutions and Organizations Across Nations*, Beverly Hills, CA: Sage.

Hofstede, Geert, and Michael Bond (1988). The Confucius connection: From cultural roots to economic growth, *Organizational Dynamics* 16, 5–21.

Hoskins, Colin, Stuart McFadyen, and Adam Finn (1997). *Global Television and Film*, Oxford: Clarendon Press.

Hutchinson, William (2003). Linguistic distance as determinant of bilateral trade, Working Paper 01-W30R, Department of Economics, Vanderbilt University.

Indian Readership Survey (2009). Media Research Users Council Hansa Research. Round 1, May. www.newswatch.in/newsblog/4171.

INRA (2001). Eurobaromètre 54 Spécial, *Les Européens et les langues*, February.

Iriberri, Nagore, and José Ramón Uriarte (2008). The language game: A game-theoretical approach to language conflict, manuscript, Universitat Pompeu Fabra, Barcelona.

Jaccard, Paul (1901). Etude comparative de la distribution florale dans une portion des Alpes et des Jura, *Bulletin de la Société Vaudoise des Sciences Naturelles* 37, 547–79.

James, Estelle (1993). Why do different countries choose a different public-private mix of educational services?, *Journal of Human Resources* 28, 571–92.

Janson, Tore (2002). *Speak: A Short Story of Languages*, Oxford: Oxford University Press.

John, Andrew, and Kei-mu Yi (1997). Language, learning and location, Federal Reserve Bank of New York Staff Report 26.

Kerswill, Paul (2006). Migration and language, in Klaus Mattheier, Ulrich Ammon, and Peter Trudgill, eds., *Sociolinguistics: An International Handbook of the Science of Language and Society*, 2nd ed., Berlin: De Gruyter.

Kessler, Brett (2001). *The Significance of Word Lists*, Stanford, CA: Center for the Study of Language and Information.

Kibbee, Douglas (2003). Language policy and linguistic theory, in Jacques Maurais and Michael Morris, eds., *Languages in a Globalising World*, Cambridge: Cambridge University Press.

Klein, Carlo (2003). La valorisation des compétences linguistiques sur le marché du travail luxembourgeois, CEPS/INSTEAD Paper, Luxembourg.

Koenker, Roger, and Kevin Hallock (2001). Quantile regression, *Journal of Economic Perspectives* 15 (4), 143–56.

Krämer, Ludwig (2010). Le régime linguistique de la Commission Européenne, in Dominik Hanf, Klaus Malacek, and Elise Muir, eds., *Langues et construction européenne*, Bruxelles: PIE/Lang.

Ku, Hyejin, and Asaf Zussman (2008). The role of English in international trade, manuscript, Department of Economics, Cornell University.

Kuijs, Louis (2005). The impact of ethnic heterogeneity on the quantity and quality of public spending, IMF Working Paper 00/49, International Monetary Fund, Washington, DC.

La Porta, Rafael, Florenzio Lopez de Silanes, Andrei Shleifer, and Robert Vishny (1999). The quality of government, *Journal of Law, Economics and Organization* 15, 222–79.

Labovitz, Sanford, and Jack Gibbs (1966). Urbanization, technology and division of labor: Further evidence, *Pacific Sociological Review* 7, 3–9.

Ladefoged, Peter, and Ian Maddieson (1996). *The Sounds of the World's Languages*, Oxford: Blackwell.

Laitin, David (1989). Language policy and political strategy in India, *Policy Studies* 22, 415–36.

—— (1994). The Tower of Babel as a coordination game: Political linguistics in Ghana, *American Political Science Review* 88, 622–34.

—— (2000). What is a language community?, *American Journal of Political Science* 44, 142–55.

Laponce, Jean (1992). Language and politics, in Mary Hawkesworth and Maurice Hogan, eds., *Encyclopedia of Government and Politics*, vol. 1, 587–602, London: Routledge.

Laurelle, Annik, and Mikka Widgrén (1998). Is the allocation of power among EU states fair?, *Public Choice* 94, 317–39.

Lazear, Edward (1999a). Culture and language, *Journal of Political Economy* 107, S95–S127.

—— (1999b). Globalization and the market for team-mates, *Economic Journal* 109, 15–40.

Le Breton, Michel, Ignacio Ortuño-Ortín, and Shlomo Weber (2009). Stability of nations and genetic diversity, manuscript.

Leslie, Derek, and Joanne Lindley (2001). The impact of language ability on employment and earnings of Britain's ethnic communities, *Economica* 68, 587–606.

Lévi-Strauss, Claude (2002). France 2 television interview, October 10.

Levinsohn, David (1998). *Ethnic Groups Worldwide. A Ready Reference Handbook*, Phoenix, AZ: Oryx Press.

Lewis, Bernard (2004). *From Babel to Dragomans: Interpreting the Middle East*, Oxford: Oxford University Press.

Lian, Brad, and John O'Neal (1997). Cultural diversity and economic development: A cross-national study of 98 countries, 1960–1985, *Economic Development and Cultural Change* 46, 61–77.

Lieberson, Stanley (1964). An extension of Greenberg's linguistic diversity measures, *Language* 40, 526–31.

—— (1969). Measuring population diversity, *American Sociological Review* 34, 850–62.

—— (1981). *Language Diversity and Language Contact: Essays by Stanley Lieberson*, Stanford, CA: Stanford University Press.

Lönnroth, Juhani (2006). The policy of multilingualism in the EU: Challenges and constraints, paper presented at the conference Challenges of Multilingual Societies, Brussels June 9–10, 2006.

MacManus, Walter, Willliam Gould, and Finis Welsch (1978). Earnings of Hispanic men: The role of English language proficiency, *Journal of Labor Economics* 1, 101–30.

Maignan, Carole, Gianmarco Ottaviano, Dino Pinelli, and Francesco Rullani (2003). Bio-ecological diversity versus socio-economic diversity: A comparison of existing measures, Fondazione Eni Enrico Mattei Discussion Paper 13.2003.

Mamadouh, Virginie (1995). De Talen in het Europees Parlement (Languages in the European Parliament), ASGS vol. 52, Institute for Social Geography, University of Amsterdam.

—— (1998). Supranationalism in the European Union: What about multilingualism?, paper presented at the World Political Map Conference on Nationalisms and Identities in a Globalized World, May-nooth and Belfast, August 1998.

Mamadouh, Virginie, and Kaj Hofman (2001). The language constellation in the European Parliament, 1989–2004, report for the European Cultural Foundation, Amsterdam.

Massey, Douglas, Joaquin Arango, Graeme Hugo, Ali Kouaouci, Adela Pellegrino, and Edward Taylor (1993). Theories of international migration: A review and appraisal, *Population and Development Review* 19, 431–66.

Mauro, Paul (1995). Corruption and growth, *Quarterly Journal of Economics* 110, 681–712.

Mayer, Thierry, and Soledad Zignago (2005). Market access in global and regional trade, Working Paper 2005-02, CEPII Research Center, Paris.

McWhorter, John (2001). *The Power of Babel: A Natural History of Language*, New York: Times Books.

Melitz, Jacques (2007a). The impact of English dominance on literature and welfare, *Journal of Economic Behavior and Organization* 64, 193–215.

—— (2007b). North, South and distance in the gravity model, *European Economic Review* 51, 971–91.

—— (2008). Language and foreign trade, *European Economic Review* 52, 667–99.

Minority Rights Group International (1998). *World Directory of Minorities*, London: Minority Rights Group International.

Montalvo, José, and Marta Reynal-Querol (2002). Why ethnic fractionalization? Polarization, ethnic conflict and growth, Working Paper 660, Universitat Pompeu Fabra, Barcelona.

Montalvo, José, and Marta Reynal-Querol (2005). Ethnic polarization, potential conflict, and civil wars, *American Economic Review* 95, 796–815.

Mosteller, Frederick, and John Tukey (1977). *Data Analysis and Regression: A Second Course in Statistics*, Reading, MA: Addison-Wesley.

Mueller, John, and Karl Shuessler (1961). *Statistical Reasoning in Sociology*, Boston: Houghton Mifflin.

Muller, Siegfried (1964). *The World's Living Languages*, New York: Frederick Ungar.

Nakhleh, Luay, Tandy Warnow, Don Ringe, and Steven Evans (2005). A comparison of phylogenetic reconstruction methods of an Indo-European data set, *Transactions of the Philological Society* 103, 171–92.

Nehring, Klaus, and Clemens Puppe (2002). A theory of diversity, *Econometrica* 70, 1155–98.

—— (2003). Diversity and dissimilarity in lines and hierarchies, *Mathematical Social Sciences* 45, 167–83.

Nei, Masatoshi, and Wen-hsiung Li (1979). Mathematical models for studying genetic variation in terms of restriction endonucleases, *Proceedings of the National Academy of Sciences* 76, 5269–73.

Nettle, Daniel (1999). *Linguistic Diversity*, Oxford: Oxford University Press.

Nida, Eugene (1975). *Language Structure and Translation*, with an introduction by S. Dil, Stanford, CA: Stanford University Press.

Nida, Eugene, and Charles Taber (1969). *The Theory and Practice of Translation*, Leiden: Brill.

Oster, Nicholas (2005). *Empires of the World: A Language History of the World*, New York: HarperCollins.

Ota, Hitoshi (2008). Indian IT software engineers in Japan: A preliminary analysis, Discussion Paper 168, Institute of Developing Economies, Tokyo.

Ottaviano, Gianmarco, and Giovanni Peri (2005). Cities and cultures, *Journal of Urban Economics* 58, 304–37.

—— (2006). The economic value of cultural diversity: Evidence from US cities, *Journal of Economic Geography* 6, 9–44.

Ottaviano, Gianmarco, Dino Pinelli, and Carole Maignan (2003). Economic growth, innovation, cultural diversity, Fondazione Eni Enrico Mattei Working Paper 12.2003.

Pande, Mrinal (2009). Hindimedia and an unreal discourse. *The Hindu*, November 18, 1.

Pattanaik, Prasanta, and Yongsheng Xu (2000). On diversity and freedom of choice, *Mathematical Social Sciences* 40, 123–30.

Penrose, Lionel (1946). The elementary statistics of majority voting, *Journal of the Royal Statistical Society* 109, 53–57.

Pfanner, Eric (2007). When brands go global, *Herald Tribune*, July 23.

Phillipson, Robert (2003). *English-Only Europe?*, London: Routledge.

Piazza, Alberto, Sabine Rendine, Eric Minch, Paolo Menozzi, Joanna Mountain, and Luigi Luca Cavalli-Sforza (1995). Genetics and the origin of European languages, *Proceedings of the National Academy of Sciences of the USA* 92, 5836–40.

Piron, Claude (1994). *Le défi des langues: Du gâchis au bon sens*, Paris: L'Harmattan.

Pool, Jonathan (1991). The official language problem, *American Political Science Review* 85, 495–514.

—— (1996). Optimal language regimes for the European Union, *International Journal of the Sociology of Languages* 121, 159–79.

Pujadas, Bernat (2006). The rules governing the languages of the European Union: Which languages and to what extent? A practical guide, www.ciemen.org/mercatorbutlettins/60-48.htm (last accessed May 2006).

La Quinzaine Littéraire (2006). La fiction, c'est l'Amérique, June 16–30.

Rao, Caluampudi (1982). Diversity and dissimilarity coefficients: A unified approach, *Theoretical Population Biology* 21, 24–43.

Rask, Morten (2004). Literature about cultural distances on the Net, http://www.morten-rask.dk/2001f.htm.

Reiss, Tom (2005). *The Orientalist: Solving the Mystery of a Strange and Dangerous Life*, New York: Random House.

Renfrew, Colin (1987). *Archeology and Language*, London: Jonathan Cape.

Reynal-Querol, Marta (2002). Ethnicity, political systems, and civil wars, *Journal of Conflict Resolution* 46, 29–54.

Ricotta, Carlo, and Laszlo Szeidl (2006). Towards a unifying approach to diversity measures: Bridging the gap between the Shannon diversity and Rao's quadratic entropy, *Theoretical Population Biology* 70, 237–43.

Roberts, Janet (1962). Sociocultural change and communication problems, in Frank Rice, ed., *Study of the Role of Second Languages in Asia, Africa, and Latin America*, Washington, DC: Center for Applied Linguistics of the Modern Language Association of America, 105–23.

Rochet, Jean-Charles, and Jean Tirole (2003). Platform competition in two-sided markets, *Journal of the European Economic Association* 1, 990–1029.

Rubinstein, Ariel (2000). *Economics and Language*, Cambridge: Cambridge University Press.

Ruhlen, Merritt (1994a). *The Origin of Language*, New York: John Wiley & Sons.

—— (1994b). *On the Origin of Language: Studies in Linguistic Taxonomy*, Stanford, CA: Stanford University Press.

Rustow, Dankwart (1967). *A World of Nations: Problems of Political Modernization*, Washington, DC: Brookings Institution.

Sapir, Edward (1970). Language, in D. G. Mendelbaum, ed., *Culture, Language and Personality: Selected Essays*, Berkeley, and Los Angeles: University of California Press.

Sassen, Saskia (1994). *Cities in the World Economy*, Thousand Oaks, CA: Pine Forge Press.

Saxenian, AnnaLee (1996). *Regional Advantage: Culture and Competition in Silicon Valley and Route 128*, Cambridge, MA: Harvard University Press.

—— (1999). *Silicon Valley's New Immigrant Entrepreneurs*, San Francisco, CA: Public Policy Institute of California.

Schulze, Christian, and Dietrich Stauffer (2006). Monte Carlo simulation of survival for minority languages, manuscript, Institute for Theoretical Physics, Cologne University.

Schwartz, Shalom (2010). Cultural distances and value orientations, in Victor Ginsburgh and David Throsby, eds., *Handbook of the Economics of Art and Culture*, vol. 2, Amsterdam: Elsevier, forthcoming.

Searls, David (2003). Linguistics: Trees of life and language, *Nature* 426, 391–92.

Selten, Reinhard, and Jonathan Pool (1991). The distribution of foreign language skills as a game equilibrium, in Reinhard Selten, ed., *Game Equilibrium Models*, vol. 4, 64–84, Berlin: Springer-Verlag.

Selniker, Larry (2001). BBC interview.

Sen, Amartya (1999). *Development as Freedom*, New York: Alfred Knopf.

Shannon, Claude (1948). A mathematical theory of communication, *Bell Systems Technical Journal* 27, 379–423, 623–56.

Shapiro, Daniel, and Morton Stelcner (1997). Language earnings in Quebec: Trends over twenty years, 1970–1990, *Canadian Public Policy* 23, 115–40.

Shapley, Lloyd (1953). A value for n-person games, in Harold Kuhn and Albert Tucker, eds., *Contributions to the Theory of Games II*, Princeton, NJ: Princeton University Press.

Shy, Oz (2001). *The Economics of Network Industries*, Cambridge: Cambridge University Press.

Simpson, Edward (1949). Measurement of diversity, *Nature* 163, 688.

Slomczynski, Wojciech, Tomasz Zastawniak, and Karol Zyczkowski (2006). The root of the matter: Voting in the EU Council, *Physics World* 19, 35–37.

Sokal, Robert (1988). Genetic, geographic, and linguistic distances in Europe, *Proceedings of the National Academy of Sciences of the USA* 85, 1722–26.

Sorensen, Thorvald (1948). A method of establishing groups of equal amplitude in plant sociology based on similarity of species and its application to analyses of the vegetation on Danish commons, *Biologiske Skrifter, Kongelige Danske Videnskabernes Selskab* 5, 1–34.

Special Eurobarometer 243 (2006). *Europeans and their Languages*, Brussels: European Commission.

Spolaore, Enrico, and Roman Wacziarg (2009). The diffusion of development, *Quarterly Journal of Economics* 124, 469–529.

Spolsky, Bernard (2004). *Language Policy*, Cambridge: Cambridge University Press.

Steiner, George (1992). *After Babel: Aspects of Language and Translation*, Oxford: Oxford University Press.

Swadesh, Morris (1952). Lexico-statistic dating of prehistoric ethnic contacts, *Proceedings of the American Philosophical Society* 96, 121–37.

Taylor, Charles, and Michael Hudson (1972). *World Handbook of Social and Political Indicators*, Ann Arbor, MI: ICSPR.

Tinbergen, Jan (1962). *Shaping the World Economy: Suggestions for an International Economic Policy*, New York: Twentieth Century Fund.

Truchot, Claude (2003). Languages and supranationality in Europe: The linguistic influence of the European Union, in Jacques Maurais, ed., *Languages in a Globalising World*, Cambridge: Cambridge University Press.

UNESCO, *Index Translationum*, translation databases: databases.unesco.org/xtrans/stat/xTransList.a?lg=1, databases.unesco.org/xtrans/stat/xTransXpert.a?lg=1.

Vaillancourt, François (1980). Differences in earnings by language group in Quebec, 1970: An economic analysis, Quebec: International Centre for Research on Bilingualism.

Vaillancourt, François, and Robert Lacroix (1985). Revenus et langue au Québec, http://www.cslf.gouv.qc.ca/publications/PubD120/D120-6.html (accessed November 4, 2005).

Van Parijs, Philippe (2005). Europe's three language problems, in Dario Castiglione and Chris Longman, eds., *The Challenge of Multilingualism in Law and Politics*, Oxford: Hart Publishing.

Van Pottelsberghe, Bruno, and Didier François (2006). The cost factor in patent systems, Working Paper CEB06-002, Centre Emile Bernheim, Université Libre de Bruxelles.

Vargas Llosa, Mario (2001). Golden globe, *New Statesman*, March 5. www.newstatesman.com/20013050033.

Vikor, Lars (2000). Northern Europe: Languages as prime markers of ethnic and national identity, in Stephen Barbour and Cathie Carmichael, eds., *Language and Nationalism in Europe*, Oxford: Oxford University Press.

Walker, John (2000). Money laundering: Quantifying international patterns, *Australian Social Monitor* 2, 139–47.

Wang, Y. (2008). The dual museum pass game, working paper, Department of Economics, University of Windsor, Ontario.

Warnow, Tandy (1997). Mathematical approaches to comparative linguistics, *Proceedings of the National Academy of Sciences of the USA* 94, 6585–90.

Weber, Max (1968). *Economy and Society*, Berkeley and Los Angeles: University of California Press.

Weikard, Hans-Peter (2002). Diversity functions and the value of biodiversity, *Land Economics* 78, 20–27.

Weitzman, Martin (1992). On diversity, *Quarterly Journal of Economics* 107, 363–405.

—— (1993). What to preserve? An application of diversity theory to crane conservation, *Quarterly Journal of Economics* 108, 157–83.

—— (1998). The Noah's ark problem, *Econometrica* 66, 1279–88.

Whorf, Benjamin (1956). *Language, Thought and Reality*, Cambridge, MA: MIT Press.

Wiener, Norbert (1948). *Cybernetics: or Control and Communication in the Animal and the Machine*, Paris: Librairie Hermann, Cambridge, MA: MIT Press.

Williams, Donald (2006). The economic returns to multiple language usage in Western Europe, CEPS/INSTEAD, IRISS Working Paper Series 2006-07, Luxembourg.

Wolfson, Michael (1994). When inequalities diverge, *American Economic Review* 84, 353–58.

Wright, Julian (2003). Optimal card payment systems, *European Economic Review* 47, 587–612.

Wright, Sue (2007). English in the European Parliament: MEPs and their language repertories, *Sociolinguistica* 21, 151–165.

Wright, Sue (2009). The elephant in the room: Language issues in the European Union, paper presented at the Conference on Language, Rights and European Democracy, University of Copenhagen, June.

Yair, Gad (1995). "Unite Unite Europe": The political and cultural structures of Europe as reflected in the Eurovision Song Contest, *Social Networks* 17, 147–61.

INDEX